Tracy Johnston

Shooting the Boh

Tracy Johnston grew up in Southern California, graduated from UC–Berkeley, and has worked as a high school teacher, ceramic sculptor, free-lance writer, and magazine editor. Her most recent job was as Northern California editor of *California* magazine. She has written for *New West*, *The New York Times Magazine*, *Playboy*, and *The Village Voice*. She lives with her husband, Jon Carroll, in Oakland.

Shooting the Boh

Shooting the Boh

A Woman's Voyage Down the Wildest River in Borneo

Tracy Johnston

VINTAGE DEPARTURES
VINTAGE BOOKS
A DIVISION OF RANDOM HOUSE, INC.
NEW YORK

A VINTAGE DEPARTURES ORIGINAL, SEPTEMBER 1992
FIRST EDITION

Copyright © 1992 by Tracy Johnston
Map copyright © 1992 by Jaye Zimet

Library of Congress Cataloging-in-Publication Data
Johnston, Tracy.
Shooting the Boh : a woman's voyage down the wildest river in
Borneo / Tracy Johnston.
p. cm. — (Vintage departures)
ISBN 0-679-74010-4 (pbk.)
1. Boh River (Indonesia)—Description and travel. 2. Johnston,
Tracy—Journeys—Indonesia—Boh Sungai. 3. Women
adventurers—United States—Biography. I. Title.
DS646.34.B64J64 1992
959.8'3—dc20 92-53825
CIP

Book design by Stephanie Bart-Horvath
Author photograph copyright © Ken Prohst

Manufactured in the United States of America
10 9 8 7 6 5 4 3 2

To my parents, Bob and Ruth Joos

Acknowledgments

This book would not have been possible without my eleven companions on the Boh River. Since we were together for only a short time, under trying circumstances, my portraits of them are incomplete. Nevertheless, everything on these pages is as true as I have been able to make it.

I also wish to thank several friends who helped me on the second part of my journey, the writing of the book: Patrick Finley, Drury Pifer, Patrick Daugherty, B.K. Moran, and my mother, who is not only a joyful traveler but a creative literary critic. They read and commented on the manuscript, and their advice, along with the enthusiasm of my agent Suzanne Gluck and the intelligent editing of Robin Desser at Vintage Books, made the experience of writing and publishing my first book more pleasurable than I had a right to expect.

For the stories about Borneo's early explorers, I am indebted to the library of the University of California, at Berkeley.

My debt to my husband, Jon Carroll, is overwhelming. He was my editor throughout all stages of the writing. I thank him for his skill and his patience; I am grateful for his love.

As you got older and felt yourself to be at the center of your time, and not at a point in its circumference, as you felt when you were little, you were seized with a sort of shuddering.

—Thomas Hardy, *Jude the Obscure*

Shooting the Boh

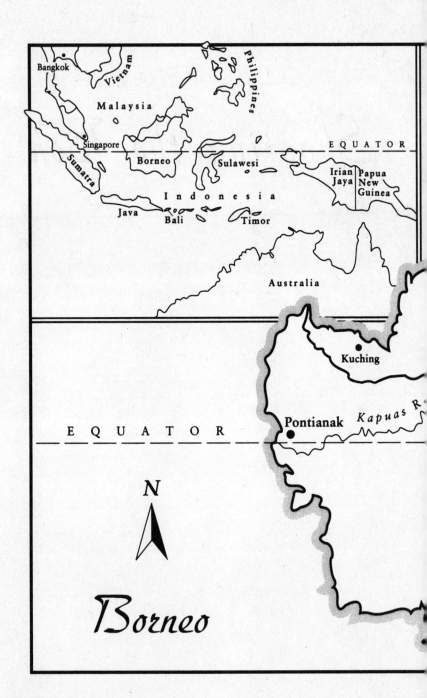

Preface

Looking around me that morning as I stood at the edge of the river, about to head into the unknown, I was reminded of the photographs I'd seen of the European explorers who came to Borneo in the nineteenth century. They were upper-class men, most of them amateur scientists, who traveled with teams of native guides and porters carrying guns, notebooks, boxes for mounting specimens, and cloth and glass beads for barter. We were three American river guides and nine thrill-seeking tourists who had flown into a village that would have taken them months to reach, and we were taking our gear in rafts instead of hiring someone to carry it. But, like those men, we stood a full head taller than the native Dayaks who had come down to the river to say good-bye to us. Like them, we had a certain smugness, as though our superior height and our modern equipment granted us special powers.

We had come to Long Lebusan, a remote village in Kalimantan, the Indonesian part of Borneo, because we'd signed up for a white water rafting trip with Sobek, an adventure travel company. Sobek hoped to open up the Boh River to commercial rafting, including an eighteen-mile section where it funneled through a steep, narrow gorge. But it needed someone to finance the exploratory run. That was us. No experience was necessary, just cash.

Sobek had planned to hire some local Dayak boatmen to accompany us, so we'd be able to hike out of the gorge if we got stuck. But now it looked as if we'd be making the trip alone. We hadn't been able to convince a single Dayak to come with us. The rapids in the gorge were unrunnable, they said. They were big, and they were dangerous. Even after we showed them our sturdy, high-tech rafts they said no, and then no again. They kept shaking their heads. Finally they told us about the river spirit, the evil, three-headed river spirit. It was in the gorge, they said, and they were afraid of it.

Although we couldn't take their warnings about the evil spirit seriously, what did concern us was the predicament their fear of it had put us in. Without a guide who knew the rain forest, we couldn't travel through it. There were no villages in the area, and no trails. That meant that once we were in the gorge, there was no turning back.

That morning the entire village of Long Lebusan had come to the river to see us off. The children fingered our white plastic helmets and red life jackets; the women stood behind them, looking beautiful and serene in their ragged sarongs; the men, barefooted and carrying long curved knives, stood on the riverbank, impatient to get back to their rice harvest.

The previous night I had given an old woman in the village a flowered pillowcase I didn't need, and that morning she suddenly appeared in front of me. I smiled, but she grabbed hold of both of my arms and held them tight. Then she spoke—a torrent of words accompanied by purposeful shakes of her head. Clearly, she was trying to tell me something. I kept shrugging, trying to indicate that I couldn't speak the village language, but she kept talking. Finally she stopped and gave me a long, penetrating stare, her eyes riveted on mine and her grip on my arms still tight. I was beginning to feel a little scared. Then she shook my arms hard, as if to kick-start some kind of understanding.

At last she sighed and let me go. As I backed away, saying,

"I'm sorry, I'm sorry," she waved, and said something that made the village children around her laugh, probably some Dayak equivalent of, "If this woman were any dumber she'd be deciduous." Then she turned and walked back up the riverbank.

When the guides finally had our boats rigged and we were ready to take off, one of the village headmen called everyone to attention. He bowed his head, waited for silence, and then gave a short, solemn speech. When he was through, even the river seemed quiet. I noticed that many of the women had tears in their eyes and was surprised to see they cared so much.

We waved good-bye until the roofs of the longhouses were swallowed up by the rain forest, and then, after a short while of leisurely paddling, we hit the Boh. The river was big and fast, and for a while we rode it in wonder and silence. Its banks were steep and choked with trees and vines, and when there were no rapids the water had a sort of bilious tinge, a murky greenish-brown, full of small bubbles and whirlpools. There were no birds, no monkey calls, no animals on the rocks, just a huge, thirty-foot-wide funnel of water cutting through the trees, curving into a canyon, heading into the unknown.

Just before we entered the gorge, we pulled into an eddy to fix an oarlock and I asked Dave Heckman, our leader, what the village headman had said.

"It was a prayer," he answered casually.

"I heard Pelanjau translate it into Indonesian for you."

"Well . . . yeah."

"So?"

Dave cleared his throat. "Well . . . actually . . . he asked God to accept the souls in heaven of the misguided white people who were going to die in the gorge. Amen."

So that's what the old woman was trying to tell me; that's why our leave-taking had been so poignant. I had read about the Dayak spirit world but this was my first encounter with it. We must have seemed so frail, so pathetic, with our pale white skin and our cameras and our sun hats, taking off to confront one of the most dangerous spirits of the rain forest with no protection other than our boats, talismans the Dayaks clearly found inadequate.

As we pulled out into the current and headed into the gorge, it occurred to me, not for the last time, that the natives of the rain forest might have had a clearer grasp of the situation than we did.

1

I first heard about the Boh River from Richard Bangs, president of Sobek. I met him at a party in San Francisco and told him about a river I'd run in California years ago, where I'd been held helpless at the bottom of a waterfall by tons of pounding water, spinning in terror, barely conscious. He looked at me with new interest and said, "You might be just the person to go on our Boh River trip."

Less than a year ago, he said, ABC television made a film of some hotshot women rafters attempting to make a first descent of the Boh River gorge. They'd abandoned the attempt because the water level was too high, but now Sobek was going to try it again, and wouldn't I like to come?

When I hesitated, wondering why he thought my fear of drowning in big rapids made me qualified for such a trip, he said the magic words: "I think Sobek can send you along for free. As a writer."

I told him I'd think about it, but in my mind I was already on the plane. Long ago I realized a disconcerting truth about myself: I am by nature a passive person who likes excitement; a person with no magnificent obsessions who loves to participate in them. The best way to solve that contradiction, I'd discovered, was to go along on other people's rides, which is probably why I became a traveler and a journalist in the first place.

*   *   *

The next day, when I checked Sobek's catalog to see what it said about the Boh River trip, I found that on a scale of I to V it was listed as a "Class III" adventure. In terms of difficulty that meant "Average." I knew there was some danger because we might run into unforeseen trouble, but I clung to that description. "Average" I could handle.

More worrisome was the back pain I had recently developed. I'd been digging in the garden when suddenly my back seemed to crumple and I had to hobble into bed. Only after several sessions of poking and prodding did my doctor, who once spent a Robinson Crusoe year on a remote island in Indonesia, give me his blessing. "Just don't lift anything heavy," he instructed, and handed over a prescription for pain pills that made my pharmacist look at me sternly and fill out a "Narcotic" form in triplicate.

It was my husband who held out the longest for common sense. He hadn't a clue as to why I lusted after adventure and I found it hard to explain.

"The last time you went on a river trip you almost died," he pointed out, "and now you're telling me you have a great idea— you want to go on *another* one."

"Well, it's my life."

"It's my life too. If you go on the trip I'll be lonely and I'll worry; and if something should happen to you, it will be my life that's ruined as well as yours."

He ended up supporting my going on the trip, but only out of love, he said, rather than understanding. And I promised him I'd take every precaution. Not only were there rapids to worry about, there were spiders, snakes, and leeches. And there were diseases—over a thousand different species of parasitic worms plus amoebic dysentery, malaria, cholera, and typhoid. An open sore in a tropical rain forest can turn overnight into a sac of infected pus; previously unexamined body parts can balloon up to the size of a small toaster.

To be safe, I bought an enormous duffel bag, put it in my

study, and gradually filled it with enough river gear to outfit a moderate-sized navy, and enough ointments and powders to obliterate an entire continent of ravenous microorganisms. I had malaria pills, antibiotics, river shoes, a repellent-soaked bug suit, pants with elastic around the ankles to keep the leeches out, shoes with a good tread for walking on rocks, a reading light, a flashlight with extra batteries, and, most important, my all-time-favorite air mattress. The bulging duffel bag was my protection; with it, I would be invincible.

A month later I arrived at Jakarta's beautiful new airport constructed of tropical hardwood. I had two hours to kill before my flight to Balikpapan in Borneo, so I bought an *International Herald Tribune* and went to the baggage claims area to pick up my duffel. The first batch of suitcases bounced down the chute so quickly and efficiently, I began to wonder if I might have enough time to hire a cab and do some sight-seeing. Then another bunch came tumbling down and circled. Then another. After a while I started pacing around, watching people stack their carts with baggage. Then I sat down and tried to concentrate on my newspaper but kept reading the same paragraph over and over again. The motor hummed, the metal slivers slipped in and out of place, and a small Indonesian boy picked up one of the remaining pieces of luggage and hoisted it high over his head, staggering like a weight lifter to remain upright.

Finally I heard a *thunk:* the metal door behind the rubber flaps clanking shut.

Impossible! I thought. This just couldn't have happened.

I stood up in the hope that a simple change of posture might somehow help, but it didn't. As far as I could see, the baggage claims area was empty. In front of me swam acres of barren tile with only a few ghostlike janitors in the distance, wielding mops. I made a mental checklist of the contents of my carry-on bag: one pair of white sandals, two sundresses, a blouse and skirt, thirty rolls of film (no camera), white cotton pants, rouge and mascara, skin cream, sunblock, underwear, and thirteen books (eight novels, three phrase books). Everything else was in my duffel bag. If I was going to make a first descent of the Boh River, I was going to do it dressed for afternoon tea in Jakarta.

I got out one of the phrase books and walked over to a janitor:

"*Say-a keh-il-angan tas,*" I said.

"*Anda perlu apa?*" he replied. "*Dari mana kamu? Kenapa kamu panya saya?*"

Great. I had thirty Indonesian words memorized, and those were not among them.

"My luggage," I said. "Lost. Where is Garuda?"

"You are American?" he asked.

"Yes. Please. Where is the Garuda Airlines office?"

"Name? What your name?"

"Tracy Johnston."

"Where from?"

"America."

"Are you single, Tracy?"

"What? Where is the Garuda office?"

"Do you have husband?"

For the next two seconds I mentally exiled the man to a strip of asphalt in the middle of a vast, boiling-hot desert, where he was forced to chew the leather straps of suitcases and drink bottles of after-shave. But then I looked at my watch and saw that time had not stopped: I had just an hour before my flight to Balikpapan.

I jogged down the terminal until I found a Garuda office with men in it and computer screens. One of the men leaped up from his chair when he saw me and I had to laugh. Was my intention of strangling him and leaving his body on the floor next to the janitor's that obvious?

"Are you missing luggage from a Garuda flight?" he asked.

"*Yes!*" I cried.

"We have it," he said.

"Oh . . . oh . . . thank God." The man was an angel. I wanted to hug him. "Where have you put it?" I asked.

"It is in Los Angeles," he said brightly. "But I will put it on the next flight to Jakarta."

"When is that?"

"Friday."

"But . . . that's three days from now."

"I'm sorry. There is no earlier plane."

I was speechless. Tomorrow I was supposed to be in Long Lebusan, a village so remote we'd be flying there on a tiny missionary airplane. By Friday we were supposed to be on the Boh, perhaps already partway down the gorge.

I walked out of the terminal into the warm tropical air. If there were options other than hysteria, now was the time to consider them. But what could I do? I could always fly to Bali, where I'd spent some time last year. It was cheap and full of people to hang out with from all over the world—surfers, artists, and expats. Or I could call up the American family I'd met on a previous trip to Jarkata and stay with them in one of their two houses staffed with entire families of servants. The only option that was out of the question, for the moment, was flying home.

Suddenly the Garuda agent popped up at my side like a cartoon genie, beckoning me back into the terminal with bent fingers. When we reached his office, he pointed to a chair and I sat down.

"Stand by," he said, holding up his hand like a traffic cop. "I think I can help you."

Then, in an instant, he vanished. Five minutes later he reappeared, his arms piled high with stuff.

"Now you can go on the river trip," he said, spilling the load on the telexes that covered his desk. "For sleep, a sleeping sack, for photos, a camera . . ." He picked up each item with a flourish, as if he had pulled it out of a magician's hat.

"You can take all of it," he said. "It's from Lost and Found, but you can have it."

I guess I waited too long to respond, because he finally shouted, as if I hadn't understood:

"Now you can go on your river trip!"

In retrospect, I think I ended up going on to Balikpapan that afternoon because I couldn't let the Garuda agent down. The shoes and almost all the clothes were too small, the camera's light meter was broken, and I had no idea how I was going to find a fraction of all the things we had been instructed to bring.

But the beaming Garuda agent was waiting for me to thank him, and I said, "This is terrific. Thank you so much." Then I stuffed an umbrella and a sweatshirt and a pair of pants and the broken camera into a plastic bag and ran off to catch my plane.

As I strapped on my seat belt and settled down to read the first chapter of *Lord Jim,* I reminded myself that one of the reasons I had come to Indonesia was to get a story. In that regard, personal suffering could only help.

2

*B*alikpapan is a sprawling, ragged, oil boom town on Borneo's east coast. When I arrived there I was jet-lagged almost to the point of stupor. I'd left Jakarta five hours earlier, and it had been thirty-nine hours since I'd left my home in Oakland. I took a taxi right to the town's only first-class hotel, where our group was scheduled to meet at seven o'clock. It was six-fifteen; I had forty-five minutes to shop.

Rattled, dazed, and unclear as to whether I was in serious denial or mid-lag paranoia, I walked out of the hotel and found myself in the middle of Third World capitalism at its most intense. The population of Balikpapan had trippled in fifteen years, and the entire city seemed in a frenzy of buying and selling. The street was lined with shops as far as I could see in both directions, each one filled with merchandise and open to the sidewalk. It was a solid mile of counters and shelves piled to the ceiling with clothes, videotapes, jewelry, furniture, hardware, lighting fixtures, televisions, radios.

I walked quickly by the plastic and polyester in search of the colors and smells of the tropics—the baskets, the weavings, the bittersweet odors that always remind me of rotting vegetation. But there was no end to the metallic ugliness: transistor radios and cassettes spewed noise into the street like a demented orchestra, and the hawkers and sellers stood behind their glass counters smiling and calling out to customers like baby birds, mouths open, arm aflutter whenever someone stopped. The men wore sunglasses and pressed white shirts, like mobsters, and the clink and jangle of cash registers rang out over the noise like a thousand tinkling charm bracelets. Posters of Sylvester Stallone were everywhere: teeth bared, neck muscles distended, Rambo as demonic god, the Shiva of the new capitalist mythology.

The idea of having to charge into this chaos with my thirty-word Indonesian vocabulary seemed about as appealing as trying to surf a tidal wave. But after a while my old bargaining skills returned, and I had a good time tossing back and forth rupiahs and numbers. I came back to the hotel with tennis shoes (too large), a flashlight (too powerful), a pair of shorts emblazoned with the words *Pacific Holiday,* a towel the size of a doily, and flowered bed sheets made out of some alien synthetic that, as I later discovered, caused sweat to gather in pools and simmer. What I didn't have was what I needed most of all: an air mattress.

I suppose all travelers have some idiosyncratic fear that makes them pack too many clothes or read too many maps. My fear is that I will have to sleep on bare ground. I have bursitis in my hips, which makes sleeping on just about anything but a mattress painful. And I'm an insomniac, which means that sleep is associated with all sorts of routines and demons. I've schlepped state-of-the-art air mattresses all over the world, carried them up sixteen thousand feet in the Himalayas, and all over Alaska, Tasmania, India, and Papua New Guinea. I like to think I can go anywhere, sleep anyplace, as long as I have a book, an air mattress, and a reading light.

In the lobby I ran into Dave Heckman, the leader of our expedition. He was a tall, handsome man, probably in his late thirties, and seemed oddly formal for a river guide. Dressed Indonesian style in pressed pants and shirt, he reminded me more of a Graham Greene character than a typical wisecracking, T-shirted boatman. I told him about my bad back and said I couldn't carry anything heavy, but he didn't seemed concerned.

"You can help with dinner or something; it will be fine." Then I told him about my lost luggage and my need for an air mattress and he was equally relaxed. "I wouldn't worry," he said. "Someone will lend you theirs. A Frenchwoman, Sylvie, was talking about leaving hers behind anyway." There was a weight limit for the airplane, he explained, and she wanted to take a video camera.

Fifteen minutes later we were all present and assembled around a huge table in the hotel's mahogany-paneled conference room. There were ten of us—six men and four women—but the two women sitting right next to Dave were so arrestingly beautiful that the rest of us more or less shut up and stared at them.

Olatz was Basque ("not Spanish"), and everything about her was intensely, exquisitely delicate: her tiny nose, her luxurious mouth, her flawless, honeyed skin. She looked like the heroine of a romance novel, with long, curly hair tumbling past her shoulders and eyes that were dark and luminous, brimming with a sort of fluctuating warmth. She was twenty-five, it turned out, and a professional model. She worked for all the big designers and traveled the world on fashion shoots.

Sylvie was French, tall and big-boned, with hair that was, if anything, even more theatrical: thick and wavy, it fell in lavish cascades over her shoulders almost to her waist. Her eyes were likewise astonishing, full of effulgent color, marbled blues and greens. She had worked as a model in Paris when she was a student, but now she made her living in New York styling models and fashion shoots for magazines and advertising agencies. I remembered what Dave had said about her possibly lending me an air mattress, and I tried to catch her eye but couldn't.

The two women were focused on Mimo, the Italian who sat between them, although what he was saying and why it was making them laugh so hard mystified me. They were talking in French, Italian, and Spanish. Mimo was tall and slender, and although his body seemed slightly soft, as if he smoked or drank too much, it was expressive. At one point, in what seemed to be a self-mocking flourish, he took a bandanna out of his pocket and wrapped it around his neck. He seemed to be a master of the bon mot, a picture of flashing self-confidence.

As the rest of us sat waiting sheepishly for Dave to begin the introductions, Mimo, Olatz, and Sylvie laughed and giggled and, at one point, started throwing things at each other like a group of show-off children. Next to their conscious display of beauty and joie de vivre, we were wallflowers, drones.

Bill and Linda were a thirtysomething couple from Florida. He was blond, freckled, and balding, a mild-mannered man I had pegged for an engineer until he said he taught about snakes and rain forests at an environmental center in Palm Beach. Linda, his girlfriend, was short and plump, with dark eyes and beautiful skin. What stood out most about her, however, was her voice: it was deep, loud, and throaty, ranging from a sexy whisper to a basso bark. She addressed most of her remarks that night to Bill, in a low rumble, but even so, we heard most of what she said. She and Bill had already been six weeks on the road, touring Hong Kong, Singapore, and rain forests all over Southeast Asia. She missed her cats. She missed her apartment.

Howard and Stuart, two young Austrialians, were from a small town near Melbourne. They didn't have much to say, and when they did speak I had trouble understanding their accent. The one word I did make out, "bee-ir," made my heart sink. I once spent a weekend with a group of beer-drinking Australians, and it was two days of nonstop tedious teasing. Howard and Stuart seemed to be relatively subdued, however, and I was glad to see that they looked strong and up for an adventure.

Finally, there was John, sitting upright in his chair and silent. His skin was pale white, his face distorted by Coke-bottle eyeglass lenses, and he wore an alligator shirt tucked into nondescript pants. Except for puffing on his pipe he remained remarkably motionless, his face set in a sleepy, puzzling grin. He was a corporate lawyer from Chicago and the only one of the group besides me without a buddy. I figured we'd be thrown together somehow.

Dave Heckman finally introduced himself: "Three of us will be leading the trip, but I guess I'm the one who will get the flak if anything goes wrong." The other two Sobek guides, Mike and Gary, were already in Long Lebusan, he said, the village near the Boh River where we would be putting in. With them was Raymond, an American client who lived in Jakarta and spoke fluent Indonesian. Raymond had volunteered to fly in to Long Lebusan early with the guides to help rig the boats and translate.

Then Dave got to the point:

"Here's what we'll be getting into. This is an exploratory trip, which means no one has run the part of the river we're going to run except for possibly a group of Dayaks. We're not sure we can do it; the river may be too high or the weather may be so bad we can't fly in. The food will be shit—freeze-dried stuff— and you'll spend at least one terrible night, maybe two, sleeping, or trying to sleep, on rocks. Maybe we'll have to sleep in the rain, or sleep sitting up in the boats. And if anyone is allergic to beestings, you shouldn't go. There is a particular kind of bee . . . when it stings you'll fall to the ground in pain. It's unbearable, we've heard."

Howard and Stuart exchanged remarks that I couldn't make out, except for the word "bloody." Olatz said something in French to Sylvie and they both laughed. I watched their thick curly hair bounce on their long thin necks and said to myself, "No problem."

That night I told the group about my lost luggage. I said I'd managed to buy a lot of things in the shops outside the hotel, but I still needed to beg or borrow one essential piece of equipment: an air mattress. I explained about my bad back, but I didn't tell the whole story—about the bursitis in my hips, about my lifelong problem with sleep. I just said an air mattress was my one, no-prisoners-taken requirement; that I couldn't go down the river without it. One by one, everyone responded. People offered T-shirts, shorts, pants, rain jackets, and then Sylvie, as Dave had predicted, said she had an air mattress.

"Oh, would you possibly lend it to me?" I asked.

"If you need it," she said.

"I'm afraid I really do need it. I've had to use one all my life. Whatever you want in return, just ask."

Sylvie didn't say anything, but later, when Mimo came to my room offering me a cotton sleeping bag as well, I couldn't believe my good fortune. I had always believed that one should travel light, without clinging to security; accept whatever comes and make it part of the plan. But as I had gotten older, "light" had become heavier and heavier. Here was my chance to shed the baggage, get rid of the deadweight, get unattached.

"I have made the right decision," I wrote my husband before going to bed. "I think all the careful packing was probably just an attempt to control the unknown. I have a feeling that I'll look back on this trip and say it was impossible to really prepare for it anyway."

I slept erratically that night, in jet-lag confusion, and finally, at about four o'clock, grouchy and lonely, I got out of bed. In the distance I could hear the muezzin, calling the Muslim faithful to prayer over a loudspeaker. Drawn to the sound, I turned off the air conditioning, threw open the window and sat on the windowsill in the darkness. The shops were closed, the city was still, and suddenly I felt the warm wet air and smelled the sweet odor of moist earth. It was the feel and the smell of the tropics— cockroaches and burning garbage, crushed fruit and sunsets. The wind in the hotel garden was rattling the palms; I could almost hear the temple bells and the gamelan music.

Suddenly I began to lose myself. The overcast sky and the opaque lights of the city began to pulse, perhaps with my heart-beat, and very quietly the windowsill beneath me faded. I floated away toward the muezzin's cry on a pagan wisp of cloud.

Master of my memories, I egged them on: I was once again in the Indonesia I had first seen a year ago: back to a house in Bali that overlooked a tiny Muslim village where my husband and I had slept so peacefully that the four A.M. call to prayer had floated in and out of our dreams like some midsummer-night spirit; back to a hot afternoon in a bare room beneath a listless

16

fan in Yogyarkarta waiting for it to cool down enough to take a walk; back to the veranda of a hotel on a remote island in the Banda Sea where I had watched a small village awaken at dawn with the sense that I was witnessing a miracle. I felt the softness of the sky, the languor of the earth, the Conradian serenity of the vast Eastern oceans. The feeling was polymorphous—all the senses piling up, without skepticism, without judgment.

Back in bed, I lay sleepless, excited by the thought of the unknown that lay before me—the river itself and also what I knew would be a more private journey. Every trip I make to somewhere remote or exotic seems to develop a personal theme. In situations of overwhelming strangeness the old rules don't apply, the possibilities are endless, and I want to say "Yes" to everything: yes I can be there, yes I can do that, yes I won't be afraid. But eventually I reach a point where I seem to be in the middle of a Road Runner cartoon, running in the air with the orange desert far below, kept aloft only by my ignorance. It is at that point, when I have to turn back, that I confront some fact about myself, some previously unknown characteristic.

Around six o'clock in the morning, after one last check of my small pile of borrowed shirts and pants, I got dressed and went down to the plush dining room and ordered strong coffee, fried rice, eggs and bacon, and some kind of rice pudding with a raw egg floating on top. When Mimo, Olatz, and Sylvie came in and took a table by themselves, I realized that there are definite advantages to being middle-aged, and one of them is delight in solitude. I was truly happy reading the *Indonesian Times* all by myself, which was just as well. I was going to be very much alone on this trip. There would be times, in fact, when I would feel desperately alone, when it seemed as if I might not see anyone again, even my husband.

3

*T*he bus ride the next morning established the tone of our group: polite, but not particularly friendly. Sylvie and Olatz had staked out the backseat, where they curled up on duffel bags and went to sleep. They napped like young children, limbs dangling and swaying with the motion of the bus. Olatz looked lovely, even beneath her baggy sweatshirt. A scarf looped through her jeans emphasized her lilliputian waist; her hands and feet seemed a miracle of creation, so perfect were they, so smooth and slender. Sylvie was more obviously sexy. She wore a floppy cotton hat that came down to her eyebrows, creating a charming Diane Keaton effect, but nothing could compete for attention with her body. She was big-thighed and big-breasted, muscular and strong. Olatz was a kitten; Sylvie a racehorse.

It was a bumpy two-hour ride to Samarinda, where we were scheduled to catch a morning flight into the interior, most of it through country that had been totally destroyed by fire. From the bus I could see only lush secondary growth—small trees, vines, and tangles of sun-loving, light green foliage broken occasionally by pockets of houses and shops. The fire, which burned for five months in 1982 and 1983, had been so immense that planes couldn't land because of its smoke as far away as Singapore. Now called the worst environmental disaster in modern history, it destroyed 13,500 square miles of rain forest, an area the size of Connecticut and Massachusetts combined.

I felt stupid not to have even heard about the fire, but Bill said I wasn't alone. Back in 1982, the only people who cared about rain forests were a few environmental scientists. In the United States, only *The New York Times* had covered the fire, and only as a small story on an inside page.

The villages we passed seemed as degraded as the forest: temporary, tin-roofed shacks built by Dayaks who had migrated to the coast. (Dayak is the name foreigners have given to all of Borneo's indigenous peoples; the natives themselves use only their tribal names: Penan, Kenyah, Iban, etc.). It was a familiar Third World scene, and one I'd viewed often from the window seat of a bus: indigenous people trying to survive on the bottom rung of capitalism; women struggling to make a home out of plastic tablecloths and broken mirrors; men either unemployed or away at labor camps; children in hot pursuit of the products they see on television.

In Balikpapan I had picked up a guidebook published by the East Kalimantan Tourist Development Board. I decided to see if it had anything to say about the road we were on. It did . . . sort of: "Land travel along the junction turns to be fascinating. Going up and down and something like snake's curb roads with virgin green valleys and hilly landscapes along the sides." It also mentioned an intriguing side trip: "Another further away following the coast road you will come to different panoramic view of sea sand at Tanah Merah . . ."

I went up to the front of the bus to tell Dave about the sea sand, but he was sound asleep.

The Samarinda airport was pretty much banana republic: inside the tiny terminal men in uniform hung around trying to look busy; outside, men in ragged pants and T-shirts hung around smoking, gossiping, and looking for work. The pilots, who wore immaculately pressed white shirts with bars and stripes, ruled the place, along with the weather. They had final say on which planes were leaving, with whom, and when.

We had scheduled a flight with MAF (Mission Aviation Fellowship), a Christian company that not only spreads the gospel in Borneo but connects various Dayak tribes in the forest with the modern world. But it didn't take us long to realize that the scheduled aspect of the flight was an illusion. Dave warned us not to get uptight. "Whatever you do, don't swear, or try to bully your way on a plane," he said. "We're depending on these guys and I don't want to upset them. Also, when Westerners get angry, Indonesians just think it's funny."

I had heard, back in Oakland, about Dave's reputation for "going native." He had lived in Indonesia for several years, spoke the language fluently, and had been in charge of organizing the 1988 Camel Cigarette Trophy Safari across Sumatra. When permits and equipment got held up, instead of pulling rank and threatening bureaucrats the way so many Westerners do, he had waited, maneuvered quietly, and found critical openings.

"He drove a lot of people crazy," said one man who was on the Camel Safari trip, "but in the end everything happened just like he said it would."

I knew what Dave meant about getting angry. Although Indonesians literally elbow each other out of line in markets, they never, ever, raise their voices. And if you get angry they just laugh. I had gotten visibly angry in Indonesia only once. I was out in the country and had an attack of diarrhea. As I headed for the bushes I noticed some young boys following me and motioned them to go away. They exploded in giggles and jumped up and down with delight. Then, in pursuit of even more fun, they came closer and closer. When I yelled at them again they spread out to surround me. Getting desperate and hoping to scare them, I tried a full-tilt temper tantrum, with screeches, shaking fists, the works. Nothing but laughter. They stayed their course and stared at me—at the crazy lady, at the comic-book witch. Finally I had to drop my pants and squat, and after a while they got bored and left.

But this morning it wasn't the kids who were pushy, it was me. We were at the airport in Samarinda, packing and weighing in, and Sylvie, like some sadistic older sister, was deliberately ignoring my meaningful looks. When I couldn't stand it anymore, I came out with it: "Wouldn't now be a good time," I suggested, "for me to start carrying the air mattress?"

She pretended not to hear me and continued packing.

There have been times in my life when I have been gracious and let things like this go, but this was not about to be one of them. I was convinced, in some crazy way, that I had to have an air mattress, that I'd been promised one. I asked her for it again, and this time she muttered something under her breath and walked off. A few moments later I heard Mimo shouting angrily to Dave. Not only did I want a sleeping bag, he said, but an air mattress as well. What was he supposed to sleep on? What was Sylvie supposed to sleep on? Were they suppposed to lie down on the dirt?

When Dave called out, "Tracy, you take the sleeping bag and, Sylvie, you take the air mattress," I just nodded numbly. Now what was I going to do? Go back to California? Give up? I tried to catch Mimo's eye but he looked away. So did Sylvie. Then I got angry. I had been pushy, out of fear, but at least I had an excuse. Why the hell hadn't the jet-setters talked to me instead of complaining to Dave?

Finally, the tiny Cessna started cranking up, and Sylvie appeared with her video camera, shooting Mimo and Olatz waving good-bye. So jolly, so free-spirited, so European. Then she got in the plane and it took off, leaving the rest of us to sit around and eat dust. In another two hours, we followed them. At least one of us was not in a good mood.

4

*F*rom the air, the city of Samarinda looked like a tin-roofed shantytown, and light flicked over the Makassar Strait as if God had stolen the aurora borealis and flattened it. The mouth of the Mahakam was a brown, braided whorl, and we spotted enormous barges in it trailing wakes of roped-together logs. As we left the coast and headed inland over miles and miles of forest, the landscape gradually crumpled into soft hills, and in the distance I could see a sea of razor-sharp peaks and mountains. I began to wonder where all the logging I'd heard about happened.

"This has all been logged," Bill said when I turned around and asked him. "It's secondary growth. See the taller hardwood trees in the canyons where they couldn't be cut?"

We kept the Mahakam on our left for a while, and I watched its brown, silty water swirl through the green lushness in immense, exaggerated loops. It is the main artery into the interior of Kalimantan, a riverine highway populated for almost three hundred miles by Chinese merchants, Indonesian immigrants from Java and Sumatra, and various tribes of Dayaks working in one way or another for the logging industry. Close to its source the Mahakam narrows and runs through some of the most remote rain forest in all of Asia, and it is there, some four hundred miles from the coast, that the Boh River joins it.

The part of the Boh we were going to run was about twenty

miles above its confluence with the Mahakam. There were no unusual villages nearby, no points of interest, no potentially enlightening artifacts, just a steep narrow gorge full of rocks, rapids, and waterfalls. Besides being a feather in Sobek's cap if we made a first descent, we were an experiment in ecotourism. If the gorge could be opened up to commercial rafting trips, Sobek could train local Dayaks to pilot the rafts and the nearby villages could begin to develop a cash economy.

After fifteen minutes or so the pilot turned north and we left the Mahakam and headed over undeveloped forest, broken only by logging roads that seemed to begin and end nowhere, and a few "transmigration" colonies: bulldozed strips of tiny, identical, tin-roofed houses perfectly spaced out in suburbanlike blocks. They had been carved out of the forest by the Indonesian government to encourage migration from the big cities: each family was issued a house, food for a year, an acre and a half of land, and enough rice to plant several crops. But the government overlooked the fact that growing rice is difficult, if not impossible, on the thin layer of soil that underlies a rain forest. And the immigrants that came from the urban slums were ill-equipped to farm in the first place. Most of them, Dave said, just ended up working for the logging companies.

As we continued east into the interior, the mist appeared, at first floating down the canyons and then gradually piling up into great cumulus clouds. Below us the forested ridges rose up like storm-tossed ocean waves and the valleys corkscrewed crazily between them. It was only when we got closer that the landscape looked monotonous, as if a great, soft blanket of vegetation had muffled it. It reminded me of the dark secrets I was reading about in *Lord Jim,* and it was a little frightening to think that we were on board a piece of metal hurtling through the clouds trying to spot a tiny dirt landing strip.

Soon the cloud cover grew as thick as a down comforter, and the forest flashed through only in tiny breaks. The pilot, without saying a word, turned the plane around and headed back to Samarinda.

At the airport we discovered that although the jet-setters had made it in, things looked bad for us. If the clouds didn't break by afternoon, we'd have to wait two days to try again. Tomorrow was Indonesian Independence Day, and no one in all of Indonesia, including the MAF pilots, worked. The terminal had perked up, however, in the hour we'd been in the air. Twenty or so black cars with smoked-glass windows were lined up at the front entrance, and dozens of military officials with walkie-talkies were positioned around the building, some in jungle camouflage, many carrying rifles with bayonets. In back of the building, near the runway, twenty girls in gold sequined dresses were darting in and out of various doorways, and on the tarmac sixty men were lined up ten abreast. They wore red pants, yellow shirts, plaid scarfs, and pointy caps, and each man carried a spear with a topknot of yellow feathers.

"Who's coming?" we asked.

"The sultan of Brunei," everyone said. "The richest man in the world."

I wanted to stay and check the sultan out. I had read about his father in *The Last Adventure* by Osa Johnson, an American adventurer who, along with her husband, established a wildlife camp on the Mahakam River in the 1930s. When Osa was staying at a hotel in Sarawak, then the British part of Borneo, she noticed a parade of beautiful women leaving trays of food each morning in the hallway outside one particular room. A hotel clerk told her that the sultan of Brunei was staying there, and that each of his fifteen wives brought him a delicacy for breakfast. Since only the sultan's "favorite" wife was allowed in his room, the others had to leave their offerings outside the door.

I'd also followed the stories about the current sultan in the press. One of my favorites was a report from a hotel in Canada, in 1987, where the sultan had booked an entire floor for himself and his entourage. Each morning, before he left his room, his male attendants would line the hallways leading to the elevator. When the sultan was ready to go out, he would open the door and ceremoniously hand over to an attendant a large sack of money. Then he'd proceed down the hallway through a sea of bowing heads.

The last I'd heard about the sultan was during the Iran-contra hearings when it was reported that he mistakenly transferred ten million dollars he'd promised to give the Nicaraguan contras into the bank account of a surprised and happy Swiss shipping magnate.

Dave was skeptical about the sultan's appearance: "The sultan of Brunei, the sultan of Brunei; it's always the sultan of Brunei," he said.

William O. Khron, an American doctor who came to Samarinda in the 1920s, wrote about visiting the local sultan, a young man who was obviously bored. The sultan couldn't travel because the British refused to let him leave Borneo, so he spent his time constructing fantasies in his opulent palace. Sometimes, he would take his vast collection of jewels out of the glass boxes where they were on display and play with them. Other times he would go for a ride in one of his three luxury cars.

There was only one small problem with driving, Khron explained: the entire island of Borneo at the time had not one road. To drive his cars the sultan would order a servant to push them onto a dirt "street" perhaps three eighths of a mile long, and then he'd get in one of them, start it up, and drive it down the bumpy path to the end. Because there was no room to turn around, he'd have to put the car in reverse and back it up to the starting point. He'd drive all three cars up and back like this, Khron reported, until he tired of it.

Carl Lumholtz, a Norwegian explorer who visited the same sultan a decade or so later, confirmed the car story and suggested that the sultan had lost some of his playfulness. His "listless pallor," he said, was probably "a result of overindulgence in spiritualistic seances."

The lesson is, you never know about sultans, and I was ready for anything. But the afternoon wore on and the soldiers meandered out of position and the guys with the feather-topped spears sat down on the grass. At last it became clear that no more planes were going to take off that afternoon, and so we gathered up our gear and headed back to Samarinda.

In the bus, Dave, Linda, and I gossiped about our own representatives of the privileged class.

"Did you know," Linda said, "that Mimo lives four months of the year in Ibiza and just travels around the world the rest of the time?"

"And Olatz," I replied, "is going to the Seychelles for some kind of bathing suit shoot after this."

"She's the real thing," Linda said. "I used to work in the fashion business in New York and I can tell."

"I think Sylvie's breathtaking," I said.

"Sylvie's a handsome woman," replied Dave, "but she's pushing thirty. She's already over the hill."

"You're right," said Linda. "She is."

I was speechless. If Sylvie was over the hill, I was a pinprick on the horizon. I wasn't just pushing forty, I was sliding down the other side of it.

5

*A*t the hotel, which sat on top of a hill and was surrounded by manicured lawns and tropical gardens, I heard Linda's stentorian laugh booming out of one of the rooms and knocked on the door to ask if she had an extra bathing suit. She did, but it was a bikini so tiny I ended up wearing a T-shirt over it and flapping around in the pool, certain that everyone thought I had some kind of skin disease. It was the first skirmish in an endless battle I was to have with myself on this trip. On the one hand I wanted not to care about what I wore, or what I looked like. Beauty, in a wild jungle setting, would come from how well I walked over boulders, or flicked a leech off my thigh. On the other hand, with Sylvie and Olatz around, I could see that men were ignoring me and I didn't like it.

I hadn't thought much about aging until a few years ago when, suddenly, it seemed, my skin had crinkled and started sprouting spots and stains. Instead of being pretty I was now perilously close to being well preserved. And now, with my back out, I could no longer rely on my body for much of anything. On this trip I was clearly the oldest and weakest. It was a state of mind and body that didn't do much for my self-confidence.

Around the pool that afternoon I had a chance to talk with Linda, who, in her tiny bikini, seemed more luscious than I had imagined. She was thirty-six, Hispanic (her mother had grown up in Puerto Rico), and full of an inchoate but passionate vitality. She was also unsure of herself in the way many women are now who have no satisfying work. Her ambition, she said, was to be a painter, but she had not seriously pursued it. In New York, before moving to Florida, she had managed a small boutique. Now she spent most of her time taking care of her mother and Bill. She fed Bill's nineteen snakes, two frogs, two large lizards, three cats, and the occasional owl, raccoon, and possum, and when Bill went off on various adventures to remote tropical outposts, she usually accompanied him. Before meeting up with us, they'd been in a dugout canoe paddling up the river Kwai in northern Thailand, on a chartered sailboat cruising Thailand's southern coast, on foot in Taman Negara, Malaysia's largest national park, and on some remote islands near the Philippines, tracking wildlife.

"I didn't know the rain forest existed before I met Bill," she said. "Now I worry about it just like he does. In fact, sometimes when I hear him talk about how fast it's being destroyed, I start to cry. I really do. It's so sad, what's happening to the rain forest. It really is just . . . so . . . sad."

We pondered the sadness for a moment as we watched the wives of visiting lumber executives play with their kids in the pool. A decade ago I would have passed judgment on them: housewives, who fiddled away their lives while their husbands raped the planet. But as a journalist I've interviewed enough women to know that all I can judge at first glance, or even at first meeting, is their style. Besides, my own profession—print journalism—has eaten up and spit out enough trees to denude a great deal of the planet.

"Bill really isn't my type," Linda continued, "but he's such a good person, and I truly do respect his character. Sometimes I think that's everything; sometimes I'm not sure. Also, he does have his arty side."

"So you can talk to him about art?" I asked.

"Well . . . no. But he likes music. He knows music and has great taste."

"What does he like?"

"Oh, modern stuff."

"Like . . . John Cage?"

"Oh . . . he has every single record ever recorded by Oingo Boingo."

Later that evening the cars with the smoked glass and the military officials with the walkie-talkies popped into my life again, this time at the hotel. A porter carrying in the luggage confirmed that the sultan of Brunei had indeed arrived. After dinner I skulked about the lobby a bit, hoping to see the sultan and maybe get an invite to the palace. The palace, built in 1984 and continuously remodeled, has 1,778 rooms and fifty acres of floor space. It has a parking lot to house the sultan's 350 cars, and an airport for his personalized Boeing 747s. If I met the sultan, I figured I'd be nice to him. He was rich; he might toss me a few thousand dollars.

But all that happened was that two middle-aged men in suits came up and introduced themselves:

"Hello, I am Mr. Jones, the minister of communication."

"Hello, I am Mr. Smith, the minister of the arts. Where are you from?"

"America."

"Oh, very beautiful. Very beautiful. What is your name?"

"Tracy."

"Very beautiful. I am sorry we must go to ceremony now, but later tonight you will have drink with us."

"I'd love to. But I'm afraid the timing is wrong. I'm so jet-lagged I can't stay awake."

"But we have booze."

"Are you with the sultan of Brunei?"

"We have Jack Daniel's."

"Will the sultan be there?"

"No, no, no. Not the sultan. The governor."

"The governor?"

"The governor of Sarawak."

Dave was right.

I went to bed and turned on the television set. The hotel had two channels—one of them CNN—and there was Dave Dravecky falling to the ground in pain, his comeback career over, and there was Leona Helmsley being interviewed on the courthouse steps. Kitty of *Gunsmoke* had just died, and Bumble Bee Tuna, a subsidiary of the Pillsbury Company, which had just been bought by Grand Metropolitan PLC of Britain, had been sold to a Thai company to pay off Pillsbury's takeover debt.

It wasn't until midnight that I was finally able to fall into a deep sleep.

At one o'clock the phone rang. It was the minister of communication:

"Hello, Tracy."

"What time is it?"

"We are having a party in room two-twelve. Ha ha ha. You must come."

"I was asleep."

"But, Tracy, ha ha ha, surely you want to have good time."

"I'm sorry, I'm too tired."

"You are not tired."

"Yes, I am."

"Just for few minutes."

"I'm sorry."

"Tracy, Tracy, ha ha ha, you must come."

"No."

"Tracy, come."

At two o'clock the phone rang again. It was the minister of the arts.

"Hello, Tracy."

"Dammit."

"Tracy, you must come to our party. Room two-twelve."

"I'm still asleep."

"Oh-h-h-h-h. Tsk tsk tsk. You must not think about sleep. You must have some fun."

I groaned.

"Tracy. Tracy. Tracy. I want to be your friend."

Again I groaned.

"We are from different cultures, Tracy. We must take this opportunity to know each other. You and me. You must come to Sarawak. It is very beautiful. I must come to U.S. It is beautiful also—no? We must become friends."

"Some other time."

"But we have only tonight. Tomorrow morning early we are leaving."

"I can't. I have to get some sleep."

"Then you don't want to become friends."

"I would if I could."

"No, you wouldn't."

"Yes, I would."

"No, you wouldn't."

Click.

Great. The only two men in greater Borneo who wanted to talk to me, and they were both obnoxious bureaucrats. I wondered if they acted like that with Indonesian women, or if they thought they could get away with it because I was an American.

I spent the rest of the night half awake, slipping in and out of a fuguelike dream state populated by old boyfriends getting horribly sick and dying while my husband, somewhere in the background, refused to help. I thought about how one of the pleasures of traveling is flirting with strangers, or used to be before I got married. I wondered how much I had counted on it when I'd traveled alone; how much I was going to miss it.

6

*T*he next morning, after several cups of delicious Indonesian coffee, I decided to take the advice of my East Kalimantan guidebook: "If you would like to roam around, you might as well practice your legs to do the walking." I staggered out in the street, confused by jet lag, exhausted from lack of sleep, and jittery from far too much caffeine. I was determined, however, to find out how Samarinda was going to celebrate Indonesian Independence Day. After three centuries of Dutch rule and three years of Japanese occupation, I figured it would be a holiday enthusiastically staged by the government, nationalism being an important psychological tool for keeping some 13,009 islands and seven hundred language groups united.

Not much was happening around the hotel: no beer (Indonesia is 80 percent Muslim), no hot dogs, no band concerts. So I decided to head for the poorest part of town where whatever was happening would be happening in the streets. There, in a market, I found knots of adults applauding and cheering and young boys competing for prizes: little boys racing to a finish line in gunny sacks; bigger boys trying to clumb up greased poles; macho boys bobbing for coins stuck in a fruit covered with fiery hot sauce. The official government parade, I was told, with floats and marching bands, would be downtown, tomorrow morning.

That afternoon I suggested to the group that we all share a

taxi and explore the city. Linda and Bill said they wanted to stay by the pool, but Howard and Stuart, the two Aussies, said they wanted to go, as did John, the pipe-smoking lawyer (his Coke-bottle glasses now replaced with contact lenses). Once we were in the car, however, I realized that neither Stuart, Howard, nor John had any idea of what to do next. Stuart was young and enthusiastic, but not an experienced traveler. Howard was shy and seemed embarrassed to ask for anything special. John expressed no thoughts or opinions on anything whatsoever, although whenever I asked him if he wanted to go someplace, he would consider it carefully and then answer with a decisive No or Yes. Not "okay," or "not really." Just No. Or Yes.

When William O. Khron (the man who'd written about the young sultan's driving habits) stayed in Samarinda in the 1920s, there were no hotels, so he took a room at a Dutch guest house that had a veranda and an expanse of lawn sloping down to the Mahakam. Next door was an opera company where he saw an opera based on a Dayak story performed by natives. The Dayak king in the opera, Khron wrote, wore "a derby hat, choker collar, blue shirt, cavalry boots and golf knickerbockers trimmed with gold lace over white tape."

Khron also visited a Dutch colonial court and attended the sentencing of a Malaysian man found guilty of stealing a piece of luggage. A Muslim dignitary was there as a "friend of the prisoner," and the judge asked him for advice.

"Cut the hand that did the stealing off at the wrist," the Muslim said.

"Some friend," thought Khron.

He was less critical of the judge.

"Of course the suggestion of the Mohammed's adviser and friend of the prisoner was but a pro forma matter, and had no real weight with the judge. It simply shows the finesse employed by Holland in its administration of colonial affairs. The mother country takes into consideration all the customs of the native inhabitants, no matter how queer and quirky they may be. This is the secret of her strength in governing her millions of subjects in colonies comprising territory fifty times her own size . . . she regards the natives as children, governs them as children, and they like her maternal attitude."

When we came to a small river that seemed to run right through Samarinda's shantytown, I asked the taxi driver to stop. It might be fun to explore the place, I said. Howard, Stuart, and John looked a little embarrassed and shrugged. I set off down a dirt path that served as a road between the rows of small, patched tin-roofed shacks, and it was as if I were walking through a tiny open-air city. I walked around people cooking, sewing, repairing baskets, mending furniture. Everyone smiled or waved. The young men were gathered in tight circles, gambling, and in back of me was the usual trail of giggling children. When the giggles reached a new level, I turned around and saw John, who had decided to brave the intimacy and was now completely surrounded. He was holding his pipe up over the children's heads and grinning. Several yards behind him I could see the white faces of Howard and Stuart rising above the crowd, like balloons in a circus.

The attention was familiar to anyone who has traveled in a Third World country: it comes from an abrupt rise in status. We were in a neighborhood where people could live for a year on the change in our pockets, and we'd descended into it from someplace they'd heard about but could never know. We were like movie stars. Or sultans.

After a while I walked over to the river and saw, side by side, on rickety piers and anchored logs, men, women, and children bathing, chatting, brushing their teeth, and squatting casually to defecate. For those who wished privacy, their were tiny outhouses built over the river at the end of wooden planks. The river was a combination backyard, kitchen, bathtub, and toilet.

As I stood watching a woman and a baldheaded boy washing vegetables, I realized that in Samarinda's shantytown I had reached one of my personal limits. I would rather have spent all night drinking with the minister of communication than brush my teeth with that water. The theme of my journey was beginning to emerge. Getting old. Getting fearful. Getting . . . smarter?

In the middle of these musings the baldheaded boy suddenly appeared at my side and offered me a glass of yellowish liquid. I took it with reluctance. It was cold.

"Water bad, *gelek*," I said to the boy, finally. Maybe I could explain. "For me, *sakit,* makes me sick."

The boy hesitated and looked back at the woman, who seemed to be his mother. She was looking at me.

"*Sakit,*" I said again, and pantomined being sick to my stomach. The boy looked at his mother again and I heard her call out to him. I stood there paralyzed for a moment, then simply handed back the glass, gave a friendly wave, and began walking off. I had thought about offering the boy money but decided his mother would be offended. Then I asked myself how bad I'd feel if the sultan of Brunei had come sauntering through the hotel lobby last night and tossed me a few thousand dollars. Pretty sure of the answer, I reached in my purse, took out a good-sized rupiah note, and walked back to the boy and gave it to him. His mother clasped her hands in front on her and gave a small bow of thanks.

I walked back to the car as the sultan must have walked through those hotel corridors—with my sack of money. If I was a queen, it was a queen of materialism.

Later that evening, when I was telling a BBC Television producer at the hotel bar about my fear of brushing my teeth with water that had turds floating through it, he commented that 34 percent of all Americans wouldn't eat a cookie if it had dropped on grass. Not dropped on dirt, he emphasized. Dropped on grass.

7

*T*he next morning at the airport we were on our best behavior. The sky was clear, the missionary pilots smoked cigarettes and drank cups of tea, the planes sat on the runway, and we politely waited. And waited. Dave sat with us, in case we got righteous and started to scream at someone about Jesus, but we didn't, and finally, just as Dave said it would, our moment came. We were waved into a plane and once again we took off, heading northwest along the Mahakam. This time the skies remained at least partly clear past the logging roads. As we flew further inland the plane bounded and shuddered and plunged in and out of some clouds. The pilot strained to see a recognizable landmark— a river, or a waterfall—and as we swooped and turned the tangle of green came closer. The rain forest now looked like a vast garden of broccoli: its texture was that nubbly and dense.

We had heard about a plane that had engine failure in this general area. It had crashed into the top of the canopy, flipped upside down, and stayed there, hanging in the trees. Everyone got out alive except for one woman who panicked, unbuckled her seat belt, and was ripped apart by a tree branch as she fell.

Eventually the pilot pointed his finger toward a ridge poking up above the clouds and we headed for it. On the other side, the clouds miraculously parted and we could see a river. "The Boh," Dave's voice sang out.

Compared to the Mahakam, the Boh River was tiny and fierce, and carved very deep into a steep, narrow canyon. I would have liked more time to study it, but suddenly it became apparent that the pilot was about to land—right in the treetops, it seemed—and I concentrated on trying to find a landing strip. I needed to see what he had in mind to make sure that his certainty of eternal salvation had not given him a cavalier view of earthly life. I looked around. Howard and Stuart, the two Aussies, were smiling and nonchalant. Linda was hunkered down in her seat studying the lock on her seat belt. Bill was looking out the window intently. John's pipe was on his lap and he was peering out the window—no, he was fast asleep.

Just as we were about to crash into the trees, we saw it: a tiny grass rectangle next to what looked like a resort—a colony of tin-roofed longhouses and several smaller wooden structures surrounded by a vast cut lawn and palm trees.

"Long Lebusan," the pilot called out. John's head jerked up.

The dark ironwood longhouse we were ushered into was like all the Dayak longhouses I'd read about: huge and raised perhaps six feet off the ground. This one was maybe half a football field in length and forty feet wide. One British explorer described a longhouse as an "enormously elongated English farmhouse on stilts"; another called it a "jungle metropolis." What it felt like to me was the set of a Hollywood western. The covered veranda, which ran the entire length of the house, could have been a boardwalk on Main Street. It was made of weathered wooden planks, and the villagers clearly used it to meet and chat. Women were husking rice on it in huge wooden mortars, and sifting the grain in round, flat baskets. Opening onto the veranda were eight doors that led to enclosed family rooms.

Long Lebusan had three longhouses in a single row, making the effective village main street almost half again as long as a football field. It felt oddly familiar. I could see the gunslingers riding into town and hitching their horses—or their monitor lizards, or their orangutans—to the tall carved wooden poles at the edge of the veranda and stomping throught the doors for a drink.

It was harvest time when we arrived, and the village men were away in the rice fields. But there were plenty of children and dogs around, and there was Mimo, squatting on the floor and shaking a winnowing basket. He was wearing a sarong around his hips and a long scarf wrapped around his head, and with his longish nose and three-day-old beard he looked a little like Yasir Arafat.

Inside the longhouse we met Raymond, the tenth member of our group and the one who had flown to Long Lebusan early, with the guides. He was busy supervising lunch and talking in rapid Indonesian to a woman who squatted over a wood fire in a tiny alcove. He looked like an English cricketer or nineteenth-century colonialist, tall and thin and dressed entirely in white: white tennis shoes, white socks, a long-sleeved white shirt, and white pants. He was American, however, in his twenties. He greeted us perfunctorily and left.

Sylvie and Olatz were also in the longhouse, similarly un-friendly. Sylvie's left eyelid was swollen from some kind of insect bite, and Olatz was packing her gear.

Then Olatz came over to Linda and me: "Look," she said, pulling up her pants to show us her perfectly shaped calves. They were covered with tiny red flea bites.

"I'm going to take the plane out. I have a job in two weeks and I can't do it if my legs look like this."

We both had to agree.

Just then Sylvie started yelling and I saw John, the lawyer, look up from his camera.

"Eef you take my peekture," Sylvie roared, "I will reep the feelm out of your camahrah!"

John just stared at her with his mouth open.

"I mean eet," she said.

"I hear you," said John, and put on his lens cap.

"How would you like it," Olatz said, "if someone tried to take your picture when you weren't looking good?"

I was astonished that Olatz or Sylvie might think a mere swollen eyelid could diminish their beauty and was about to make a joke to that effect. But then I looked at Sylvie and saw that she was truly upset.

Moments later Raymond appeared again, announcing lunch.

"It's not very good," he said, "just rice and some kind of vegetable. I don't know what they eat here. We couldn't get even this much until they sent for a Chinese woman from another village to come and cook."

The food was fine with me: I like rice and greens. Also, I had read about what the natives of Borneo ate: rats and monkeys, porcupines and lizards. One tribe mixed the flesh of a dead animal with certain barks and herbs, packed it in the hollow lumen of a bamboo shoot, and buried it for six to eight months. The result, when exhumed, was a jellylike mass of necrotic material that was served up especially for visitors.

Sometimes it's good not to ask for special favors.

8

*A*s we were staking out our sleeping spots in the longhouse, mostly on the floor of an open communal area, I noticed that not only did Sylvie have an air mattress, so did everyone else. I told myself to stop worrying about it, that no one ever died from loss of sleep. But, the fact is, the thought of waking up on a hard rock bed with my hips and back hurting night after night rekindled some of the old insomnia terror. I hadn't realized how quickly the sleep monster could be summoned.

Then Dave appeared with the two other Sobek guides and introduced them: Gary Bolton and Mike Speaks. Gary, in his middle thirties, was tall, slender, and bearded; if I'd seen him in another context I'd have pegged him for a biologist. When he introduced himself he seemed hesitant, speaking in small bursts and stops as if he were searching for the right word, the right image. It wasn't what I'd come to expect from river guides, who tend to be almost theatrical free spirits—storytellers and tricksters who ward off their clients' fears with a joke. Gary was serious. So serious, in fact, that the jet-setters, who'd spent two days in Long Lebusan with him, had already dubbed him "the priest." I suspected he had some intellectal passion: writing plays, collecting birds' nests, composing nocturnes.

But then Gary said that for seventeen years he'd worked as a guide and manager of a rafting company on the Colorado River in the Grand Canyon. The Colorado is one of the truly great rivers of the world, so I was impressed. But I also was surprised that he'd been chosen for an exploratory trip. The Colorado is a big river, but the run through it doesn't change much. On an exploratory trip we'd need people familiar with all kinds of white water, someone who could deal with the unexpected.

Mike, the second boatman, was Gary's opposite. He looked as if he belonged outdoors, as if he would be at ease lashed to a tree in a howling thunderstorm. He introduced himself briefly, saying he'd led river trips all over the world, particularly in Alaska and Africa, but what lingered with me most was his accent. He was from Alabama and his drawl was slow and seductive. He also had a beautiful well-muscled body and an extraordinary physical grace, the kind of physicality you have to be born with. He wore a headband, which he claimed was only to keep the hair out of his eyes, but along with his wire-rimmed glasses the look was classic: a sensitive outlaw; an outlaw athlete.

Sylvie, I noticed, paid him particular attention. I heard her ask Mike to look at her eyelid, which he did, smoothing her hair away from her face with his hands.

"It will be gone by tomorrow," he said, as Sylvie looked up at him with her great flashing eyes.

Later I heard her video camera whirring and saw that she was shooting Mike standing in the doorway, in the light.

By early afternoon the village had quieted down; most of the men were still out in the rice fields, and the women had gone down to the river or were farther down the longhouse in their family rooms. A few were on the veranda husking rice with a heavy seven-foot-long wooden pestle. They pounded the pestle into an ironwood mortar and brushed the grains back into place with their bare feet. I tried out some of my Indonesian phrases on one woman, but she didn't understand. Long Lebusan was a Kenyah village and only a few of the villagers—all of them men—spoke Indonesian. But the woman seemed friendly and confident and I liked her. We got along by smiling and watching the children, and after a while she handed me one of the big wooden pestles and I tried husking rice while she laughed.

Eventually, the slow *thump, thump, thump, swish, thump* of the pounding was soporific. Dogs lay curled up on the wooden floor, and the sunlight came down on the large grass field in front of the longhouses through a misty haze. Gary said that for three days preceding our arrival, the villagers had been out on the grass, cutting it with knives. The resulting lawns along with the palm trees were what made the village seem so familiar, as if there must be some archetypical blueprint for tropical paradise.

Mimo appeared from somewhere to tell us that he and Sylvie and Olatz had gone in a dugout canoe yesterday to see the gorge and that it looked bad, with no place to sleep, let alone camp. "If you're worried about your back . . . ?" he said, looking at me.

I'm not good at apologies, and hadn't really thought this one out, but I forced myself to take a big breath and plunge ahead: "I want to apologize about the air mattress," I began. "I certainly didn't mean to leave you with nothing to sleep on. It was . . . a misunderstanding. But . . . I know I was rude. I guess I'm just terrified that my back will go out and you'll have to leave me lying by the side of the river."

"You know," Mimo said, "I'd think twice if I were you about sleeping on those rocks."

For a moment I wanted to hit him. Was he ignoring my noble effort? Or, worse, was he trying to get me off the trip? But the moment passed, and I realized he might actually know something I didn't. In his turban and sarong he certainly looked the part of a native savant.

A little later I overheard Mike and Sylvie talking about whether she should fly back to Bali with Olatz. Sylvie had initially signed up for this trip along with a group of five friends: Mimo, Olatz, Sylvie's boyfriend Richard, Laura Steinberg (the ex-wife of New York billionaire Saul Steinberg), and a friend of Mimo's, a "wild and crazy" Italian. Steinberg and the Italian had dropped out months ago, and Richard had canceled at the last minute when he got a job working for Warner Bros. Records. Sylvie had come anyway because last year she'd rafted the Zambezi River in Africa and loved it. But now she wasn't sure. She hadn't liked what she'd seen at the entrance to the gorge and hated not knowing what to expect.

Mike told her to do whatever would make her happiest. Then he said that if she was feeling scared now, she should probably turn back. "Don't test yourself," he said. "Not on this trip."

For some reason I thought Mike's warning had nothing to do with me. Sylvie might be a princess; Olatz might be a princess; but I stayed the course and went the distance. Also, I was stubborn. Too stubborn to come this far and turn back.

Raymond, who now seemed to be everywhere, towering over us all like a lofty white ghost, was doing a lot of work for a paying client: organizing meals, working on the boats, planning our activities with the village leaders who spoke Indonesian. But every now and then, if we asked him a question, he'd go out of his way to make us feel stupid. He was either socially inept, I figured, or arrogant. Bill insisted he had guide-in-training status until Raymond told us directly that he'd paid Sobek his $1,950.

That afternoon Raymond made arrangements for a local boatman to take us down to the beginning of the gorge so we could see it for ourselves. We thanked him, and Stuart asked if we'd need to take a daypack. "How should *I* know?" Raymond snapped.

On our way to the river we ran into Sylvie and Mimo again, walking to the airstrip. Sylvie had decided to fly out, she said.

"Oh, then, could . . ." I stopped in mid-sentence and watched her walk off. In the duffel bag slung over her shoulder was an air mattress.

There it goes, I thought to myself, and then, almost perceptibly, I began to relax. I had made the decision to stay and face the night; now I could concentrate on making the best of it.

The river that ran right in front of the village was not the Boh, it turned out, but a tributary. We went down it in a dugout canoe, watching in vain for birds and monkeys and wildlife. It was my first inkling that a rain forest—the ecosystem with the most life per square inch of any place on earth—could seem like a monotonous blanket of green vegetation. Where were all the birds? Where were the monkeys and toucans? When we hit the Boh, which was much bigger but still calm, our boatman turned upstream. We indicated we wanted to go downriver toward the gorge, but he refused to turn around. He tried to tell us why in the Kenyah language but we couldn't get it, and finally he gave up and pulled over to a sandbar. The jungle was ten feet away, and I decided to check it out.

I made my way overland without much problem, sliding through the bushes, grabbing hold of vines, climbing over fallen trees. The big trees had been cut down here, but there were plenty of creepers and woody vines, called lianas. My first surprise was how much of what I touched was rotten. The vines cracked off the trees, logs crumbled in my hands, and the earth was more like compost than dirt, hot and oxidizing. The tree canopy wasn't closed up over my head, so I knew I wasn't walking in primary rain forest, but the world around me was nevertheless a maze of leafy tangles.

After I had gone inland about fifty yards, I realized that everything looked the same and I should probably turn back. I remembered the line from Tom Harrisson, the British paratrooper who had parachuted into the jungle during World War II: "Take two steps off the trail, get disoriented, and no one will ever see you again." I wasn't worried since I had headed in only one direction, away from the river; nevertheless, I turned around and started back, threading my way through the forest litter. But when I came to the river, there were no people and no boat, only the sound of the water lapping at the riverbank. I could see up and down the river for about twenty yards, and there was no sandbar.

I called out but no one answered, so I started making my way upriver, moving as fast as I could. When another turn revealed more monotonous, jungle-covered riverbank, I realized I had no idea if I was above or below the boat. My instincts were obviously wrong; I could be heading further and further in the wrong direction. Suddenly the jungle was hot and it seemed as if the creepers and the leaves were stealing my air. My T-shirt got caught in a prickly creeper and I had to use two hands and my teeth to get it unstuck. I was lost.

I decided to turn around and retrace my steps, but then I arrived at a straight stretch in the river and as far downriver as I could see, there was no sandbar. Maybe what I had come to was another fork of the river and not the one I had started from at all. Maybe I had gotten completely turned around and . . . and . . . maybe . . . ohmygod! Maybe I was covered with leeches. Quick check. Nothing. Moving fast now, and panting, I headed inland to take a shortcut where I saw the river take a bend, trying to remember landmarks—a tall tree, a fallen tree—and then, finally, I heard:

"Tracy! *Tracy!*"

"Coming!" I cried. It was Howard.

"It's amazing in there," I said when I rejoined the group, sweating, breathless. But no one asked me what I had seen. It didn't matter; I was thrilled. Part of the urge to explore is a desire to become lost.

9

*B*ack in the longhouse we saw Sylvie negotiating with a local woman to buy a beaded baby carrier. She'd decided not to fly out with Olatz because the pilot had to stop in another village to pick up a sick woman on a stretcher. If he took Sylvie as well, neither she nor Olatz could bring any luggage.

"I'm sorry about the air mattress," I began, embarrassed that all my conversations with Sylvie seemed to be about the same subject.

But Sylvie wasn't listening. She turned away and started twisting her hair into a coil and then she fastened it in place with a pencil. I decided my apology could wait.

After dinner that night (more rice and greens), we noticed that some of the old men of the village had spread out mats on the floor in our section of the longhouse. They were talking and laughing with each other and with some old women who were hovering nearby. We weren't sure what was going on until Dave pointed out the wooden objects in front of them. The men were hoping, he said, to sell us some handicrafts. I was surprised to see this bit of commercialism in a village that had never known tourism, but when I went over to look at what they were selling, I realized that none of it had been made for us. There were some old bamboo cases for carrying flint, holders for carrying poison arrows, a long blowpipe, some old carved boxes, and a few worn woven skirts for dancing. I wanted to buy something but was hesitant to bargain.

"The prices are Balikpapan prices," Dave to us. "One of the local women who migrated to the coast married a Brit—a guy named Dave Ferguson. He's told them just what to ask."

The old men didn't speak Indonesian, so we started talking to them with our fingers. Five hundred rupiahs? Two hundred? Two for five hundred? Five hundred for three? I felt uncomfortable because there was none of the laughter and joy that usually accompanies hard bargaining in the marketplace. Picking up some of the objects to look at them under the kerosene light and then rejecting them seemed rude. But the men were quiet and had great dignity; the old women were the ones who looked at us and said with their hands and their eyes, "Come on . . . Buy. Buy."

I ended up buying a poison-arrow holder filled with poison-tipped arrows and stayed with the men awhile afterward, hoping, I suppose, that one of them would suddenly burst out speaking perfect English. The men were Kenyahs, one of the tribes that had fought alongside the Allied soldiers who parachuted into the interior of Borneo in 1942 and forced the Japanese down the rivers to the coast. They had participated in one of the great chapters of world history and I wanted to learn something from them. They had been headhunters in their youth—all the Dayak tribes had hunted heads until the 1940s—and had lived in the jungle before missionaries and motorboats. Now they were watching their grandchildren head for the coastal cities and assume Muslim names. They were a generation that had seen the world become transformed at a pace that modern Americans, fretting about future shock, could not imagine. I wanted to ask, in a thousand different ways, that classic primal question of journalism: what it is like to be *you*?

But after an hour or so of talking and laughing among each other, the men rolled up their mats and stood up. The room quieted down as they started walking out, looking small, suddenly, and hunched over. Then, at the door, one of them called out something funny and the longhouse rocked with laughter. Afterward, I went up to one of the old women and gave her the pillowcase that had come with my flowered bed sheet. She grabbed it and held it to her chest and nodded and thanked me with a toothless smile.

At around nine o'clock, Pelanjau, the assistant headman of the village, came to announce that the "show" the villagers had prepared for us was almost ready. Dave translated for us and explained that the main headman of the village had walked to another longhouse to celebrate Independence Day. Pelanjau was an animated, impish man with a crooked smile and easy laugh. He looked a little like an elf, or a mime. He was also the man I remembered Richard Bangs writing about in his book on Indonesia. He had volunteered to show Bangs a *palang*, and had taken him to the schoolhouse, closed the door, pulled up one side of his shorts, and let him look at the rattan dowel that was stuck crosswise through his penis. It was three inches long, Bangs said, and pierced the flesh near the tip. Other *palangs*, Pelanjau had explained, were made of deer horn, or pig bristle, or gold, silver, and copper wire. Recently, some had been fashioned from the shear pins on outboard motors.

The reason Dayak men underwent this painful operation, Pelanjau told Bangs, was because the women wanted them to. "They like it," Pelanjau had said.

Bangs had also told me about Dave Ferguson, the Brit who had convinced the old men to ask high prices for their artifacts. He was a British expat, a university graduate from Ipswich who'd taken off on a trip around the world and never returned. He was working for a French seismic company in Balikpapan when he met his wife, a woman from Long Lebusan who had migrated with her family to the coast. When he came to Long Lebusan to meet her relatives, he fell in love with the village, and although his wife continued to wear Western clothes, he stripped down to a sarong and changed his name to Taman Kahang.

Ferguson had been dismayed to discover that Long Lebusan was losing population and might eventually have to be abandoned, so he devised a number of schemes to help the village out. First he took a collection of wood carvings made by the village men to Balikpapan's finest hotel—only to discover that no one was interested. Then he took the carvings to England and returned even more disappointed. His next plan was a bit more ambitious. He proposed creating a Dayak theme park complete with natives dressed in traditional hunting attire stalking wild boar and deer in a fenced-off area near Balikpapan. Along with this living diorama he envisioned a shop where native men carved wooden figures, and a cultural display with a video of the Kenyahs in their true environment. There would be a zoo with orangutans, crocodiles, bears, and snakes, and a restaurant serving natural jungle food along with Dayak coffee and sugarcane juice.

Alas, there were no takers.

Ferguson's third idea was the one that got Richard Bangs interested: a "Dayak Overland Guide Service." Ferguson had written to individual tour operators all over the world, inviting them on a trek from Long Lebusan to a nearby village, and in 1987 Bangs took up his offer. While they were trekking, Ferguson mentioned the Boh River and the gorge that had never been run, and here I was at the end of a chain from Ferguson to Bangs to me, a chain that was pulling me into the gorge of the Boh.

In my journal that evening I tried to figure out why I had been so determined to pursue this adventure despite the decreasing odds of actually enjoying it, but all I could come up with was the fact that I have always been excited by uncertainty, hated the notion that something predictable lay ahead. It was as good a reason for coming to Borneo as the one given by Mr. Carvath Wells, an Englishman who had come to Samarinda in the early 1900s. On the first page of his book he explains:

"One morning in May, after getting out of bed on the wrong side and making the baby cry, I determined to quit my job of Assistant Professor of Civil Engineering and look for something dangerous."

Before we walked down to the middle of the three longhouses

for the evening's performances, Dave announced that the guides had decided the river was at an acceptable level to run. The water level had come up and gone down a couple of times since Gary and Mike had been watching it, but it hadn't rained in two days now and was substantially below its high-water mark. It was lower, the villagers said, than when ABC had scouted it.

"Are we going for sure?" asked Bill.

"If the water level holds overnight, we'll be putting in early tomorrow morning."

"How early?" asked Linda. "Can we get some sleep?"

"I don't know," said Dave. "There's a party."

10

*D*ayak parties were one of the reasons almost all of the modern adventurers had fallen in love with Borneo: they were drunken and hilarious. Most had a spiritual purpose that became clearer after a lot of *tuak,* or rice wine, but there was always plenty of dancing and silliness. Anthropologist Peter Metcalf writes that a Dayak party without noise, confusion, and laughter is considered a failure because the whole idea of it is to demonstrate spontaneous vitality. Sexual license, he explains, restores a village's vigor. Exuberance breaks a village free from the grip of death.

American adventurer Eric Hansen first came to Borneo in 1976, and was invited to a party at an Iban village that started off with him having to participate in what must surely be one of the world's strangest party games. He was given a live rooster and told to hit every man, woman, and child in the longhouse over the head with it. He started out giving people little taps, but one woman took the rooster from him and demonstrated how to do it right: grab the bird by the legs and swing it like a tennis racket. She demonstrated sizzling backhands and overhead smashes. By the time Hansen was finished, everyone was roaring with laughter and the rooster was dead.

And that was just the beginning. He was encouraged to drink glass after glass of *tuak,* and as the evening progressed young men grabbed old women and pantomimed humping them for laughs, young girls were made to sing and then grabbed and smeared with pot black, and one old man went so berserk he had to be tied to a post with jungle vines. Guns were fired into the jungle; men, women, and children got sick over the longhouse railings; unmarried men and women went off into the jungle in new couplings; and finally the entire longhouse caught fire.

The party that made James Barclay, a British writer, decide to spend a few months walking across Borneo began with him being pinned down by a bunch of Iban girls ("a wild bunch of Amazons") who tore off his shirt, put a bottle of liquor in his mouth, held back his head, and forced him to drink. From then on, by his account, the party got even more vivid:

". . . all along the common room, swaying in the oil lamp-lights, were hundreds of contorting bodies; from a distance they resembled a heaving mass of maggots inside a long dark piece of putrid flesh. . . . In moments of fleeting sobriety it made a memorable scene. The great longhouse, surrounded by jungle, with the small river winding among the trees in front, the occasional glimpse of the moon through the rolling clouds, the continual reverberating throb of the drums and gongs, the excited shrieks, screams and shouts of the people, the hot, sultry weather and the pleasant muzziness induced by the hooch."

The late-nineteenth-century explorers did not admit to getting drunk themselves, but they seemed to have attended the same wild parties. When Spenser St. John, a British naturalist and "Her Majesty's Counsel-general in the great island of Borneo," went into the interior of Borneo in 1858, he attended a three-day party to initiate priestesses. The village women, he said, painted coconuts, dipped them in soot, and ran up and down the longhouse, tossing them through the rafters like hot potatoes. When their skin became almost completely black with soot, the young women starting "howling dolefully" around an altar, and the old women climbed up to the rafters and mounted some crude swings. For three nights the villagers danced and sang while the women cavorted and the men beat drums, and in the middle of it all was a display of publicly induced catatonia so strange that St. John had no explanation for it. The village children were made to lie down on the floor of the longhouse, then loosely tied up and covered with a cloth. There they remained prostrate, "like a row of logs," while the celebration continued throughout the night.

In 1952, Malcolm MacDonald, governor-general of Malaysia and British Borneo, described a typical evening of revelry at a Kenyah village during which an event occurred that I can only think of as a form of alimentary rape. MacDonald, like Hansen and Barclay, spoke of it with some fondness. Selected male guests at such a party, he wrote, would be given, one by one, a rattan straw and urged to suck enough *tuak* from a large urn to reduce the level by two inches. The man would protest that he couldn't possibly drink that much, but then the prettiest young girls in the village would walk up to him, put their arms affectionately around his waist, and push and prod him until he succumbed. "The man," wrote MacDonald, "flattered by their deliciously friendly attentions, would allow himself to be led to the pot, as an innocent lamb might be led with music, garlands, and laughter to the slaughter.

"With a self-confident smile he would put his lips to the rattan and start sucking at the liquor. After a while his powers of in-bibing began to flag, and he would try to disengage himself. Sweet female voices would then tell him that his task was not yet finished, and that he should persevere a little longer. If he sought to lift his head from the straw, the pressure of their hands on the back of his neck would increase. Indeed they forced him to stay where he was."

And while all this was happening, the pretense that everyone was participating in a flirtatious, friendly game was kept up; the women would giggle shyly and let their hair brush against the man's face, and the audience would cheer and demand that he drink.

Eventually, said MacDonald, the poor fellow would try to indicate how seriously miserable he was by shouting and trying to twist his body around to escape. But the women, still stroking his shoulders and caressing his cheeks, would strengthen their grip on his head and now grab firm hold of his shoulders and his wrists. If he grew more impatient, they would actually kick him on the shins or give him a smack on his behind. The bottom line was that unless the man wanted to try to actually punch out the young village girls, he had to do what they said. It was, as MacDonald pointed out with some relish, "an unequal struggle."

My modern guidebook mentioned only one Dayak celebration—the kwangkai traditional ceremony—but it didn't sound as if it would be much fun.

"The term 'kwangkai,'" it said, "is often misinterpreted as 'buang bangkai' (throwing the corpse). This is not true since in the ceremony itself there is not any corpse to be thrown.

" 'Kwangkai' traditional ceremony is a formal occasion on reburying (the second time) the remained bones of the corpse which was buried in the ground or kept inside lungun (wooden coffin). The ceremony is still actual for Dayak Benuaq and Dayak Tunjung tribe. It usually lasts 1 x 7 days, 2 x 7 days, 3 x 7 days and more depend on family's ability to accomplish the ceremony . . . The climax of this ceremony is witnessed by thousand of spectators coming from neighboring villages, the sacrificed animal is killed by some people using lances or stab at it with sharp weapons until the animal is helpless."

I hoped it wasn't a kwangkai traditional ceremony that we were about to witness: I've never relished the idea of digging up tropical corpses and I hate arithmetic.

11

*F*or better or worse, it looked as if our party was going to be more of a performance than a free-for-all. Christian missionaries had come to Long Lebusan (the village now had two churches, one Protestant, one Catholic), and there was a ban on alcohol.

We walked to the main longhouse, where over one hundred people were arranged in an orderly semicircle on the veranda, creating a stage. When we took our seats the village children shifted to sit facing us, as if we were the main attraction, and we kept them giggling and falling on the floor in laughter as we took photos, made faces, and in general tried to achieve a polite combination of silliness and respect. Then Pelanjau came out on stage and gave a signal for silence.

It was a show, all right, and he was the master of ceremonies. Although we didn't understand a word of what he said, it was fun to watch him work the crowd. There were the warm-up jokes, a "seriously, folks" part, and finally two prayers, one Christian and one Kenyah.Then, with a burst of gongs and drumbeats, the first group of dancers came out.

These were the most beautiful young women in the village, dressed in stunning costumes of sequins, velvet, feathers, and bone. Their movements were simple, but their figures were perfect, their carriage erect, and their necks and fingers swayed subtly to the drumbeat. The point was their beauty, and we applauded. Then more groups of women came onstage, in different costumes, equally beautiful. It was pleasant enough, but after an hour or so I began to think fondly of coconut tossing and rooster bashing. When Eric Hansen visited Long Lebusan in 1982, he attended a party that was beginning to sound similar to this one. It was given for a much-disliked guest of honor, and was so interminable he decided it must be a "subtle form of revenge."

But then, just as I was floating off in my mind, rising up over the longhouse to some point in the sky where the moon turned the earth silvery white and the longhouse, way down below in a tiny clearing, throbbed with the slow rhythms of gongs and "the heaving mass of maggots" Barclay wrote about, a single dancer came onstage. He was dressed in tree bark, animal skins, feathers, and shells, and carried a painted wooden shield and a *mandau,* or headhunting sword. He remained poised in an intense crouch for perhaps thirty seconds, and then suddenly gave an animal leap that caused all of us to gasp.

It was the beginning of the famous Kenyah headhunting dance. The dancer was a beautiful man with a well muscled body, and in an absolutely still pose he looked like a bird, or a bronzed Hindu god. With his first movement it was clear we were about to see some extraordinary dancing. Slowly, he twisted into an attack position—knees bent, fingers and toes spread out, neck in conscious counterpoint—and then he whirled as if in flight, or battle, keeping his intense muscular control but capturing a feeling of frenzy or abandon. He crossed one leg in front of the other and spiraled downward, seeming to make two complete revolutions; then he froze again and slowly began to uncurl. The dance was a perfect translation of violence into grace. It reminded me of palace dances in Thailand, court performances in Java, and temple dancing in Bali. I wondered if it went back to the Mongolians, the first people to migrate to Borneo in 5000 B.C.

There was another extraordinary solo hunting dance after that, and then it was time for the Hornbill Dance. The hornbill— a beautiful, long-tailed, large-beaked bird almost as big as a swan—is one of the most spiritually important birds of the rain forest, and many of the Dayak tribes have a dance in honor of it. A woman appeared onstage with a clutch of the hornbill's eighteen-inch-long tail feathers spread out between her fingers, and like the stately, leisurely flight of the bird, she twisted and dipped in measured movements, using her entire body to simulate the bird's grace.

It was midnight when we were shocked into attention by a loud blast of Indonesian pop music and three young village women prancing onstage wearing shorts, T-shirts, sunglasses, and curly wigs. They looked both silly and lascivious. They started dancing wildly—wiggling their behinds, flinging their arms and feet out like rag dolls, and making goofy faces—while a young man with an immense boom box carried it onstage and sat down with it blasting amidst the now stilled gongs and drums. It took us a minute to realize what was going on and why everyone was snickering and giggling: then we got it. They were dancing like Westerners, like rock-and-roll stars. They were making fun of us.

Soon the children were jumping up and down, and the villagers were holding their sides and doubling up with laughter, and it didn't take long for us to become equally hysterical, laughing with the kind of abandon that comes from suddenly perceiving that everything, including oneself, has a role in some grand, cosmic joke.

Then the three bewigged women came into the audience and grabbed Dave, Gary, Mike, and Raymond, and led them up onstage. No one was drunk, but the Kenyahs weren't going to let that stand in their way. And all the Americans, even Raymond and Gary, got the point and started dancing like monkeys, dancing like acid freaks. The girls started to trip them, and pretty soon they were all falling down and laughing and wriggling, and we were all laughing and laughing with them. In the end, dancers and spectators alike had tears in their eyes—Kenyah tears, American and Italian tears, French and Australian tears. It was a moment of grace.

By the time the show ended at about one o'clock in the morning, Long Lebusan felt very familiar, like a small town in America before television and radio. I noticed some of the evening's "costumes" on the floor and went over to examine them: there was a long, soft, scarflike material made of tree bark and a headdress of feathers and shells and stones. In a place of honor was a clouded leopard skin, the black-and-white pelt of Borneo's most beautiful and elusive animal. I imagined it must have been killed by a very great hunter.

Suddenly the old woman to whom I'd given the pillowcase appeared and took my hand and pressed it softly and briefly to her cheek. We smiled and I took her hand in mine, and then we parted. There was a sweetness in the air, and a warmth that felt like church.

Before bedding down for the night I walked to the river to pee, stepping on God knows how many forest creatures and at least one outraged chicken. As I stood in the water in complete darkness, I heard other people moving quietly in the distance—in the river, in the forest. Mostly, however, I heard the quiet rush of the river and my heartbeat amidst a cacophony of insect calls.

12

At four-thirty the next morning the dogs began howling and then the roosters kicked in. By five all the infants in the village were wailing, and by five-thirty the older kids were running along the veranda on the loose, clanking floorboards. It was like sleeping courtside in a basketball gym. Finally I gave up trying to ignore the racket and sent a prayer of thanks to the missionaries. At least I didn't have a hangover.

By eight o'clock we had eaten a quick breakfast of oatmeal and canned milk and assembled at the river where the boats were inflated and rigged. There were three boats—two larger oar boats and one small paddle boat—"Avons," river runners call them. Most of the time they look like immense inflated bathtub toys, but here on the banks of the dark green river they seemed completely alien, like some kind of futuristic space capsules, comfortingly invincible.

They reminded me of a story I'd heard from an old man who had trekked high in the Hindu Kush in Pakistan. At one point he came to a river that had no bridge. As he stood there, bewildered as to how to get across, a young boy appeared and asked, in sign language, if he wanted to get to the other side. He nodded, and the boy ran down to the river and picked up a goatskin covered with maggots. The goat had been gutted entirely through one of its legs and could be inflated like a balloon. The boy brushed off the maggots, blew it up, tied it off, lashed a platform made of branches to it and—*violà!*—a raft.

Our boats had the aesthetic of running shoes, all turbo-hydro-psycho-dynamic. Made out of nylon covered with neoprene covered with hypolon and inflated with a foot pump, they were battleship gray with yellow stripes. Our food and gear were strapped to a pontoon in the middle of each; passengers straddled the outside tubes.

While we all waited, the guides tied our provisions to the boats: first the food and tents, then our own personal dry bags for clothing (made of heavy rubber folded over and buckled), and on top of that, white plastic helmets and extra life jackets. Finally, they roped on our "ammo boxes": sturdy, waterproof, metal boxes for our personal use. They were just big enough to fit a camera, some suntan lotion, mosquito repellent, and a crumpled sun hat.

Sylvie had made a friend in the village who didn't leave her side that morning: a particularly beautiful Kenyah girl, about seven years old. She had come to say good-bye dressed up like a Western doll. Her dress was ragged and full of holes, but her silky black hair was curled (we had seen it last night wrapped around rolled leaves and tied with pieces of rattan), and she and Sylvie combed each other's hair and held hands and touched each other's clothes and hugged until it was time for us to get in the boats. When Sylvie started to go the girl began to cry quietly, and Sylvie took a scarf from around her wrist and knelt down and arranged it like a ribbon in the girl's hair. It was a sweet moment of universal girltalk.

Before we got in the boats, Pelanjau orchestrated the closing ceremonies. Thank yous were given, prayers were offered, women cried, and the old woman tried to speak to me. As we pushed off into the river I looked at my watch (10:15) and noted that in a few hours we would be entering a part of the world that perhaps only twenty humans had ever seen.

*   *   *

There is a definite physical hierarchy in serious adventuring, and it's wise to know your place, which in my case was close to the bottom. When Dave had asked us to choose which boat we wanted to be in—either the fun boat where everyone paddles or the wimp boat where a single boatman oars—I felt as if a ghost had suddenly joined me there on the shores of the river, a dark voice telling me to get cautious. I'd done quite a bit of back-packing and trekking, but most of it was over six years ago. And just a month earlier I had abruptly entered a world of doctors, physical therapists, and talk about chronic back pain. I had no idea if paddling would hurt my back or help it, no idea of how careful I had to be; I just knew that for everyone's sake I had to err on the side of caution. Pushing my body on this trip would not be courageous; it would be stupid.

There were two oar boats, which Dave had assigned to Gary and Mike. He would command the paddle boat, which could hold as many as six people. When Dave asked who wanted to go on the paddle boat, Howard and Stewart, Bill and Linda, and Mimo raised their hands. I was embarrassed not to choose the paddle boat, but not embarrassed enough to pretend. A glimmer of sanity here and there; a reward for actuarial creep.

Raymond was going in Mike's boat, the lead boat, because he and Mike had been together on another rafting trip and they could work together on rescues. That left Sylvie, me, and John.

Dave asked which one of us was a good swimmer, and to my surprise John put his pipe in his mouth and raised his hand.

"Swimming is one thing I can actually do," he said, and went off to the lead boat with Raymond and Mike. Sylvie and I looked at each other. It was us, the river, and Gary, the priest.

The main difference between a paddle boat and an oar boat is how they are controlled. An oar boat is controlled by a single boatman who sits in the middle and does all the work with two long oars. Passengers sit up front, facing forward, toes jammed under one of the tubes, and stay in the boat by holding on to guide ropes. In a paddle boat, everyone on the raft paddles and the boatman, sitting in the stern, uses his paddle as a rudder and barks out commands: *Right, Left, Backpaddle, Stop*. Paddlers hook the toes of one foot underneath one of the tubes and hang their bodies over the side of the boat so they can dig their paddles straight down into the water. A paddle boat is smaller and more maneuverable than an oar boat, and much more fun to be on, but it is also more likely to flip.

When we hit the Boh, Gary said, it would be big and fast but there wouldn't be any rapids until we were in the gorge, where rocks had piled up in the river creating a chaos of hydraulics. As he paddled leisurely downstream, he recited the rules of river rafting, which are simple: hang on in serious rapids, lean into big waves, and fling youself over to the high side of the raft if it gets tilted up against a big wave or a rock. And after the rapids, bail like crazy. Mike's oar boat and Dave's paddle boat were self-bailing. They had separate bottoms attached to the boat by webbing so that whenever water came in, the weight of it would force the floor down and let it out. A self-bailing boat could completely empty itself in five seconds, which made it safe in long rapids because it never got too heavy to control.

Our boat, "the bathtub boat," was the only one that was not self-bailing, which is why we were going last: theoretically there would be two boatmen at the bottom of each rapid to throw us a line in case we needed help. The idea after running a rapid is always to oar or swim out to an eddy, a place at the edge of a river where the fast water of the rapids runs into the slower water of the main current and some of it backs up into a quiet pool.

We entered the gorge almost without realizing it. Suddenly the canyon was narrow and at times the tree canopy completely enclosed us. The walls grew steep and a thick tangle of vegetation spilled down to the highwater mark. Mostly, the river flowed right up against the walls of the gorge; occasionally, it skirted piles of boulders. As Mimo and Sylvie had warned, there were no beaches or sandbars.

That morning rapids were not the problem; boredom was. We were moving downriver at about twenty yards an hour. Since no one knew what lay ahead, the guides had to stop at every rapid and scout it. That meant we had to get the boats into an eddy, tie them to a tree or rock, and wait while Dave, Mike, and Gary took off downriver to study the white water and come up with a plan for running it. It was hard work for them, and tedious for those left behind, but it was absolutely necessary. Boredom is the enemy of caution; we needed to be careful.

Even though the river looked calm, it was big, and something as simple and inevitable as a drop in the gradient or a rockpile could create a deathtrap. We might turn a corner and discover a twenty-foot waterfall, or slide into a keeper hole and get trapped by a back-wave. My own particular nightmare was a sieve, where the current strains through a pile of rocks or debris underwater. You can be pressed flat up against a sieve and held there forever.

The rest of us stayed behind on these long scouts mainly because we couldn't keep up with the guides, who would literally run over the rocks and boulders, pick their way across what seemed like sheer vertical rock walls, and climb up and down the gorge, traveling from rock to mud to jungle at a breakneck pace, occasionally stringing ropes and rappelling. At times they had to hack their way through wet creepers and vines with machetes, which they also used to whack the leeches off.

When we stopped for lunch on some rocks, we had our first taste of Dave Heckman's river cuisine: peanut butter, jelly, Kraft processed cheese, and some pale slabs of pressed animal product that tasted more or less like candy-coated industrial carpet. "Deng deng," Dave called it.

"Jesus," said Raymond with genuine annoyance. "I could have done better that this in just a couple of hours in Jakarta."

The rest of us teased Dave more gently. We were becoming a determinedly amiable group.

After lunch the guides came back from a long scout and motioned us to get into the boats. Gary told Sylvie and me to unstrap the white plastic helmets and put them on. "This is a big one," he said. "There are two big drops, about twenty feet, but it's impossible to portage around it and we think we can run it." Later he told us that when they were scouting, Dave had said, "Let's run it before we get scared."

So Sylvie and I buckled up, grabbed the ropes around the side of the raft, and prepared to do the only thing we could: hang on. This might, after all, be fun. We were going to take the rapids with a very good boatman; it could be like sitting on the shoulders of a competition skier as he made a difficult run.

And we hung on, all right. We braced our feet and hung on as we glided around the bend, still in calm water. We hung on when we spotted the paddle boat ahead of us in the white water and saw it hit a wave, fly up in the air, and land upside down. We hung on as Gary positioned us at the top of the run, and we hung on as we bounded down a chute, ended up too far to the right, and hit a rock wall at a 45-degree angle and began to fly. We were still hanging on in midair as the boat started to turn all the way over.

I let go and took a big breath before I plunged into the water. Curiously, it was not painful. The initial trauma was psychological, a feeling of overwhelming fear and powerlessness.

13

Something powerful happens to the brain in moments of sheer terror. Adrenaline is the ultimate amphetamine. Impressions come in at record speed and are magnified and made exquisitely lucid. Details that usually whiz by in a blur drift around like cartwheeling spaceships.

When I hit the water this time, all it took was a few seconds for all the images to flood in from that spring afternoon in 1982 when I'd taken a swim in the Kern River in California. Everything felt familiar: the incredible force of the pounding water; the fear that my legs and arms were about to be ripped off; the conviction that I was going to pop up momentarily; the anger when I didn't. I could even see the ghostly images of the boats on the Kern, feel the sun on my back, sense the unexpectedness of the danger that seemed to loom up out of nowhere, like a nightmare. I could see the line of my life unraveling—spinning like a ball of yarn down the side of a hill. I could see the end, the last frayed, ragged fiber.

I had joined a small group of magazine employees for a two-day run of California's most challenging stretch of white water: a section of the Kern River in the Sierra Nevada Mountains that shoots through a high granite gorge called the Forks. Don Peterson, a photographer, and I had driven down from Oakland as last-minute replacements for two people who had canceled.

The river was higher than any of the guides had ever seen it, and by the second day we were all a little scared. Even one of the boatmen was scared, which didn't do much for our confidence. It was late afternoon and we were coming up to the Carson Falls, the last and most serious rapids on the river and the one place we had been told we might have to portage (unload the boats, roll them up, and carry everything down to the bottom of the rapids). Then, up ahead we saw the first of our three boats bouncing in the rapids, upside down. The river around us was still calm and the rapids weren't supposed to be there; they didn't even have a name. I saw Don Peterson's face in the water, and from almost twenty yards away I could see he was in trouble. His mouth was open, he was gasping, but he wasn't swimming and he wasn't looking around for help. Only his life jacket kept him from going under.

I could see, too, the faces in our boat: Andy, our guide, a strong, experienced boatman, master of the raised eyebrow, the no-comment shrug; Scott, a magazine editor, blond, quiet, intense; Debbie, a shy fact checker, baby-faced and sweet.

Andy had stood up in the boat, trying to see what had caused the boats in front of us to flip, and then he grabbed the oars and took us through the middle of the rapids, right over a boulder. My stomach was in my throat as we dropped down about ten feet and hit the wave at the bottom with a bone-pounding smack. We were still upright, though, and started cheering until we saw Andy's face, still contorted as he strained at the oars. He was pulling hard and going nowhere.

Finally he stood up, let his oars flop in the oarlocks, and yelled: *"We're in a hole! Everyone highside!"*

All I had known about holes was that they were one of the most dangerous traps in a river. They happen when water, falling off a rock or a log with great force, creates a wave coming back in the opposite direction. If it's a "keeper hole," the boat can't be oared out of it and is stuck, whirling and bouncing helplessly.

We'd been told that one of the advantages of the sheer amount of water flowing down the Kern was that the current was so strong it would carry us through any holes. But here we were, in one. Our boat was bouncing wildly and slowly spinning, tipped at about a 30-degree angle.

"*Highside! Highside!*" Andy cried again. And again we followed his orders, flinging ourselves to the new high side of the boat as it spun at a tilt toward the water. "*Highside! Highside!*" Andy yelled, and we kept scrambling, flinging ourselves to the high side over bodies, bailing buckets, food bags, and oars.

The water roared around me, the boat tipped slowly in its whirlpool, and I heaved myself from one side of the raft to the other, trying not to panic, trying to follow instructions. I knew the situation was serious by the way Andy kept leaping on top of us with the full force of his body. I quivered beneath him in darkness, in a tangle of human flesh and ropes.

After maybe two exhausting minutes, I began to try and think for myself. We were highsiding, just as Andy had instructed us to, and it wasn't working. We were doing everything he told us to do, and we were still whirling around in what felt like some nightmare circle in hell. I was afraid of being caught and held under the boat in a tangle of ropes. I took a second to look at the raft and our situation and counted bodies. "Where's Debbie?" I shrieked. "*Where's Debbie?*"

"She's out of the boat," Andy shouted back. "Don't worry about her, she's all right."

Suddenly I wanted to be out of the boat with her. I felt like diving into the water, flinging myself into the air, doing anything to stop the fear and chaos, anything to get free of the whirling. The rapids looked terrifying, but they were an escape.

Whether I deliberately let go or not I still don't know; in any case it happened in an instant. I was sucked down under the raft and carried about twenty yards downstream. It was like being tumbled by a huge ocean wave and then shot out of a cannon. I popped up, gasped for breath, and went under again, fighting to try to stay upright, to keep my feet downstream so they would cushion any collisions I might have with a rock. I was under the second time forever, it seemed, but then popped up, went under, and finally emerged in calm water. I lay back on my life jacket for a moment, just riding with the current, trying to recover. I knew I would have to gather strength to swim out before Carson Falls, but I hadn't thought of the possibility that there would be no eddies in sight. There was nothing but brush on the sides of the river, and we'd been instructed to stay away from it since the current might press us up against it and pull us under. Up ahead, the river took a curve, and beyond that I couldn't see anything.

Then a voice—I remember it as sounding crystal clear—called out behind me: "Tracy! *TRACY!*" I looked around and saw Andy and Scott in the raft, coming up on me. I started to swim toward them, but after a few strokes I realized that I couldn't get anywhere at all. I was a strong swimmer, but I was no match for the current. Then Andy somehow got the raft right behind me, and Scott leaned over and heaved me in. "Can you bail?" he gasped. "Sure," I gasped back, and took the bucket from him. I felt as if I were outside my body at that point, and I coached it: take deep breaths, maintain a rhythm, move efficiently. It had taken only one look at the situation to realize that Andy was in trouble. He had only one oar, and the boat was swamped with water. It was almost impossible to maneuver.

"How did you get out of the hole?" I asked, but Andy just yelled back at me. "Bail! Bail! We have to get rid of the water!"

Then we saw Debbie. She was standing in some brush on firm ground at the side of the river. She looked terrified, but she was safe. Andy tried to get the boat over to her but couldn't do it. He tried to make another eddy after that and didn't make that one either. He wasn't saying anything, and his face was in a grimace as he strained at his one oar. The only thing he wanted from us was help. "*Bail!*" he kept yelling. As if our lives depended on it. "Bail! *Bail!*"

Finally Andy got us close to the right side of the river, and we all saw it coming up—an eddy. Andy strained at the oar, and Scott leaned out and grabbed a tree branch, and suddenly the river was still. We let go. The water gurgled pleasantly around us. Even the breezes were calm. We got out of the boat and stood in the water, speechless. Then I heard a low roar coming from downstream. "Where's Carson Falls?" I gasped.

"I didn't want to tell you," Andy said, his lopsided grin re-establishing itself, "but it's right down there. This is where we eddy out to scout it."

We had made it out of the river on our last chance.

I drove home with Don Peterson late that night, flying along the empty roads. I had been right when I thought he was in trouble on the river, he said. He had swallowed so much water that he was nauseated and almost unconscious. It had taken three men to finally lift him back in the boat.

A week later, a friend called to tell me that the night before, Don had gone to a party where he drank a lot and fell asleep on a back-room couch. For some reason, in the middle of the night, he woke up and decided to go for a ride. He drove his van to the Alameda navy base, speeding past the security guard, and when the guard got in a car and started to chase him, he drove faster and faster, toward the bay. At about three-thirty, he drove off a pier and landed a hundred yards into the water. The guard dove in to try to save him and saw Don inside the van trying to get out, but the doors wouldn't open and the guard couldn't break the windows. At about three-forty, Don Peterson drowned.

14

After my initial rush of terror and panic, time cartwheeled slowly as I spun helplessly at the bottom of the Boh, pounded into place by great walls of water. For a while I tried kicking and flailing my arms, trying to get upright, but it soon became clear that I didn't really know which way was up. Gradually I realized that I was more in danger of running out of breath than plunging downstream and hitting rocks, so I stopped fighting the river, stopped trying to get upright, and told myself to relax. Gary had said something about going into a "reptilian mode" underwater, and I remembered that and let myself go limp, hoping one of my legs or arms would catch a current and shoot me downriver.

Even at the time, I found it remarkable that I had coherent thoughts. I wondered if it was Sylvie's foot I felt when I first fell out of the boat, and whether or not we could have avoided the flip if all three of us had highsided. I debated the pros and cons of gulping more water and determined that for some reason it seemed to have helped when I did it earlier. I even had time left over to remember my most recurring childhood nightmare: I would be playing in the sand on a beach in front of an amusement park, and the tidal wave would rise way off in the ocean and get bigger and bigger until finally it curled up over my entire world—the beach, the hot-dog stands, the couples on the boardwalk, even the Ferris wheel. In my dream I would run away from the wave, up the beach and down a street until I felt water licking at my feet, and then I would turn around and feel myself being sucked backward, up, up, up the funnel of the wave and over the tops of the houses.

Perhaps this time I wasn't going to wake up, I thought. Perhaps this time I'd crash and end up draped over a pile of rocks like an old nightgown.

All of a sudden I shot up toward the light and my head broke water. I gasped some air before I was sucked under again, but now I was careening downriver, tumbling and tumbling, like Alice falling down the rabbit hole. Then the nightmare started all over—I ran out of air; I couldn't reach the light; my lungs felt like they were going to explode. I remembered, finally, to blow out some carbon dioxide, but then I gasped again and choked down more water. It worked! Of course! I thought. Frothing water is full of air.

Then the water around me began to darken, and I realized that instead of rising to the top of the river, I was being pushed down. It occured to me that there might be a series of rapids, not just one, and that I had missed the first eddy and was now in a part of the river the guides hadn't scouted. But just as I had this thought I popped up above water again, and suddenly, almost like magic, I was out of the rapids and in calm water. It was a small eddy, and after a few strokes I stood up, thigh deep in the water, heaving, coughing, blowing water out my nose, and trying to hold on to a slippery rock. I looked up and saw an upturned raft bouncing down the other side of the river with Gary climbing on top of it and Sylvie trailing behind, holding on to the bowline. I watched them go around the bend.

And then I was all alone. Behind me was a steep rock wall. My instinct was to swim to the other side of the river where I could get out of the water and make my way downstream over some boulders. But I knew I probably couldn't make it across before I rounded the bend, and since there might be more rapids ahead, or a waterfall, I made myself wait.

I waited long enough to relive the rapids I'd just been through; I'd spilled at the top of the first waterfall and had gone down it and then down the second one. Then I waited while I tried to think of what to do next. If the boats had all flipped and no one had been able to get out of the river for a mile or so, the guides might not be able to get back to me.

Or maybe someone had gotten hurt and there was no time to hike back upstream.

Maybe I'd have to wait where I was until they got off the Boh and down the Mahakam far enough to call for some kind of helicopter rescue. I might be stuck where I was for days: thigh deep in water in a part of Borneo that perhaps only ten or twenty people on earth had ever seen, without food or dry clothes or even a place to sit, let alone sleep.

I looked around at the dark green water, the black rock wall in back of me, the rank tangle of trees and leaves and vines over my head. My legs in the water looked like little twigs; my knees were quivering. I felt very much alone.

I smelled the mold already in my life jacket and fingered my arm, which was red with deep scratches, and realized that this loneliness might not be just in my head. It might not be romantic or metaphorical; it might be ugly and real. I might have to try to climb up the wall, find a place to sleep in the jungle, and live on . . . something. Leaves and berries. I felt as if I were looking down a dark well into my essence, but I couldn't see it. I couldn't see what to do next. I couldn't even see how to get out of the goddamned water.

It had all been very naïve, my idea about how safe it was to go on a river trip with world-class boatmen. I hadn't thought about what would happen if a wave suddenly reached out of the river and flicked over the boat. I'd been on my own in that white water. As had everyone.

And then . . . I heard a voice across the river calling, *"Tracy, Tracy,"* and I yelled back, *"Here! Here!"* It was warmth, it was music. Whoever had come to get me, I loved him.

It was Mike, in his headband and wire-rimmed glasses, waving from the other side of the river; strong, lovely Mike with his bulging biceps. He tried to tell me something, but the water was too loud and I couldn't hear, and then he held out his palm, indicating that I should stay put, and I smiled and laughed and gave him the okay sign. "I'm fine!" I cried. *"Fine!"*

I was still shaky, but the adrenaline was pumping, and after a minute or so of waiting I became impatient and examined the rock wall behind me with a climber's eye. I saw a route and decided to try it. Moving deliberately, checking my strength, I traversed the wall, making my way downstream, feeling strong and high. I've never discovered anything that requires more concentration than rock climbing—more centering of mind and body, more awareness at every nerve ending—and I felt a rising ecstasy as the handholds materialized, roots appeared around corners, ledges held firm. When I rounded the bend I looked up as if to applause, but there was only the dirty-brown Boh, the river taking another quick curve.

It was an easy boulder hop around the next bend, and then I saw the boats. Two were still overturned, and everyone was busy trying to get them upright. I yelled, but no one heard me, and finallly, when I was right across the river from everyone, Dave looked up and saw me waving. He waved back and continued fixing something on his boat.

It was something of an anticlimax, not having anyone falling to their knees with thanksgiving for my safe arrival, but I took it in stride, and finally, after the guides huddled together for a moment, I saw Dave cup his hands and yell:

"We're going to throw you a line. Try and catch it."

I braced myself against a rock, held out both arms, and tried not to think about being dragged across the current. The "rescue line" or "throw line" was a rope in a small canvas bag that uncoiled as it sailed through the air. I watched Gary's throw arc across the river toward me and fall short by about twenty feet. Then I watched Mike's throw land upriver in the current and sail by far out of reach. The guides went into another huddle, and soon Gary and Sylvie got in our boat and took off. Gary strained against the current, oaring into it at a 45-degree angle, and made it across just a few feet before the river disappeared around a bend.

"I want you to know," said Gary, when I reached the boat, "that I've been rafting for nineteen years, and this is only the fifth time I've flipped a boat."

I was impressed.

While we waited for the other boats to put in, Gary described the rescue. It had been frantic, he said, but well done. Luckily, Mike, Raymond, and John had made it through the rapids safely in Mike's boat, and Mike was ready to throw a line to the paddlers who were coming down in the water. Mimo caught the line and clipped it to one of the boat's metal rings, and Bill grabbed the paddles that floated by him in the water. Then, just as Mike and Raymond were pulling in the paddle boat and the swimmers were safe in the eddy, Gary came down the river on top of his overturned boat, Sylvie trailing in the water behind him. Gary had managed to reach under the boat and unclip the throw line, which he hurled at Bill, who had just pulled himself up out of the rapids onto a rock. Mike yelled at Gary, "Bill can't hold it up there," but somehow Bill braced himself and did. Then Mike ran up and together they pulled the boat in.

Gary asked if I had seen the MAF pilot who had appeared out of nowhere just after the rescue. He did a wing stand in his Cessna, circled, and left. Amazingly enough, I hadn't.

Sylvie and I exchanged "swimming" stories. She, too, had been pounded underwater, but when she popped up she felt something bump her softly on the head. She opened her eyes and saw that she was in complete darkness; the water all around her was black.

"I knew then," she said, "that I had come up underneath the boat."

She tumbled down the river helplessly for what seemed like minutes, trying to stay upright and swim out from underneath the boat. When she opened her eyes a second time, and again saw nothing but blackness, she gave up.

"I knew that I was going to die. I had already swallowed water, and now I couldn't stop it. I kept swallowing big gulps of water. I couldn't get any air."

She had flipped on the Zambezi River in Africa, she said, but she'd never stayed underwater long. There she had worried more about bashing into rhinos or crocodiles than actually drowning.

"All I could think" she said, "was 'Shit, I'm going to die because of this stupid river trip.'"

For some reason I couldn't keep the grin off my face. I was still flushed with the euphoria of having survived. I also wanted a moment to send off an apology to my husband. "I'm sorry, lover," I said to the river and the wind. "No more dangerous rivers. Really."

When we finally took off again and I strapped on my life jacket and grabbed the ropes, my mood abruptly changed. Suddenly I felt numb. Blank. Confused. Gary and Sylvie were also quiet. Sylvie clutched the ropes, and Gary stood up to try to see ahead.

I took my position, legs braced, hands secure on the ropes, but it felt futile. I noticed I was shaking, and suddenly I was cold. I was two degrees from the equator, on calm water, gliding through a tropical wonderland, but everything had changed. As Peter Matthiessen once wrote, the earth had nudged me. This little adventure had turned serious.

15

*T*he Sobek Adventure Travel Company catalog had pictured the Boh River trip as mostly a cultural experience. We would hang out with "Borneo's reputed headhunters" who would dance and sing for us in their longhouse and then escort us down the river for a rafting adventure "highlighted" by the white water of the Boh River gorge. The trip description didn't mention that the "reputed headhunters" had already told Sobek the gorge was too dangerous for anyone to go down, or that this was an exploratory river trip, the most perilous kind of river running. It was a "Class III" adventure, the catalog said. Mimo had considered bringing his eleven-year-old son.

The more thorough trip itinerary we'd all received from Sobek did say that ABC had filmed a team of women called ALLWET (All Women's Exploratory Team) abandoning an attempt to get down the gorge after scouting it with a helicopter. But even this material labeled the trip a "Class III."

I'd asked Richard Bangs before I left about the ABC film, and he said it had been his idea, a scheme to get Sobek publicity as well as finance a first descent. He wanted to put native Dayaks, who thought women didn't belong on the river, together with the experienced ALLWET rafters and film the two groups learning to work together as a team. It was an idea, he thought, whose time had come. And sure enough, American Adventure Productions at ABC had bought it.

Then, three days before the ABC film crew was scheduled to fly into Long Lebusan, Dave Ferguson, who had been the point man in the village for ABC, casually mentioned to Bangs that a few weeks earlier he and four village men had gone down the gorge themselves. It had been in extremely low water, Ferguson said, and they had used a Zodiac, a small inflatable raft with a wooden floor. Bangs was furious, as was ABC. The premise of the film was that ALLWET would be making a first descent, and Ferguson knew it. But finally, after a flurry of faxes and phone calls, ABC decided to go ahead with the shoot, and in the spring of 1987 a film crew of eight, plus show host Diana Nyad, met the six women from ALLWET in Long Lebusan.

There they discovered that the Boh was a more ferocious river than they had imagined, especially at high-water level. It had rained for over a week when they arrived, and the river was big enough to frighten everyone. Bangs had given me a videotape of the ABC program four days before I left, and my husband and I watched it with more than a little amazement. The helicopter scout showed the women looking down at the white water in the gorge and saying things like, "Oh, my God," and "That's instant death." Finally, we see them portaging the gorge instead of running it and then leaving to try for another possible first descent in New Zealand.

The Dayak boatmen who were supposed to be part of the film were not shown, or even mentioned.

The ALLWET team did sound convinced that the gorge could be run in lower water, but it was now dawning on me that they really couldn't have known. High water can conceal keeper holes, logjams, and even waterfalls, and since much of the river was covered by tree canopy, they hadn't been able to see all of it.

After four hours on the Boh I had found out enough to know that there was a gap between the trip's description and its reality, a breach I wanted to fill.

"What else don't we know about this gorge?" I asked Gary.

"We don't know if we can get through it," he said.

"But . . . we could always portage. Right?"

"Not really."

"But the ALLWET women portaged the entire gorge."

"Oh, no. They portaged about sixty feet of it, just for the television cameras. Then they flew out in helicopters."

"But Ferguson and Pelanjau and two others did make it through the gorge, right?"

"Well, after talking to Pelanjau we aren't really sure. He said that they had to carry the boat upstream for two hours and then portage over a big mountain. So they didn't really go down the entire river corridor. And some of the things he said just didn't make sense. He showed us a Polaroid of the part of the Boh they supposedly portaged, but it looked to us like a tributary stream, and the photo was taken from extremely high up. In fact, you could see the strut of an airplane wing. Also, Dayaks have a thing about women not being in the gorge. We decided Pelanjau was probably just trying to scare us."

"What about the three-headed river spirit?"

"Ferguson says Pelanjau saw it, but Pelanjau told us that Ferguson saw it. From what we could gather, Ferguson may have gone off the deep end. When they portaged the mountain, Pelanjau said Ferguson had to be carried up it, strapped to a pole."

"Do we at least know how long the gorge is?"

"Well . . . thirty kilometers we think. About eighteen miles."

"Do we have a map?"

"We went to the Department of Highways in Samarinda because we found out they have aerial photographs. But all we could get was a map of the upper Boh, with no topographical features, no villages, just a blue line on a white piece of paper marking tributaries and turns. We're not sure we can read it. The reason there are no good maps of the interior, we discovered, is that the Indonesian government has outlawed them. It doesn't want them to get in the hands of the wrong people."

"Criminals?"

"Guerrillas. There are Dayaks who resent being ruled by Jakarta, it seems."

"Do we know if there's anyplace we could hike out to if we get in trouble—if someone gets hurt?"

"We know there's a village toward the bottom of the gorge, three days' walk from the river, but we couldn't possibly find it without a guide who knows the forest."

"So . . . no one really knows what we're going to run into."

"Right."

"And the only people who ever—maybe—scouted the river—the Dayaks—told us it's dangerous."

"Right."

At least I knew the truth now, and, strangely enough, it made me feel better. I understood the impulse to discount bad news. Part of the fun of adventuring is going places and doing things people tell you not to. I even liked the idea that we didn't really know what we were getting into on the Boh. Partly out of confusion and partly out of laziness, I've always thrived in an atmosphere of uncertainty. Whenever I take the random chances that come my way, life suddenly gets interesting. Besides, it's hard to lead a deliberate life, I've discovered, harder to create a challenge than to accept one. And I hadn't completely given up the sense of security that seems to come as a birthright to Westerners: we'd paid our money; we had our return tickets; surely no reputable company would send us anywhere truly dangerous.

16

Almost as soon as we recovered from our "swim," we noticed that bees had begun to circle around the boat: humming, buzzing honeybees, the familiar stinging kind with striped, bull's-eye rear ends and black heads.

"Jesus," said Gary, taking off his hat to fan his face.

"*Merde,*" said Sylvie, reaching into her ammo box for a sarong, which she wrapped around her legs.

"Shit," I said, wishing I had my own bottle of insect repellent and hesitating to beg.

"Get the bucket out and throw water at them," said Gary. "Throw it everywhere. Let's try to drown them."

For a while it was fun, flinging the water in the air and on each other, watching it arc and sparkle in the dull green light. But after ten minutes or so, even when dozens of dead bees were floating in the water around our feet, the number of them in the air still dive-bombing and buzzing us had not diminished.

It was beginning to feel a little like a Hitchcock movie. Repellent kept the bees off our skin for about ten minutes, but they didn't go away, they just kept circling.

"We must have run into a nest or something," Gary said.

"Let's get out of here!" Sylvie cried.

"There's Mike's boat up ahead," I said, "under a waterfall."

We headed over to the fall, and Gary maneuvered the boat

right under it. The water pounded down on our heads and filled the boat again, but when we pulled out of it and looked up, the bees were still there.

"Olatz," Sylvie said, "wouldn't have been able to take this. She is allergic to bugs. She would be dead."

"It's good we sent her home," agreed Gary.

"I thought she left because of her swimsuit shoot and the flea bites," I said.

"She had an insect phobia," Gary explained. "Mike said she almost overturned a dugout just to get away from a dragonfly."

All three boats were surrounded by dark clouds of bees now, and the only thing we could think to do was try to outrun them. The guides started to oar and paddle faster, but when we pulled into camp—a pile of rocks, as Dave had predicted—they were still with us. In addition, small stingless sweat bees now started to crawl all over our bare skin. We put on long pants and long-sleeved shirts, but after fifteen minutes the sweat pouring down inside our clothes was as irritating as the bees. Mimo hung a mosquito net over a tree branch and secured it with rocks on the ground. But before he could seal it off, about a dozen bees flew inside and somehow more kept coming in. For a half hour or so, Mimo valiantly tried to read while the bees piled up at the top of the mosquito netting, in great, dark, seething, humming clumps over an inch deep. But he soon burst out of his tent, cursing mightily in Italian. I saw Mike say something and heard Mimo roar angrily back at him.

Later I found out that Mimo had unwittingly constructed what's called a miasma trap, a French device used by entomologists to attract and capture bees. It is like a pup tent made out of mosquito netting, with a vertical net panel at the center. The bees are attracted to the netting, crawl up the panel to the top of the tent, and eventually reach an exit that funnels them down into a jar of formaldehyde.

What it reminded me of was the fort I had built as a child with a girlfriend. We spent days constructing it in the dry hills behind her home, cutting away the underbrush, stringing up blankets, filling it with candy and comic books. We had invented a new language, and our plan was to speak it only in our fort, in secret. But when construction was finished, all we could think to do was have a tea party, and so we set up our pretend table, got out our pretend cups and saucers, poured our pretend tea, and pretended that we were having a good time gossiping. It all felt pretty stupid, and luckily an amazing creature came waddling across the blanket just then—an enormous, ugly, monster bug. It was oozing some kind of sticky juice, and its body was a ghostly, translucent white. Out of its head arose two long red eyestalks, each topped by a rolling, pale pink eyeball.

It never occurred to us to pull off its legs or set it on fire, as it might have, had we been boys. We just screamed and screamed, and then we ran.

The next day we discovered that an ant colony had taken up residence in our fort, as had several lizards, and we gathered up our comic books and went back to my friend's cabana beside her swimming pool.

It was a man, much later, who taught me how to explore nature, to follow lizards and bugs, investigate stream beds, turn over rocks, watch and listen for sounds and movement. I took to it so readily it puzzles me why, as a young girl I could only run away from it.

Besides the bees and the unportageable rapids, the other bad news of our first day in the gorge was that when Gary's boat had flipped, the rubber dry bags in it had taken in water. John and I were sharing one bag because we'd both brought such a pathetically small amount of clothes, and when I reached down to the bottom of it I felt a pool of wetness. Half of us that night— the ones who hadn't thought to pack their clothes in Ziploc plastic bags—had nothing dry to wear or sleep on.

By sundown we had spread out our wet clothes on the rocks, found places to sleep, and cheered as the last bee left camp with the dying sun. We built a fire using a fire starter and damp wood, ate a meal of rice, freeze-dried vegetables, and Indonesian peanut sauce, and drank some of what would turn out to be an enormous stash of rum and vodka. The river was only about twenty feet away from us, as it would be every night we spent in the gorge, but it was calm—a murmur in the night, a dark rustle—and the coolness coming off it was soothing.

Talk around the campfire was about the rapids; it was hard to think about anything else. Our jobs, our personal histories, our dreams for the future all seemed irrelevant. Interestingly enough, Dave, for the first time, was relaxed. He was shoeless and shirtless, and although he was quiet he was very much present. He was a tall man, with handsome brown eyes and a lanky, well-proportioned body. Unlike Gary and Mike, who had full beards, he shaved regularly and trimmed his mustache. I noticed that his hair was receding and remembered his remark about Sylvie being "over the hill."

In many ways Dave had remained an enigma. He wasn't playful, but neither was he earnest. I couldn't figure out whether he had great depth or deep apathy. He was a sober trickster, I finally decided; a man who made his own quiet jokes. Somehow he deflected questions about himself and kept much of his character hidden.

Tonight he told us that he had known the rapids we flipped in might cause problems, but had decided to run them anyway since a portage was impossible and he had scouted far enough to see the "rescue pool" at the bottom. Mike, he said, had come up with a name for the rapids: "Bee no portage."

At what must have been about eight o'clock we went to bed. Howard slept on a wooden platform he'd constructed out of branches on the top of some rocks; Bill and Linda piled their air mattresses and sheets together to make a very bumpy double bed near the edge of the forest; and the rest of us lay, like solitary animals, curled up in various positions around rocks.

I had carefully tucked Mimo's sleeping bag into an eighteen-inch-wide strip of sand in a gully between two rocks, and surprised myself by going to sleep quickly. But an hour or so later I woke up with my entire body on fire, tingling all over as if I'd somehow bedded down in a huge tray of hot sauce. I got out my flashlight and saw thousands of tiny black dots crawling all over my right arm, ants so tiny I couldn't even feel them as I frantically brushed them off my hands. I grabbed the back of my neck and checked my hand again with the flashlight— hundreds of them were speeding around like tiny Pac-Men. Finally, I lifted up my sheet, aimed the flashlight inside, and saw the worst: my entire body was crawling with ants. I'd heard that ants and termites make up one third of the total weight of animal life in a rain forest, and that in a ten-foot-square area of leaf litter scientists have discovered no less than fifty different ant species. Now I believed it.

I jumped up, flung aside the sleeping bag, and aimed my flashlight on the patch of sand. There they were: billions of them coming out of a hole in a dark, seething stream. It looked as if the earth itself were moving.

I spent a miserable hour or so carrying all my stuff to an ant-free rock, brushing the ants off everything, and finding a new place to sleep. My new bed was on a flat boulder that sloped at a 15-degree angle directly into the river. I figured I'd just stay awake all night and hang on.

I wrapped myself in my damp sheet again and looked up at the stars, which seemed very distant in the slice of sky at the top of the gorge. My back hurt, but not too badly, and at least the ant episode had allowed me to shake out the kinks in my hips. The night air was warm and tropical, and I basked in it for a while, listening to the river, which seemed very immediate. Before long I began to feel exquisitely sensual, as if phenomena were just pouring through me, as if my entire body was responding to light and darkness, rippling breezes, the sounds of the river, whisperings in the treetops. The forest behind me seemed sheathed in its own wetness and I felt it at my back, breathing and wet and alive. I had always envied the poets and writers who flung themselves on mountain meadows and had epiphanies. Perhaps here, in the world's most highly evolved ecological system, I, too, could somehow connect with the earth in a new way.

But just then I heard a curse with an Australian accent. About twenty feet away I recognized the *swish swish swish* of someone trying frantically to brush off insects.

17

*T*he next morning Dave appeared with a swollen eye. Just before dawn, when he was half awake, a bee had come out of nowhere and stung him right on the eyelid. We laughed because he looked so lopsided, but by the time breakfast was over we all felt as if we were in some kind of horror movie. We tried covering up, we tried insect repellent, we tried walking around in frantic circles. But after a while, when nothing worked, we realized we were stuck with the bees and would have to come to terms with them. The only possible relief was going to be mind control. We had to learn to let the bees crawl all over us. I comforted myself by remembering that although the bees did sting, at least they weren't the kind Dave had warned us about, the ones whose stings make you lie down on the ground and chew your tongue off in hopes of losing consciousness.

We also discovered that morning that all our clothes were exactly as wet as they had been yesterday afternoon when we spread them out on rocks. Bill told us to think of the rain forest as a kind of moisture bank, holding water everywhere: in rivers, moss, leaves, and rotting vines. The moisture evaporates, but mostly swirls around in the mist for a while and then falls back down in the form of rain. Some of it blows away to water the rest of the earth, but half stays behind in a continual exchange between earth and sky.

Already my clothes were smelling of mildew, and I realized that although I had launched a successful counterattack against ants, the two hundred billion invisible microorganisms in my socks and T-shirts were still multiplying exponentially. There wasn't much I could do about it. I could hope for the sun; I could hope for the end of the gorge.

Just after breakfast Bill asked me if I'd heard gibbons earlier. I hadn't. Gibbons are a form of ape, he said, and their cry is haunting and sad, a mournful *whoop, whoop, whoop.*

It took at least an hour to pack and load the boats each morning, a time that became my least favorite in the day because I couldn't lift the heavy bags and carry them to the boats; I couldn't even lift and carry my own bag, mine and John's. Poor John; poor me. He wasn't used to carrying a load over slippery rocks, and I wasn't used to being a weakling. In fact I used to be impatient with weakness. Now I had to ask for patience myself.

It was John who provided the next surprise of the morning. When I climbed into Gary's boat he was sitting in it, in Sylvie's place. He was wearing long pants, a long-sleeved shirt, hat, a safari-style vest with 107 pockets, wraparound sunglasses, tennis shoes, and socks. He looked as if he were ready to spend the afternoon in a cave. Sylvie had asked him to switch boats, he said.

I couldn't imagine why he had agreed. Mike's boat was the only one that had made it through the rapids yesterday without flipping, and Mike was so mellow and so physically strong that he inspired confidence. Most of us believed he could single-handedly right his boat if it started to overturn.

John was the least agile member of our group, but he was also the most uncomplaining. I was beginning to suspect he had remarkable inner resources.

As it turned out, we didn't have to worry about running any rapids that day. The very first one we came to was so horrendous—two hundred feet of continuous, boiling white water—that the guides decided to play it safe. We would line the boats down the rapids rather than run them. And so they tied ropes to both ends of each boat and began the arduous process of getting them downstream by pushing and pulling them along the edge of the water. In eddies they would simply pull a boat downstream, and when there were no eddies they'd push it into the current and pull it out again with the ropes. Occasionally they'd have to lift and pull a boat entirely over a rock or log.

We made a little under two miles that day.

It was clear the guides wanted only Raymond, Bill, Stuart, and perhaps Howard and Mimo to work with them on the lining. That left me, Linda, Sylvie, and John back at camp. If my back had been better I might have protested, but as it was, I understood. Getting the boats downstream was dangerous work. The men had to stand on slippery boulders and hold a boat against the current; they had to lift and carry the heavy boats while walking blindly over sharp rocks. All of them returned with skinned knees and ankles.

Waiting, however, was not much more fun. We spent our time staring off into space and swatting bees, coexisting separately but peacefully. Linda would occasionally try to start a conversation—complain about something, or crack a joke—but the heat and the humidity made us languid and sluggish. Nothing seemed important but how bored or scared we were, how damp and mildewed, how hot and insect-crazed. Because none of us wanted to complain, we simply stopped talking.

Sylvie mostly lay on the rocks with her eyes closed, turning now and then to perfect her tan, and I amused myself by gazing at her as I would a beautiful bird or animal. John, in his full jungle outfit, passed the time by sitting absolutely still except for his right arm, which moved up and down with his pipe. He looked like a eunuch in a maharaja's court: bored, discreet, and loyal. I imagined his pipe full of opium, his thoughts in the form of a sonnet.

I did work up enough energy that morning to walk into the jungle to see if the bees would follow me. Sure enough, about twenty feet in, they left. I was sweating more than ever—my

18

Camp that night, our second on the Boh, was another rock pile at another bend in the river, only a couple of miles from where we started.

Because our boat was last, all the decent sleeping spots were taken. On other trips I'd been on, people often left, or shared, choice camping spots. But not here. Not on the rocks. John and I were doomed to sleep on bumpy rocks, slanty rocks, rocks pocked with water holes, rocks with tree roots wrapped around them.

I laid out all my possessions that evening and took inventory. I had two pairs of long pants: one made of thin white cotton, already filthy and ripped, the other (borrowed from Mimo) damp and smelling of mildew. In addition to the pants, I had underwear, two pairs of thin summer socks, two wet, dirty T-shirts borrowed from Dave and Linda, one dry, long-sleeved shirt borrowed from Dave, two pairs of wet shorts (one from Dave and one from my jet-lagged shopping trip), one pair of city sandals, one pair of tennis shoes, and a tiny towel.

It wasn't much, but according to our schedule we had only one more day in the gorge. By nightfall tomorrow we would be on a river taxi cruising down the Mahakam.

"I can feel it," said Bill, around the fire. "We are almost out of this gorge."

"Well . . ." said Gary.

"If not tomorrow," added Linda, "the next day."

"I wouldn't lay odds on it," said John.

It was possible that John knew something we didn't, but he wasn't the kind of guy you'd ask. He had pretty much established his role on the trip after the first day. He was the space cadet; he was present and took up space. While Sylvie, Mike, and Mimo were larger than life, John was almost nonexistent. Since he and I were the only members of the group without a buddy, in Samarinda I had suggested that we look out for each other. But now I was worried because he never seemed to take care of himself. At one point I noticed he had put his camera, packed only in a leather bag, on top of the dry bags on the boat.

"You have to put your camera in an ammo can," I said.

"I didn't get one," he replied.

"Ask for one," I told him. "I know we're all supposed to have our own, especially for a camera. You could put it in mine, but there isn't room with my notebook."

He didn't answer, but in a few days the camera got wet and was ruined. He didn't seem to mind. While the rest of us worked on drying our clothes, plunged into the river to get rid of the bees, or rigged up various contraptions involving mosquito netting and air mattresses, John sat on a rock, absolutely still. His presence wasn't dour; he smiled often. But it was a smile requiring a minimum of muscle strain, a grin that came on slowly and lasted a long, long time. Sometimes I'd see him sitting by himself, smiling into the distance, and realize that he just hadn't bothered to rearrange his face after one of Mimo's jokes.

That night, as we were stuffing clothes and towels into rock crevices to try to construct a halfway comfortable bed, John made history in our little group for taking passivity to a new level. He wasn't going to bother, he said, to blow up his air mattress. I looked at him in disbelief.

"Can I borrow it?" I asked.

"Sure," he said. "I don't really need it."

Suddenly, John was a saint, an utterly benign river god.

"I can't thank you enough," I said.

He shrugged. "I'm a good sleeper."

I wanted to hug him but refrained, thinking it might scare him.

A little later, when I went back to the fire, I overheard Mike and Gary talking about rafting in Africa.

"I thought you just lead trips on the Colorado River," I said to Gary.

"That's in the spring and summer."

"He's run rivers everywhere," Mike said. "In Nepal. In South America. In Australia. In Papua New Guinea. He's done the Franklin in Tasmania, and . . . didn't you do the world's highest put-in?"

"And you've only flipped a boat five times?" I burst out.

"You were there for it," Gary said.

Now I really was impressed.

That night I woke up to find ants in my bed again, and again I had to find a new site in the dark. But this time I didn't mind. The air mattress was a heavy canvas one—the kind you can blow up six inches high, section by section—and with it I could sleep on almost anything. I looked at John, who lay sleeping in the ant pile next to me, and decided not to wake him. He was lying on his back, draped over some uneven boulders, and breathing so quietly I had to trust fate that he hadn't expired. I carried the mattress to the river's edge again, and when I lay down it was like snuggling into a warm, firm waterbed.

Once more I lay awake in the middle of the night, feeling sheer pleasure at being in a place where few humans had been before me. The trees overhead that let the stars through in little flecks were trees that had survived centuries of storms and pestilence. The gap in the canopy where the gorge widened was like the earth's opening eye.

That night I relaxed enough to explore my actual rather than my carefully controlled emotions and wondered why I had been determined to continue on this trip despite numerous chances to turn back. Why had I dismissed Mimo and Olatz's warnings? Why, back in Jakarta, had the idea of flying home to Oakland, and a life I love, seemed so awful?

I thought once again about being a passive person who likes excitement, a person who goes along for other people's rides. But that didn't explain why, even as a small child, I had an unusual love of going new places and trying new things. One of my clearest early memories is of my mother, a good swimmer, encouraging me to dog-paddle behind her when I was five years old out beyond the boat dock of our beach house in Southern California and into the open sea channel. The water was dark and shimmered in places with oil slicks; far below was another realm, teeming with strange and scary creatures.

"Isn't it nice," my mother said, "that we can stay right on top?" I gasped for breath and flailed my scrawny arms and legs even harder, but I loved her for taking me out there to commune with something thrilling and mysterious.

I have never, I realized, been sorry for taking a risk; I've never been pulled under when I was in over my head. If I was growing too old to risk my body, I should probably start thinking about risking something else. Perhaps my ideas, or my emotions.

But how? And where?

I pulled up my sheet and said a prayer of thanks to my husband. He thinks I'm crazy but he also thinks I'm sexy. I hoped we'd meet again in this lifetime.

19

*T*he next morning the guides were subdued when we gathered to eat instant oatmeal and coffee. "We hear something," Mike said, nodding downriver. "A sort of thudding sound. Maybe a waterfall." They took off to scout, warning us that it might be a long one, and we drifted apart to wait. We were beginning to feel the effects of what Dave had identified as "insect stress," especially Mimo. That morning he woke up with a fever, and because he was so sweaty, he was under attack. The bees swarmed around his face in a buzzing black cloud, following him everywhere. Finally, in desperation, he stood right in the smoke of the fire with a scarf over his nose and mouth. When he emerged, he was cursing and coughing, his face black with soot.

"You look like the Wild Man of Borneo," Linda said.

We all laughed because we'd heard the phrase repeated ceaselessly before we left ("So you're going to Borneo, huh? The Wild Man of Borneo, ha ha ha.")

I had been surprised to find out that the Wild Men of Borneo did, in fact, exist. They were two American brothers—odd-looking, mentally retarded dwarfs—who were put on the freak show circuit in 1852 by an American showman, Lyman Warner. The brothers, Hiram and Barney Davis, grew up on a farm in Ohio, and when they were in their twenties, Warner came to see them and asked their mother if he could put them on exhibit. She refused, but when Warner came back with a washpan full of gold and silver and dumped it in her lap, she decided that if her sons could make that much money on the road, she ought to let them.

Warner changed their names to Waino and Plutano, had them grow their hair down to their waists, and billed them as savages so "wild and ferocious" they could easily "subdue tigers." They became the main attraction in a dime museum, where they were bound in chains and displayed against a painted jungle backdrop, snapping and snarling at the audience and talking gibberish. When the brothers, who were actually very sweet-natured and capable of speaking perfect English, couldn't keep up the pretense of savagery, they became the *tamed* Wild Men of Borneo: proof of mankind's innate goodness.

The career of the Davis brothers lasted over fifty years, and they were beloved by audiences all over the world. They passed through every large city in the United States several times and toured Europe with the Barnum and London circuses. It wasn't until they were in their late seventies and eighties that they retired and settled down in Massachusetts with Lyman Warner's son Henry and his wife.

There were, for a short time in the 1920s, real Dayak "wild men" on exhibit in America. Sam Gumpertz, the Coney Island freak show czar, imported 150 Borneo natives and billed them as the "authentic wild men from Borneo." But little is known about them—whether they survived, whether they were exhibited in cages, who they were, or where they ended up.

Mimo was in no mood to be laughed at, and since none of us would get within ten feet of him and his buzzing entourage, he went off to sit by himself in the shade. My heart went out to him because his misery was so transparent; his face almost a caricature of self-pity.

Mimo, I'd gathered, had one of those fathers whose very presence was intimidating: rich, powerful, a big game hunter, and of course an extremely successful businessman. He was in retail manufacturing, and for a while Mimo had followed in his footsteps, coming to New York in the seventies to open Diane Von Furstenberg's line of clothing. Von Furstenberg was a family friend, but the business had ended in a tangled lawsuit (Roy Cohn had been Mimo's lawyer), and Mimo had "retired," as he put it. He was a globe-trotter now, going from one adventure to another, staying in touch with his son, who lived with Mimo's ex-wife in New York, and rendezvousing all over the world with Olatz.

Bill, I noticed this morning, went into the jungle with Linda, carrying his snake stick. Borneo has more snakes than anywhere else in Southeast Asia, many of them unique to very specific, remote mountain areas. It was possible that Bill would come across a new species of snake—one that had evolved in the gorge and was still in the first millennia of its earth-life. Or he might find an old species that had become extinct everywhere else. In Long Lebusan, Gary had seen a king cobra, the largest poisonous snake in the world. It was crossing the river, he reported, and its head was about the size of a dog's head.

"Those snakes can attack a boat," Gary said, but Bill shook his head.

"An English writer wrote about being attacked by one," Gary insisted. "Right here, in this part of Borneo."

"Well," said Bill, "I've never heard of it. King cobras are one of a handful of snakes that can be aggressive—they do protect their nests—but I don't think they attack boats. A lot of people have a snake experience that somehow, in their heads, becomes an attack. I don't see how a cobra could even raise its head that high in the water."

I knew the story Gary was talking about. James Barclay, in *A Stroll Through Borneo,* wrote about coming across a king cobra in 1983. He was traveling upriver in a native longboat when some of the boatmen suddenly started beating furiously on the water with their paddles. Barclay looked in the water and saw a twelve-foot snake heading straight toward him.

"I had a split second to see its head rearing towards my leg with a big white patch on the underneath of its mouth before I flashed my umbrella between my leg and its head. Its head struck the umbrella, and I jumped up and very nearly out of the other side of the boat."

I believed Barclay, mostly because no writer, I figured, would tell a blatant lie about a place where there was no shortage of true horror stories. Also, Eric Mujoberg, a Swedish naturalist traveling in Borneo in 1920, wrote that the king cobra "has been known to follow human beings over stock and stone for a distance of three and a half miles." The only possible way to escape, he said, is to run as fast as you can while ripping off all of your clothing. The cobra will stop to viciously attack the tossed-off scarf, T-shirt, or pair of underpants.

Somehow I've always found snakes silly, especially when I discovered, in the sixth grade, that they had two penises and boys seemed more afraid of them than girls. But an experience on an island off Papua New Guinea had recently caused me to take them seriously, at least as images. I had gone out on a warm, clear night to the beach with a local diver who said he wanted to show me something beautiful. We stopped about thirty feet from the water behind an old shed, and he put a finger to his lips and held up his other hand. He crept up to the shed and silently opened the door. Then he aimed a flashlight inside and ran backward. I watched the light and within seconds saw a writhing mass of enormous black poisonous sea snakes oozing out of the door. They slid across the sand, glistening black in the moonlight, each at least twelve feet long and maybe six inches in diameter. As they traveled toward the water they writhed together like long, silky, gelatinous ropes, twisting and pulsating, entwining around each other in seeming slow motion. It was a beautiful sight, an image of sensuality and horror.

Osa Johnson, the woman who described the sultan of Brunei's breakfast trays in *The Last Adventure*, also wrote about a rather gruesome encounter between a pig and a giant python on the Mahakam. She and her husband had set up a camp on the river where he filmed documentaries with her wearing tightly fitting, beautifully tailored dresses in front of battling monitor lizards and mating orangutans. One day, off camera, she saw a twenty-seven-foot, two-hundred-pound python slither down a tree trunk and sink its teeth into an unsuspecting wild boar.

The brutal struggle began. It was a fight to the death. Both creatures rolled over and over in the slimy swampy earth. The squealing boar sank his sharp ivory tusks into the thick unyielding skin of the snake as the python slowly but methodically wrapped himself around him.

Tugging, pulling, and squirming, with water and mud flying all about the arena of death, the boar tried to get loose, but the hold of the python was too overpowering. The python did not make a sound. With deadly silence he went on with his intended purpose of killing the boar. In contrast, the boar squealed and grunted futilely as the reptile wound himself around him. The fight continued. Large gaping wounds now covered the snake's body. Blood and mud covered both combatants.

The boar rolled over and over in the slime in an attempt to crush the snake, but his efforts were in vain. He tried to run, but the weight of the immense snake about him was too great and he fell. He rolled into deep water as if he were trying to drown the python but rolled out again as the attempt failed. His movements began to slow down. He was tiring of the fight. The tremendous pressure of the snake encircled about him was too much. His squeals and grunts stopped and all movement ceased. The battle was over and all that could now be heard was the cracking of the boar's bones as the python went about his grim job.

It was a disturbing image, especially the part about the bones cracking. But still, I was rooting for Bill to come out of the forest with something monstrous.

And he did, sort of.

"I couldn't find any snakes," Bill said when he returned. "Just a podlike thing that I picked up because it had a covering that looked exactly like a snakeskin."

"Where is it?" I asked.

"We didn't bring it back," he said. "I felt a kind of tingling in my hand when I picked it up, but then I showed it to Linda and she must have grasped it harder than I did. She dropped it suddenly and looked down at her hand: there were hundreds of tiny, stinging-nettle-like things embedded in her skin. She tried to take some of them out with her teeth, but then she got them on her tongue."

Linda's tongue, it turned out, hurt for a day and a half.

20

When the guides returned from the scout they were covered with mud and trickles of blood where they'd cut off leeches (Dave swore that one leaped onto him from a tree). They had now identified three different kinds of leeches: the large brown common ground leech I had seen, a tiny brown leech about a quarter of an inch long that got between their toes, and a leech with a green stripe down its back that stung when it bit. All three men looked like extras in a horror movie, their legs and arms smeared with gore. But they brought good news. The water downriver was "classy," they said. The rapids were big, but there was a route through them and we should have a good Class IV run (Class III is average; Class V is the highest level considered runnable).

Just as the boats were all rigged and packed and we were ready to take off, Raymond, who still dressed entirely in white and had remained something of an apparition around camp—a tall and fleeting presence popping up occasionally to offer food to Sylvie and bark an order at the rest of us—suddenly called out to Mike and pointed to his boat. It had sprung a slow leak. We couldn't go anywhere until it was patched.

Patching involved heating up some glue and spreading it on a piece of rubber, then applying the patch to the boat and letting it dry. The whole process took an hour, which we spent mostly in silence. Howard got a beesting, or some kind of bite that made his entire arm swell from his wrist right up to his elbow. Dave looked worried and gave him an antihistamine and then asked if he wanted a painkiller. Howard just laughed. Howard was the descendant of pioneers. He grew up on the same Australian sheep station as his father and his grandfather and his great grandfather before him. It would take a lot more than a ballooning arm to make Howard ask for help.

Howard looked boyish, with curly brown hair and a wide, open face, but in matters physical he was supremely confident. So confident, I would later find out, that he didn't even bother to tell us that the cheap tennis shoes he'd bought in Bali turned out to have no traction on the rocks. All we knew was that he fell a lot.

When the patch was dry and we were ready to take off, I reminded myself that river running can be a lot of fun. But then, as Gary pulled out into the current, I saw the white line in the water up ahead that signaled the beginning of rapids, and my stomach began to twist into a knot. It was the nightmare all over again: the wave, the Ferris wheel, and little Tracy crashing down.

Gary was also nervous; he'd lost control of an oar in some rapids yesterday and had flipped his boat the day before, and he wasn't a man who liked to make mistakes. Sometimes I wished he would dismiss the danger the way Mike did, so John and I could keep from dwelling on it, but Gary, despite his careful and precise manner of speech, was honest. Today he would be damned if he didn't take these rapids right.

After Mike's and then Dave's boat took off, Gary oared out to catch the current and positioned us at the top of the rapids. As the current caught us, we bounced through some waves, shot through a center slot in the white water, and came right up to an enormous, frothing hole. As John and I stared down into it, expecting the worst, Gary did a back twist with the boat and we took the monster right on its edge. Next we powered straight through a big wave, which slapped us right in the face, and then slid down another wave sideways. Finally, Gary pulled hard to the left to avoid a log and we ended up in an eddy, cheering. It had been a classy run and a classy performance.

The rest of the morning was stop and go, but the rapids were runnable—turbulent but thrilling and without serious danger. John and I hung on, took some hard splashes, leaned into the waves, and cheered. Well, I cheered. I had started to have a good time.

"This is what river running should be," Gary said. "This is the kind of water the boats were meant to be on."

Just before stopping for lunch we took our first stretch of riffles—easy, Class II rapids—which meant the gradient of the gorge had reduced and the water wasn't falling downhill so fast. And then the rock walls opened a bit and the river flattened out. It looked like a chance to clock some mileage.

"I hate to jinx it," said Dave, "but this might be the end of the gorge. We may be almost out."

"And here comes the sun," said Mike.

We ate a relaxed lunch—peanut butter, jelly, crackers, and processed cheese. Stuart took a bite of the deng deng, made a face, and stuffed it back in the food bag. While the guides went on another scout we talked for the first time about our plans for the following week.

John was going to Bali to shop for textiles (he was president of the Primitive Art Society of Chicago, which was how he got into adventure traveling in the first place). Raymond was going to Benjarhassen (the Venice of Borneo) for the weekend and then back to work for Exxon. Stuart was going directly home to Australia, where he managed the hardware section of his father's farm machinery and hardware store. Howard was going to Malaysia and then back to Kuta Beach in Bali to drink and party for one more week. Sylvie and Mimo had plans to fly back to Bali and hook up with Olatz at the house Mimo had rented in Sanur Beach.

I was going to Sumatra to explore a hill town and then fly to

Penang to lounge in an old colonial hotel (hence the eight novels). After that I was going on another Sobek trip, this one a luxurious float down a river in Sumatra.

Bill was the only one with absolutely pressing plans. He had to be back in Balikpapan in three days to catch a series of flights that would end up in Palm Beach. He was already missing registration week at the extension of Florida Atlantic University where he taught. If he was delayed at all he'd miss his classes.

The talk was animated for a while. Then it dawned on us that the scout was getting to be a long one—never a good sign—and we grew silent, stupefied again by the heat and the bees. And sure enough, when the guides finally returned, they reported that there were all sorts of obstacles downriver: a rock pile, some logs, and lots more rapids. They had decided we could run them, they said, but there wasn't enough daylight left. We'd have to make camp early and spend at least one more night in the gorge.

Camp was once again on some rocks with no room to set up tents. This time we were just a few feet from the river, right next to a freshwater stream that tumbled down the canyon in back of us. Rather than heading out of bee territory, we seemed to have gone farther into it. We had three different kinds now: two that looked like honeybees—one medium-sized, one huge—plus the sweat bees. The sweat bees didn't sting, but we all swore they bit us. They were evidently attracted to the sweet odor of rot that we exuded, the tang of tasty waste products. They normally lived on feces and carrion, Bill said, and were champion survivors. Scientists had found fossils of sweat bees from the Cretaceous period along with the bones of dinosaurs.

Since we couldn't get rid of the bees, we endured, and fanned, and inevitably got stung several times a day—when one got in our armpits, or on the back of our thighs when we sat down, or when we tried to brush it off our neck. And we swore. Oh, how we swore. Sometimes it was low and pathetic, occasionally it sounded like a cacophonous angry drumbeat: *Piss! Merde! Shit! Damn!*

We took off our sweaty T-shirts and life jackets and put them in a ring around camp, hoping to keep the bees at the perimeter. But although they did gather on the sweaty clothes—in black swarms, several layers deep—there were always more of them. Where they came from and what they lived on when we weren't around was a mystery.

Occasionally we'd get desperate from bee stress and run into the river, rub ourselves all over with soap, and come out covered with lather. But the sweat would make its way through the soap in about five minutes.

Five sweet minutes. I'd have stayed in a lather continually, but I had to borrow the soap and already I was tired of asking. What had seemed to everyone like excess baggage at the beginning of the trip was now a bare minimum. The group was growing possessive; no one wanted to lend foot powder, or soap, or batteries, or dry socks. If I wanted anything at all, I had to beg. I was beginning to feel like a whiner, like the trip's dependent. I thought back to my joy in the hotel when I realized I'd shed my baggage and would have to travel light. How romantic that seemed now. How silly to think I'd gain something by making things difficult.

Only John never changed strategies for coping. At one point, sweltering in his long pants, shirt, vest, and hat, he lay down on a rock, closed his eyes, and remained motionless for a couple of hours, except for his hand, which languidly waved back and forth, conducting space music. I assumed he was waving away bees like the rest of us, but later he told me he'd been asleep.

21

*T*hat evening Howard found a giant centipede. A monster centipede. It was about eight inches long and iridescent in the sun. It moved by wriggling like a snake.

Dayaks consider centipedes one of the worst omens in the forest, so malevolent that in the old days anyone who saw one had to abandon whatever he was doing and run. If he was harvesting rice, he would abandon the field forever; if he was hunting heads, he would run back to his village and give up headhunting for at least four years.

Bill and Howard played with the centipede for a while with the snake stick, and then Bill tossed it in the river. I was glad to see it go, although as I watched it float off with the current I wondered if it would return to haunt us. By now it didn't take much suspension of disbelief to conjure up a few bad omens.

The early European explorers in Borneo who had to travel with native guides and porters all complained about the Dayak spirit world. Evil spirits were so omnipotent, and demanded so much attention, that it was hard, they said, to get anything done.

"The very air was peopled with a thousand malignant devils," wrote one frustrated explorer. "A sudden breath might engulf a spirit. An awkward step might crush one. Any man who stubbed a toe or stepped on a thorn immediately fell into a paroxysm of terror, convinced that he had offended the entire spirit world."

Charles Miller, a Hollywood cameraman who traveled up the Mahakam to a Kenyah village near Long Lebusan in 1942, said he wasted a full twenty days out of thirty avoiding bad omens and waiting around for good ones.

"A bad omen might hold us in some mudhole for a week," he wrote. "It would keep us from starting, make us go to the right or left side of a river needlessly, or wait to continue for a full moon."

It's hard to know whether or not to trust the Westerners who first observed Dayak culture. They called the natives "boys," after all, and treated them as children. But they also voluminously recorded what they saw and heard, and the number and variety of rituals and omens they came across was indeed astonishing. Consider, for example, the cloud of ritual and belief that surrounded pregnancy.

A pregnant woman had to go to the rice fields and work each day so the evil spirits wouldn't suspect her condition, but at the sight of certain birds and animals and even cloud formations, she had to run back to the longhouse and hide. And during a rainstorm, when the spirits were out in full force, she had to remain awake in case they tried something sneaky, a real problem during the rainy season when it often rained all night.

The woman's husband also had to perform wearisome rituals. In particular, he had to spit (a sign of respect for the spirits) each day in one thousand different directions. He would start spitting early in the morning, spit until he hadn't a drop of saliva left, hide in the bushes until he got his saliva back, and then resume his spitting. In addition, every time he threw a piece of wood in a fire or cut back a vine, he'd have to spit to calm down the spirits that were released. The poor fellow had to spit so much that expectant husbands could always be identified by their swollen tongues and cracked lips.

In addition to protecting herself from evil spirits trying to harm her unborn child, a pregnant woman had to obseve more symbolic taboos. She could not:

Gather or split firewood (so her child wouldn't have a harelip or double thumbs);

Cut off the limbs of an animal (so her child wouldn't have stumps for arms or legs);

Open the head of a fish (so her child wouldn't be born without ears);

Stretch up either arm to take food from a hanging tray (so her child wouldn't come into the world arm first);

Make fish hooks (so her child wouldn't be born doubled up in the wrong position);

Nail or tie up anything, or lock a trunk (so her child wouldn't remain in the womb and kill her);

Put a handle on a *parang* (knife) (so she wouldn't attract the attention of violent spirits);

Put a cork in a bottle or a cover on a bamboo basket containing rice (so her child wouldn't be born without eyes or ears, and with its nostrils open);

Split bamboo sticks for making mats (so her child wouldn't be born with some of his fingers grown together);

Tie garments around her neck when feeling hot (so her child wouldn't be born with the umbilical cord around its neck).

As I watched the centipede float into the current, I wanted to believe that a centipede is just a centipede. But I wasn't sure if my Western pragmatism applied anymore. I had traveled enough to know that the "truth" about the way the world works is localized, that although a centipede is just a centipede in Oakland, it might be more on the Boh.

When I spent time in Bali, Thailand, and Nepal, I accepted the presence of spirits with gratitude. They were a realm of the imagination that seemed peaceful and gentle, and far from limiting the way people conducted their lives, they enhanced it, inspiring music, dance, sculpture, and art. The spirit of the centipede, on the other hand, seemed the opposite of transcendent. It was pure random evil, like monsters in a nightmare. I hoped I wasn't going to find out too late that we should have dropped everything when we found the centipede and attempted to hike out of the gorge.

I had always imagined that someday, like Leda and the swan, I'd encounter some dark knowledge, glimpse some ancient, godless truth—a sudden blow, the great wings beating still, little Tracy held helpless, breast upon its breast.

But not death. When I was tumbling underwater, at the mercy of the river, I'd felt exactly like Sylvie did: Shit! What a colossal mistake. How stupid to die on this half-baked, harebrained, no-class river trip.

22

We all doubted that our third night in the gorge would be our last, but since our itinerary had us on the Mahakam the next morning, we pretended to believe it. Mimo had taken a great turn for the better (his fever was gone), and of all of us, he seemed most unhappy to sit still. He continually set small tasks for himself: cooking, gathering and chopping firewood, writing notes in bottles and sending them down the river, stringing up tarps and mosquito nets. Between him and Raymond, there weren't any camp chores left for the rest of us. That evening he built a fire and strung a clothesline next to it. He was going to personally burn the forest down, he said, if that's what it took to dry his clothes.

With visions of dry T-shirts and underwear, hot and mildew-free, I washed just about everything I owned. All evening I sat by the flames—blowing, fanning, rearranging, fighting for space close to the heat. But when it started to drizzle at about nine o'clock, almost nothing I had washed was dry and some of it was dripping wet. I folded the clothes carefully and put them in the carry-on cloth suitcase I'd taken with me on the plane. It was a little like putting fresh cheese in a bag full of fungus. My suitcase smelled like the essence of rot, like a thousand filthy basements, like a cave filled with decomposing rodents. It was so bad I had to laugh.

Like the jungle, our very persons were becoming a hotbed of silent, unseen organisms. Gary announced he had developed a bad case of foot rot, and it was getting painful just to walk. He had left his wet tennis shoes in the longhouse in Long Lebusan for four days and theorized that something particularly virulent had set up housekeeping inside them. Foot rot is a common ailment among boaters, but neither he, Mike, nor Dave had seen it develop this fast. Within a day, the areas between Gary's toes went from pink to red and cracked, and he had a band of flaking skin around the sides and back of both feet. Dave told the rest of us to keep our feet dry, or the fungus would spread. We laughed. Nothing was dry. Not our shoes, not our socks, and certainly not our feet.

"We'll be okay once we get on the Mahakam," Dave replied.

"That's supposed to be tomorrow night," I said.

"Fourth night on the Mahakam," Bill muttered darkly. "That's what they told us."

That night around the light of the fire, we toasted the possibility of making all of our airplane connections to places we would rather be, and stayed up talking later than usual. Howard and Stuart, who had heretofore seemed almost interchangeable— both in their late twenties, both modest and independent—finally began to take on distinct personalities. Howard didn't talk a lot unless he had something to say, but that didn't keep him from being absolutely pigheaded in his opinions. He was not a racist or a bully, but he was a product of four generations of farmers and sheep ranchers and so committed to common sense and personal independence that it was inconceivable to him that anyone might look at the world differently. When John mentioned anything having to do with the law, he made snide remarks about lawsuit-happy Americans; when someone mentioned missionaries he gave a short, passionate speech about the arrogance of imposing on others one's own beliefs. When Bill talked about the plight of the rain forest he fell asleep.

His pride in himself and his culture was rock solid. He brought pictures of his farm and the house he had built by hand on the family property and passed them around. He and his brother were managing the farm, he said, which was over nine thousand acres and had been in the family almost one hundred years.

I assumed his background was Scottish; he certainly looked it. His hair was curly, his skin was fair, his body stocky and strong. And he did have one particularly endearing trait I associate with Scotsmen, the one that had brought him to Borneo. He scoffed at bourgeois materialism and the encumbrances of modern life. He wanted to escape it by traveling, by being a romantic voyager. He had a girlfriend back home, he said, and because they both wanted to be independent they had talked seriously about not having children.

Howard had possibilities, I thought. He might someday encounter the unexpected and respond unexpectedly.

Stuart was a few years younger than Howard and his opposite in many respects: he was slender, talkative, interested in exploring ideas rather than expressing opinions. Although neither of the two Aussies was jaded or cynical, Stuart was more open-minded. He had never gone to college, but he was interested in history and ecology and knew he had a lot to learn.

"I'm very different than Howard," Stuart emphasized, wanting to dissociate himself mostly from Howard's conservative politics. He and Howard had not been close friends growing up in their small town and ended up coming to Borneo together only when they happened to meet by chance one day in a pub. But the two mates had grown close and took care of each other. As far as I could see they made absolutely no demands on anyone.

Stuart was the biggest drinker of all of us, and sometimes repeated himself and talked too much when he drank. We forgave him because he was unassuming and had a good heart. One time, Mimo told him to shut up, and Stuart apologized. My worry about the Aussies being macho was unfounded.

Raymond was the only one of our group who remained hard to like, mostly because he was so completely uninterested in the rest of us. He didn't seem particularly proud of working for Exxon; in fact the one thing he made sure to tell everybody was that he was taking a year's leave next year to do volunteer work for an Indonesian environmental organization. But other than that, he was closemouthed. None of us found out much about him, even Sylvie, with whom he seemed by now clearly besotted.

On the surface, Raymond was a pile of contradictions. He claimed to love Indonesia and Indonesians but complained continually about both the country and the people. He reminded us frequently that he wasn't a guide but barked orders more often than Gary, Dave, or Mike did. From time to time I sensed that the real Raymond was a prisoner of his intellect, that something generous inside him was trying to get free. But then I'd realize that he never said anything nice, never spoke about anything or anyone with warmth, was rarely even minimally polite. Although I was curious about him because he was competent and smart, I finally lost interest. His sense of hierarchy was unshakable: he patronized everyone but those above him in the pecking order, the jet-setters and the guides.

Mimo was our genuine jet-setter, a citizen of the world, a bon vivant. He was forty, and clearly accustomed to wealth, but seemed happy to sleep on a dirty wood floor in a longhouse. He was also able to have fun doing the grungiest of tasks. Sylvie said he'd been on a lot of adventures, including treks in the Sahara with "some of his crazy friends." He threw great parties, she said, all over Europe and America—in New York, Paris, Rome, and Ibiza. That night he told us that when he was nineteen years old his father divorced his mother and married a girl of sixteen.

"Jesus. How did you feel about that?" Linda asked.

He shrugged. "What could I feel? It didn't make any difference what I felt."

Here on the river, Mimo was our wild man. Although he was a smoker, and not terribly strong, he did seek out danger, even seemed to relish it. Bill said that every adventure trip he'd been on had one person who pushed for more and more thrills, and on our trip it was Mimo. He asked Bill to take a picture of him at one point, calling out: "Take a picture of me being a hero."

"He was joking," Bill said, "but still it says something about him."

That night, for the first time on the trip, we started to form a bond based on our growing hatred of the rain forest. Far from feeling reverential toward it, we were beginning to find it repugnant. Rather than a tropical garden, it seemed to be a single impenetrable organism of insects and tangled greens. Where were the monkeys? Where were the pheasants? Where were the orchids? And as for the river experience, it was mostly boredom punctuated by brief moments of terror. The point of running it—simply because no one had ever done it before—now seemed ludicrous.

Linda, who was the most miserable of us all, was torn between her growing hatred of the rain forest and her loyalty to Bill.

"The rain forest is fine," she said. "We're just not supposed to be in it."

"I'll never be so glad in my life," Bill conceded, "to see a logging camp."

The complaining was strangely desultory, however, even when the sand fleas came out, even when, moments later, it started to drizzle. And although we griped about Sobek's labeling the Boh a Class III adventure, none of us was truly angry. None of us had what Conrad called "the soft spot, the place of decay, the determination to lounge safely through existence." At this point we still accepted the adventure code of travel: go with the unexpected and make do with what you get.

23

One of my travel fantasies has always been to go someplace so remote that I'd be transported to another reality, the one that flourished on earth before the evolution of human technocrats. The only person I know to have done that is Eric Hansen, who spent seven months in Borneo traveling in the rain forest as the natives do—setting up temporary shelters, hunting and gathering food, adapting to the rhythms of the jungle as well as the villages and longhouses.

When Hansen finally reached a logging camp near the east coast, he was ushered into the bathroom of a missionary pilot and confronted by a "a brand-new bar of Dove soap, a white porcelain washbasin, and a blue terrycloth handtowel with matching washcloth." His response was an almost uncontrollable urge to leap out of the window.

"The ultimate trip," I wrote in my journal that night—our third on the Boh—"would be to get that far out; far enough out there to be scared by a bar of soap."

I'm not sure where I got this longing for other worlds. It doesn't have anything to do with being unhappy, as my husband fears. I suspect it's because I'm a dreamer, and as a child I read a lot. Also, in some strange way, I think I inherited this longing from my parents. My father is a man who, since I've known him, has been content with a circumscribed life. Pleasure, he says, is the absence of pain. But there was a time when he journeyed out into the world in search of adventure and a time when he found it. In his early twenties, on summer vacations from college, he pitched hay on a ranch in Cuba and worked his way to South America on a freighter. In Miami he was thrown in jail as a vagrant; in World War II he was a naval officer in the Pacific. My father is not a sentimental man; in fact, he is prone to understatement. But those are the experiences he refers to when he says, now, that he has lived a full life.

My mother, who is as ready as I am to be ravished by new experiences, has always supported my traveling. Except for her intolerance of filth, we have the same tastes. If I'm going somewhere that may be dangerous, she worries, but at the last minute she always writes a note or gives me a call: "I understand, Tracy," she says. "I know you just have one life."

I lay awake a long time that night, watching the gray, starless sky through the gaps in the canopy. The outside world felt very far away, and I felt very sealed off from it. The gorge had turned opaque, damp, and airless, as if it were inside a giant Tupperware box. And everything was hot. Either hot or wildly hot. About once an hour I would start to sweat so profusely I'd have to flap the sheets to try to dry off.

These heat episodes were beginning to come with such uncomfortable regularity that I could no longer ignore them. I couldn't talk about them; in fact, I could barely think about them. But I knew what was happening. The rain forest wasn't changing temperature in an hourly cycle, I was. I was entering menopause.

I hardly knew what menopause was. None of my friends had ever talked to me about it, and people my age were still, occasionally, bearing children. But before I left, my doctor had told me that it was coming. And here it was. The heat seemed to begin in my face, spread to my neck and chest, and stay there for about five minutes. Fanning made my skin feel better, but nothing reduced my internal temperature much. Only time. After a few minutes I'd start to feel better, and in another five minutes or so I was back to normal.

My instinct was to talk to someone about this newest indignity, but I realized I couldn't. It was too personal. Too terrible. I was too ashamed. I slept very little that night, waking up every now and then in a pool of sweat, and then, just before dawn, I witnessed a surprising tableau. I heard someone rustling in the dark and recognized Mike's silhouette. He was starting the morning fire. Then I heard another voice, a woman's. Sylvie!

I sat up and in the dim light saw her taking things out of the food bag and cleaning off the slab of wood that served as our table. Had she somehow been assigned to breakfast detail, I wondered. Should I get up and start helping her?

Then, suddenly, I understood what was happening. Sylvie and Mike must have woken up together, which meant they'd slept together last night. In the midst of the leeches and bees, the fear and the foot rot, they had managed to become lovers.

"They had to mate," Linda said later. "They are both just too gorgeous."

The affair did seem inevitable, but it made my hormonal state even more humiliating. I thought about the one joyful Dayak spirit I'd read about, a female spirit who lives in rivers. I had seen her several times in flashes of glorious cliché: a glimpse of flesh in a deep pool; a face with white teeth in a waterfall; hair streaming over a dark rock. I did not imagine her as anything like me. I used to feel connected to sex symbols; even comforted by them. But no more.

24

*T*hat morning, our fourth on the river, was hot, clammy, and beautiful. Eerie clouds floated through the canyon and drifted down the steep rock walls; in one place the mist blew back on itself like waves in a Japanese painting. For the first time, I imagined myself not just in a rain forest but in a genetic hothouse, a place where there was enough uninterrupted water and sunlight for continual evolutionary experiment. The soil was old and weathered, and had lost much of its mineral content, but every single nutrient was used, and in terms of sheer bulk there was an extraordinary amount of life.

Then I discovered nature's latest little gift to me: a sore in my mouth, a red spot on my gums where something or other had found a home. I just hoped it wouldn't turn out to be one of those virulent tropical diseases—Gary's foot rot squared.

Gary's foot rot had not only increased exponentially, it was now making all of us nervous. In just one night it had spread all over his feet, and he was afraid that if it continued spreading, he might not be able to walk. Dave and Mike were powdering their feet feverishly.

Only Sylvie was keeping up appearances. This morning she was dressed in a miraculously clean blue-and-white-striped pedal-pusher outfit, looking very French. Underneath was another bathing suit, half a bathing suit, really. When she undressed to run in the water, I saw that it revealed just about all of her tan, well-muscled bottom. She was built like an athlete, with broad shoulders, solid haunches, and a tiny, firm waist. Linda, who was pretty sexy herself, complained bitterly: "I could take off all my clothes and run around naked and no one would pay any attention."

I'd completely given up comparing myself to Sylvie. I had no clean clothes, no shampoo, no brush, no scarves. My hair was flat and stringy, my legs were covered with welts, my T-shirts smelled like rotten milk, I wasn't even bothering to put on my one, moldy bra.

Our first bit of good news that day was that the rapids, which the guides had named Boh Dacious, Boh Derek, and Boh Diddley, were runnable. And in the morning we actually sped a couple of miles down the river, past flocks of butterflies on the riverbanks and a waterfall that looked like a cross between a Gauguin painting and an electric beer sign in a bar. Sometimes, when the river was calm enough for us to look at the scenery, it seemed like a Zen koan, a deep, deep thread that managed to clarify the jungle chaos. At other times the river was a rodeo or shivaree, whereas the jungle was dark and quiet.

Although we took most of the rapids without our helmets, Dave continued to give us warnings, stray bits of good advice. "If you feel yourself just swimming around in white water but not getting anywhere," he said, "reach up and feel for a rope. If we see you, we'll be trying to throw you one." I imagined the likelihood of a rope brushing my fingers as I spun around in a hole. I was not encouraged.

And then, about two hours into the morning run, we heard the unmistakable roar of white water. We pulled into an eddy and sat in the boats, silent. Gary knew he would have to do some hard walking to scout the river and was tight-lipped and furious. But he gathered his water bottle and knife and went off with Dave and Mike. Mimo went with them for a while but returned looking dejected.

"It looks impossible to me," he said. "Around the corner the entire river funnels into one tremendous waterfall."

"Our world," I wrote in my journal, "has basically narrowed down to the river. Everything else seems irrelevant—the incredible butterflies, the jungle, our careers back home, even the bees. Our lives depend on holes, eddies, keepers, cheats, haystacks, waterfalls, pinballs, gradient, volume, running-right, running-left, highsiding, pull, harder, *Pull! Harder!*"

"Whose idea was it to run this river?" said Bill a little later. "I hope he's fired."

25

*T*his time the wait seemed endless; after three hours we knew our hopes of getting out of the gorge that day had been naïve. For the first time we began to discuss the rescue Dave had told us about. He had left a deposit in Balikpapan for a helicopter to come and search for us if we were more than a week late.

"I don't think a helicopter could rescue us here," Mimo said. "There's no place to land."

"Don't they have baskets and big hooks or something to scoop you up?" I asked.

"I hope not," said Raymond.

"Even if they had, they might not be able to get to us," said Bill. "The gorge is pretty narrow and the tree canopy is impenetrable."

"I can't believe we didn't bring a radio," Linda said.

I walked into the forest a few feet and sat on a log. I had decided to trade the bees, and now tiny black flies as well, for leeches. My plan was to give Dave's leech techniques a try and let them balloon up with blood until they dropped.

Although the sweat still trickled down my back, I felt cooler in the shade, but then I put my hand down on the log and leaped up. Something incredibly slimy was living on the rotting wood; its entire top side was glistening with a silvery ooze. I tried to wipe the stuff from my hands on a nearby vine, but it was sticky and viscous. When I looked at it I gagged: it was exactly like snot. Then I felt the seat of my shorts with my other hand and gave a scream: I couldn't even feel the cloth through the goo. It took me about two seconds to get in the river, and ten minutes to rub my hands and butt in the sand until most of the muck had disappeared. My shorts were still slimy when I took them off that night.

"If I am to die on this adventure," I wrote in my journal, "it won't be sudden. I'll just lie down in the rain forest and rot."

The guides sensed our gloom when they finally returned. They tried to be upbeat, but the rapids ahead were over a mile long, with one hundred feet of drop. There was a short calm section at the end of it and then more big water as far as they could see. It was definitely dangerous for a nonbailing boat. The good news was that we didn't have to portage; Dave decided to send the boats down without passengers, just kick them into the rapids. He called it "ghostboating." The danger was losing a boat, either in an unreachable eddy, a hole, or some kind of logjam.

While we endured the heat and the bees, the guides whacked a trail through the tangle of vegetation that somehow managed to flourish right on the steep sides of the gorge. They had to go almost a mile before they came to an eddy large enough to retrieve the ghostboats. We could see them climb maybe thirty feet up the gorge and then cut a traverse, popping in and out of the trees as they made their way downstream. The trail looked difficult, but I was ready for action. I was tired of waiting, tired of feeling superfluous.

Bill walked upstream for a while, in search of snakes. Many of them lived in the trees, he said, but he figured he might flush out something hidden in a log pile or under a rock. Mimo unwrapped some chocolate he and Sylvie had brought for themselves, and started a playful food fight with her. Sylvie got out her video camera and told him to throw things at it. I lay back and tried to doze.

Bill returned twenty minutes later to report that he'd seen an entire troop of red-leaf monkeys. He'd also found a tiny sandbar with tracks of a monitor lizard, a dinosaurlike creature with two clawed feet and a dragging tail. It was probably about four to six feet long, he said, and much more common in Borneo's inland rivers than crocodiles, which had been mostly hunted out.

The Dayaks used to catch crocodiles with a device so ingenious all the explorers who saw it described it in detail. It was a fifteen-inch stick, sharpened at both ends, with a length of rattan attached. They ran the stick through an animal carcass, bent the stick and carcass in half, wrapped it up with a strip of rattan, and suspended the entire contraption from a branch over a river. An unsuspecting crocodile would smell the tasty morsel and swallow it whole, whereupon the Dayaks would pull on the rattan rope, causing the pointed stick to snap back open inside the hapless crocodile's stomach. Since the animal couldn't thrash around in this condition, the Dayaks could haul it ashore and leave it to die in the sun, thus avoiding being personally responsible for upsetting a spirit should the crocodile have eaten anyone.

The way the Dayaks killed monitor lizards was a little less elegant. Jim Slade, a Sobek guide who traversed Borneo in the seventies, told me about hunting on a river not far from the Boh. The Kenyah boatman he was with signaled that he saw some game, jumped out, and started walking upstream in the water with his spear raised. Jim couldn't imagine that anything a person would want to eat would wait for someone to walk through the water and spear it, but the man suddenly hurled the spear into the water and stabbed at something on the bottom over and over again. Finally, after much blood and turbulence, he reached down and pulled up a huge monitor lizard. He stabbed it some more, squished the spear around inside its head, and then heaved it into Jim's boat, where it lay bleeding profusely in front of him for the next hour as he continued paddling to a downstream village. The reptile was clearly dead, Jim said. Absolutely motionless. He swears most of its head was gone.

After they pulled into the village and started a fire, one of the men went to the boat to get the lizard for cooking. While he was walking back with it, staggering under its weight, Jim saw the lizard's head move. He didn't believe it at first, but then he saw a long forked tongue flick in and out of its mouth. Suddenly the lizard came completely alive, flailing and thrashing so much the Dayak had to drop him. And when he did, the lizard, still without half a head and holes in him the size of a pocketbook, started to attack, rearing up, opening its jaws, and lunging.

About three o'clock in the afternoon, Mike sent the first ghost-boat down, and we all watched it pilot itself through a series of huge pourovers and head for the big drop—the Boh Constrictor, Mike had named it. It took the drop and disappeared in a sea of roaring turbulence. I could only glimpse flashes of gray and yellow bouncing around in the spray. But then it popped out, upside down, and caught a current that took it careening down-river until it landed in an eddy alongside a high rock wall. In some eddies the line between the slow water that's backing up and the fast water from the rapids actually forms a ridge high enough to keep a boat in it. This was one of them, a keeper eddy, boatmen call it. There was nothing to do but try to get to the boat and kick it out into the current.

Gary and Dave were waiting below the rapids, so Mike took off by himself, doing a belly crawl underneath a fallen tree, ("Evidently," said Bill, "he's not worried about snakes"). He made it to the top of the rock wall above the boat and climbed down some slime-covered boulders to a point where he could string a rope to an overhanging tree branch. Then he grabbed the rope and, like Tarzan, made a flying leap, kicking his legs out to gain momentum, then snapping his torso forward to land on the boat in a crouch.

"Like in the movies," Howard said.

Standing on the boat, holding the rope, he walked the boat like a treadmill to the point upstream where the eddy wall was lowest. Then, with a final thrust, he kicked it into the current and swung back to the boulder. The boat danced in the turbu-lence for a bit and then went over another drop only to get caught in another eddy. Again Mike climbed the rope back up to the forest, made his way downstream, and repeated the performance.

"I haven't seen that much courage in quite a spell," Howard said afterward. It was high praise.

While Sylvie was filming Mike's final Tarzan act, I found a piece of chocolate on the ground—the chocolate she and Mimo had split between them. It was dark chocolate, wrapped in tinfoil, and I thought about giving it to her for all of ten seconds.

If there's anything better than sitting in the sun on a rock by a river and eating a piece of dark chocolate, I couldn't think of it.

26

"*Eeeee, Eeeee, Eeeee!*" There was a certain cicada that seemed to awaken regularly at six o'clock every evening, fifteen minutes before sunset. Its call soared over the noise of everything else, even the rapids: an unforgettable, high-pitched, keening wail that sounded like a cross between glass bells and screeching brakes. Tom Harrisson, who organized an expedition to Borneo in 1932 with a group of Oxford and Cambridge men, dubbed it "the gin and bitters bug." For us it signaled a rush to get prepared for darkness. After we heard it, we knew the sun would sink in the sky like a stone. We were almost on the equator, where there were twelve hours of daylight, twelve hours of darkness, and almost no dawn or dusk in between. The cry had particular significance for me since the flashlight I'd bought in Balikpapan had proved to be worthless for the long haul. It had a beam that lit up the entire tree canopy, but required four fresh American batteries every fifteen minutes. I had only one half hour of light left.

Tonight, the insects were already making their last call when Gary, Mike, and Dave came back from tying up the paddle boat downstream. They were exhausted. And tomorrow they would have to send two more ghostboats down, meaning we weren't going to go anywhere at all until late afternoon.

Gary's feet now looked almost necrotic. The skin was peeling off in chunks around his toenails, and the sides of his feet were fiery red. He rubbed antifungal ointment on them, borrowed a pair of my thin socks to wear with his thongs, and after dinner went down to the boats to brood. Dave also went off somewhere to tend to his feet, which were cut and scratched as well as red.

Mike sat by the fire directly in front of Sylvie, who wrapped her legs around his legs in a hug. She massaged his shoulders and forehead and when she spoke she leaned forward and brushed her lips against his ear. Her hair fell down his shoulders; he took his glasses off. Although Mike remained relatively low-key, Sylvie was constantly nuzzling and fondling him. It was outright, blatant lust. After trying not to stare for a while, I finally gave up and watched them openly. I decided to enjoy the show. We all did, I think, which is why we were able to sit around for hours at night without saying much of anything.

Sylvie's boyfriend, Richard, was not forgotten—Sylvie and Mimo often brought up his name when they were talking together. But even Mimo, who was one of Richard's good friends, seemed to accept the notion that a romantic liaison in a rain forest in Borneo is something an unmarried woman is not expected to resist. And so Mike and Sylvie and Mimo became a threesome, two lovers and a friend. It all seemed complicated but not deceptive. Very French. The only element that tilted this stable triangle was Raymond, who still seemed to be pursuing Sylvie. At one point I saw him stroking her face and running his fingers through her hair as she lay on her side next to the fire. Sylvie didn't encourage him—she seemed only to tolerate the attention—but it gave the affair poignancy. As competent as Raymond was, he wasn't sexy, not next to Mike. Mike was blessed with a slow smile, a gorgeous body, and enough sense not to spoil the effect with too much talk.

John and I were becoming pals more or less by default. He had to carry our joint bag full of clothes from the boat to a campsite, and we ended up sleeping next to each other at night. Little by little he began to talk. He had a girlfriend back in Chicago, he said. She was vice-president of a company that made inflight audiotapes for airlines. They had been seeing each other exclusively for twelve years.

"Do you live together?" I asked.

"No. Although she does now have an apartment. She lived with her mother until six months ago."

"Are you going to get married?"

John gave a tiny flash—just a hint—of frustration and anger. "I don't know," he said. "She's still making up her mind."

It was a start.

"How long can you wait for her?" I asked.

He shrugged. "Until I get tired of it, I guess."

That would be, I knew, a long, long time. If John was anything at all, he was patient.

I felt the first raindrops after dinner when I was trying to find a place to pee without using my flashlight, and when I came back to camp everyone was busy constructing shelters from tarps and rope. We had tents with us, but there was no rock-free space in which to pitch them. I asked where the tarps were and found only a ragged piece of plastic. The rope had all been taken and the guides were off somewhere tending their feet. I sat down to have a small fit.

Eventually I searched for Dave and found him staring at the sores between his toes. He told me it probably wouldn't rain very hard and to just put the plastic over my face and go to sleep. I was shocked. Everyone else was rigging up elaborate structures; what if we *did* have a downpour? But in a few minutes he went down to a boat to get some twine, and I thanked him and went back to camp. I managed to rig a three-sided shelter, strung from trees and secured to a rock, and remembered that I could take care of myself. It wasn't the greatest shelter—that was always constructed by Howard—but it would more or less keep the rain off. And so I wrapped myself up in my sheet and listened to the boulders tumbling in the distance. For the first time, I knew we wouldn't make it out of the gorge the next day. What I didn't know was what happened to rivers in Borneo when it rained.

27

I awoke at dawn the next morning in a small pool of water, last night's drizzle plus an intense series of hormonal sweat attacks. Strangely, I was happy. A slow, soft hum was in the air along with the distant roar of the Boh and the calls of unseen insects. The heat intensified the smell of the river and the forest, creating a perfume of stagnant mud and rotting vegetation: the smell of the tropics. It was a sweet smell of riches and fecundity that had seduced many a sailor and traveler, the latest in my memory being James Hamilton-Paterson. In *Playing with Water* he'd called it a "tropical opiate," awakening "memories of things which have never happened and foretelling things which will never be." The smell brought back for me now, as it had in Balikpapan, memories of sensual languor. I threw off the sheet, stretched, and noted how strange it was that here, this very morning, bitten and stinking and tired from a terrible night's sleep—with little to look forward to but another day of terror or boredom—I was content. I reached up sleepily to scratch my face and . . . Ouch!

The bees had come early that morning, and soon all of us were up early, waving our hands and prancing around like a bunch of goofy two-year-olds practicing bye-bye. The sun was out and last night's mist was rising off the rocks like steam, but the bees managed to keep us from enjoying it. Our group good humor began to break.

Mimo was the first to speak the obvious: this wasn't much fun. His problem was not the rapids, or the unknown, but the waiting.

"I wouldn't mind this if we were actually running the river," he said, "but we're crawling it. We've spent a total of about two hours in the rafts."

"Right!" Howard said. "I get so frustrated when we have to stop at four o'clock each afternoon. I say let's get on with it. Let's push."

"I keep thinking," Linda said, "what if something happens to one of us? What if we get sick, or break something? What if we get bitten by a snake? We could die on this trip. I don't think there are emergency plans."

"Dave said a radio was too heavy to bring," I commented, "but how heavy is something like an airplane signaling device? You can carry it in your pocket."

"If Laura [Steinberg] had come," said Mimo, "she would have . . . I don't know, gone crazy. She couldn't have taken the bees. The *sight* of a spider freaks her out."

"What amazes me," said John, "is that Sobek would send a lawyer *and* a journalist on this trip."

"Look at it this way," said Bill. "If something happens to one of us, you'll get rich."

Although I had thought a lot of these thoughts, even written them in my journal, hearing them spoken out loud made me uncomfortable. I had seen fear turn into outrage and righteousness before, and once I'd watched a group disintegrate because two of its members insisted on trying to make the reality of a trip conform to how it had been packaged.

In Nepal my husband and I had been invited to dinner with an adventure travel group that was a day away from the Mt. Everest base camp. We were having chocolate pudding in their kitchen tent when the leader announced that at least half of the group wanted to skip the base camp and explore a reputedly more beautiful side canyon. He'd decided to split the group in two so everyone could go where they wanted. He'd lead the base camp group, and the head Sherpa would accompany those who wanted to hike into the canyon.

There was a moment of excited conversation while people discussed the pros and cons of both trips and then one man, a lawyer, rose to speak. As far as he and his wife (also a lawyer) were concerned, he said, the entire group had a responsibility to stick with the original base camp plan. The trip was sold on the basis of that itinerary; there were dangers in splitting a group in two (which group got the trip doctor?), and although he personally had no opinion as to which was the better route, he and his wife would expect a full refund of their money if the itinerary was changed.

It would have been funny if the evening hadn't ended up with shouting. And the lesson was clear: sometimes it's better to leave behind preconceived expectations and go with whatever will produce the most good feeling. When I thought of what might happen to our group if anyone started to turn on Dave, Gary, or Mike, the rapids and the bees seemed like minor irritations.

Also, truth be told, I had mixed feelings about the trip so far. There had been plenty of moments when I'd felt scared, lonely, or irritated, but there was also the increasing joy of being on what had become a genuine adventure. I was beginning to feel as if I'd found that alternate reality, that I was having another life. There was something about being so remote and alone that heightened my sense of self. I could see myself in focus, as usual, but I could also make the picture widen as I became part of a group, and then part of a group by a river in a forest, and then just a flicker of color on a vast blanket of primal green vegetation. Eons had passed here, unregarded, and now we were stealing minutes under the nose of eternity. Our three rubber boats bounced at the river's edge like time capsules. I liked the image; I even, at times, liked the reality. We all did.

*　　*　　*

It was the bees that were breaking our spirits. Coexisting with them this morning wasn't enough; they seemed to be angry, deliberately tormenting us with a little inferno of noise. The sound of them was like the sound of torturers, cackling and sneering as they danced around our brains.

"What I don't understand," said Bill, "is why *honeybees* are after salt."

"Because they're hungry?" Gary suggested.

"But there's nectar in the tree canopy. The only explanation I can think of is that there's some weird kind of salt deficiency in the gorge."

"Do bees feed on other animals?" I asked.

"Not honeybees. And where *are* the other animals? I haven't seen much evidence of them. There's definitely something strange about this place."

"Maybe the bees have driven the animals away," Linda said.

"Maybe the bees are in cahoots with the evil river spirit," Bill replied.

"Maybe . . ." We all looked up. It was John. "Maybe the bees *are* tiny little evil river spirits," he said.

Just then Raymond appeared. Secretly I would have been glad by now to see him humbled in some particularly humiliating fashion—attacked by giant leeches, say, who suck the blood out of him until he shrinks down into a wrinkled old dustrag and has to ask for help in a tiny little voice like Vincent Price in *The Fly*. But I forgave him everything that morning when he came up to us with a beautifully decorated plate of food: Pringles carefully arranged in a circle around what looked like a heap of black beans, hot red peppers, and peanuts.

"Fantastic!" we all cried.

"Where did you get this?"

"Who's been hoarding the food?"

But then Bill started to laugh, and Mimo and Sylvie both shrieked and shouted something in French. I took a closer look at the plate. *Bees!* It was the first good laugh I'd had since Linda and I realized we'd each gone down to the river and washed our crotches after making fun of Sylvie for doing it.

The beans were bees, about six cupfuls of dead bees. Raymond had scooped them up from a sweaty T-shirt, drowned them in a bucket overnight, drained them this morning, and created a master salad.

"On the menu this morning is composed bee salad," Mimo announced in dulcet waitperson tones, and while those with cameras ran off to get them, he arranged a few bees on a Pringle and passed it around.

When Sylvie came back with her video camera, Raymond opened his mouth wide and actually arranged a couple of dead bees on his tongue. Then, sensing the aesthetic possibilities, several live bees arranged themselves attractively on his face and neck. I wished I had my camera. I liked him better at that moment than at any other time in the trip.

28

*T*he plan this morning was for Mike to send the last two ghost-boats down the river while the rest of us climbed partway up the side of the gorge and made our way downriver through the vegetation. If luck was with us, the boats wouldn't get stuck and we could conceivably sail out of the gorge by late afternoon.

I was looking forward to the walk. I wanted to seize the initiative, take some action on my own, do something. Anything. Also, I love traverses. Since I'm not afraid of heights I have no problem standing on tiny ledges hundreds of feet above the ground. Even when I was a kid I could terrorize my mother by standing on the edge of cliffs or walking along high walls. She'd wave at me frantically and shout for me to get down, but because she was afraid to actually come over and grab me, I could watch her quiver and bite her fingernails until I relented and came running into her arms. I loved the power then, and I suppose I must love it now.

Packing that morning was a new form of torment. First of all, the bees were crawling all over my sweaty clothes, and every time I tried to roll or fold something I crushed a few. I had developed a kind of hop-wave-jerk-swish routine, but it was only marginally successful and I got stung twice before I finished.

Even worse than the bees were the fashion decisions: we had to decide what to wear for the jungle walk. Should we completely cover up with clothing in an attempt to keep out the leeches? Or should we go with our usual shorts and a T-shirt in order to see the leeches and rub them off? Yesterday I'd noticed a leech come toward me, stop in mid-sniff, wave its head about, and then turn away, as if disgusted. It had given me hope. Perhaps my outer layer of slime and mold had camouflaged me as a bloodless, rotting carcass.

Dave had warned us that not only do leeches crawl up your boots and find their way into your warm body parts, they make flying leaps from trees and hurl themselves off vines and rocks. So in addition to the image of leeches loping along the ground and catapulting themselves onto my shoes, I now had to think of leeches as little aerialists, waiting for a chance to practice their trapeze acts. At least leeches couldn't kill me, I told myself. Not like flying snakes.

Osa Johnson wrote about taking a walk near her Mahakam River camp and suddenly seeing poisonous snakes fly through the air "like arrows of death." One moment she was taking a stroll at the edge of a clearing and the next moment fifty snakes were in the air, heading right for her. She had a pretty terrible three seconds until she realized they were actually heading for a tree just behind her.

Osa also wrote about a flying monkey that had taken to hanging around her camp. It was a species that could jump from tall trees into the brush by spreading its arms and legs and letting its skin act as a sail. One night it got into her bedroom, climbed up to an overhead beam, and had the bright idea of sailing down to the top of her mosquito net. It leaped off, whooshed down, and crashed through the net, landing on top of her and knocking her wind out.

Osa, I decided, probably flicked mere leeches off her thighs like sow bugs. Hell, I would brave the rain forest in shorts.

But just when I finally had everything packed, Dave announced that we had to prepare an emergency bag, things to carry with us on the trail in case one or both of the ghostboats couldn't be recovered and our personal gear was lost. I stared at the heavy rubber bag that contained all of John's and my possessions for several minutes, trying to think. I was blocked. Somehow I'd developed a disturbingly personal relationship with that blue monster. Some primordial instinct for cleanliness overwhelmed me whenever I dug down into it to retrieve my moldy cloth suitcase. I must have started to carry that stinking canvas fungus farm down to the river to give it a good wash a dozen times before I remembered that it wouldn't dry. Then there was the matter of John's wet socks. He'd put them at the bottom of the bag and now they smelled like the vomit-ridden stairwell of a train station in India where I'd once seen a man coughing blood. If I dug too deep, the fumes would come rocketing up.

But finally I braved the odor and dragged out my glasses and contact lenses, my journal, a tube of sunscreen, my bottle of pain pills, a long-sleeved shirt, and a pair of long pants. Then I realized that I had forgotten to buy a daypack. I wandered around and asked if anyone had an extra, which, of course, no one did, and eventually Dave had to stuff my things into his daypack.

When I was at last ready to go, I noticed Sylvie sitting on a rock down by the river, plucking some stray hairs from her thighs. It seemed completely inappropriate, taking comfort in such grooming, but then I remembered that the Dayaks also pluck out body hair. They believe hair saps their strength, and have been known to remove even their eyelashes. As I watched Sylvie set the mirror down and fiddle with her hair and a large blue plastic clip, it began to dawn on me that body care is not just an invention of Madison Avenue or the cosmetics industry. There was grooming before there were grooming aids. Sylvie's profession had taught her to keep clean and dry, and treat every sore and blemish. It was a skill that might prove extremely valuable in a sodden, bacteria-ridden rain forest.

29

On the traverse, I was surprised all over again at how spongy and rotten everything was. The entire forest floor was being devoured by ravenous microorganisms. Our progress was slow but constant, mostly a matter of finding firm foot- and handholds. Dave had warned us about rattan, which is a long (up to five hundred feet), flat liana edged on both sides with sharp thorns. Now it was everywhere. A quarter of the things I touched had thorns or sharp spines and the rest were covered with ants. At times I had to go through maddening contortions to remove the spiny vines from my clothes and hair, twisting and lifting them off while standing on the practically nonexistent trail.

But I hiked mostly with a sense of exhilaration, passing John, then Linda and Bill, then Howard; in retrospect I remember my first walk through the jungle as a race. I had a tremendous urge to get somewhere without stopping, to reach a destination, to feel my body working well again.

At times the edge of the trail dropped straight off to the river and I had an uninterrupted aerial view of the rapids that had stopped us. They seemed both monstrous and splendid. Although it was not terribly steep here, the gorge had narrowed down to a width of about twenty feet, and the river was funneling through it with tremendous force. In the middle was the keeper hole. It was a churning whirlpool, its center sunk perhaps five feet below its rim, and on either side were logjams and rock piles. I could see why Dave had said it was impossible to line the boats.

I could also see why he'd decided not to portage. The trail was fine without a load, but it would have been extremely difficult to carry the heavy bags of food and equipment on it, not to mention the deflated and rolled-up 130-pound rafts. And some parts of the trail were dangerously exposed. A fall could mean a plunge into the rapids, or an abrupt splatter on the rocks.

Finally I saw the end of the trail, a point where it took a nosedive down the side of the gorge to a pool where the river was calm again. Gary and Raymond were waiting down at the edge of the water to catch the ghostboats. I made a quick leech check—nothing so far—and decided to stay put a while and watch the others emerge from the trees.

Howard came first; sturdy, silent, and self-sufficient. One of the reasons nobody on the trip talked seriously about suing Sobek, I realized, was Howard's strong opinions about litigation-happy Americans. He said it amazed Australians that Americans expect the world to be made safe for them. "Americans will sue," Howard complained, "if they take a walk in the woods and a tree branch falls on them. And if there is a sign warning them that a tree branch might fall, they'll say someone should have made them read it."

John nodded in agreement. "All this talk about protecting rights and so forth is just a bunch of lawyer talk," he said. "Most people sue because they want to get money."

After Howard came Bill and then Linda, who was now barely managing to keep her good humor. She was clearly the most emotional member of the group, and Bill was sticking close to her. She seemed to need his help. It occurred to me that he was a good mate—calm, steady, and kind, but also passionate enough about his own work to keep Linda interested. He lacked charm, but he was, at his core, an original.

Finally John appeared—sliding down the trail on his butt. I had to laugh. He had become the trip's comic-book character. He was two-dimensional. We could see him, we could hear him, but we had no clue as to his depth. His stance toward life was singular, one of quiet bemusement. At first I had thought he was suffering in silence, but now I wondered if he was suffering at all. I remembered what Gary had said about going into a "reptilian mode" in the rapids: it seemed to apply to John. He was so undemanding, so unwilling to cause trouble that I began to worry he'd attempt something too difficult simply because it was easier than making a fuss. I'd see him staggering up a path, carrying our mutual dry bag, slipping, grabbing hold of rotten vines, falling down in the mud, and feel guilty about not being able to help. He managed, however, and I think he was pleased with himself.

Everyone made it down the rope, including John, and for a brief moment, before it was my turn to descend, I looked longingly at the rocks down by the river, which were glistening in full sun. I saw a route down to a flat rock in the water, and imagined lying down on it, drifting to the sound of the river and the feel of the heat, dangling my feet in the cold water and then rolling over to let the sun bake my thighs and chest.

The California river fantasy lasted until I heard the buzzing. The goddamned buzzing. The pissant, goddamned, I-don't-believe-this-get-away-from-me-you-little-shits buzzing.

30

Clearly, insect stress was all a matter of attitude. The two or three beestings I got each day were painful, but brief. What I had to do was learn to accept the idea of bees, the sound of bees, the feel of bees on my skin. As I sat by the river waiting for the ghostboats, I decided to see if I could psych myself up, just once, to actually enjoy the sensation of tiny moving insect feet. I sat motionless, letting the bees gather on me, then imagined someone tickling me sensuously with his fingertips. H-m-m . . . oh-h-h-h . . . Yuk!

I had forgotten how much tiny insect feet make you want to scratch.

I told myself to think of bees as tiny pets, cuddling up and buzzing with affection, but that lasted about thirty seconds before I started to laugh. I even tried some experiments in noble self-sacrifice. The bees were an endangered species doomed to perish from the face of the earth unless I offered up my sweat. The bees were a torturer's test: hot pokers would be driven up the fingernails of my stepchildren unless I kept perfectly still while they crawled all over my face.

But lying to myself didn't work. I hated the bees. They were like little furies. If they didn't have stingers I would have picked them up with my fingers like snails and crushed them.

The minutes went by—ten minutes, twenty minutes, a half

hour—and Dave got up with a curse. Somehow the primitive but foolproof communication system he'd set up had failed. He could look upstream and see Stuart; Stuart could look upstream and see Mimo; Mimo could look upstream and see Mike, back at camp with Sylvie, waiting to send the boats down. What had happened?

While Dave hiked back upriver I checked my feet. I'd gotten a leech in my shoe during the jungle walk, but the only sign of it now was a dark ring about an inch in diameter. Worse were the small lesions between my toes along with some tiny bumps. On my calf was a long line of red spots that felt like the beginning stages of poison oak. The time had come to swallow my pride and beg for antifungal medication or powder. Since Bill also had foot rot, I figured he'd sympathize.

I found him and Linda dusting their feet behind a rock with a big bottle of medicated powder and decided that it was paranoid to think they were hiding from me. When I asked for some, Linda handed me the bottle, but when I began to shake a little of it on my feet she shouted for me to stop. "Don't use it all up," she snapped. "Shake a little into your hand and rub it on. This has to last."

"I'm sorry," I said, and took the tinest amount.

All of us had raw nerves. It seemed that bees from all over Borneo were now pouring into the gorge.

Upriver, Mike was also having problems.

In order to get the boats started on a good run through the rapids, he had to release them from the other side of the river, which was essentially a vertical rock wall. The only place where he had a chance of standing upright was a half-submerged boulder, and to get to it he had to swim across the current. His plan was to hook together both boats, tie a rope to them, stuff the rope into a throw bag tied to his shorts, and swim hard with the rope trailing out behind him. Sylvie would stay with the boats and push them into the river when he was ready to pull them across.

On his first attempt he ran out of rope just before he got to the boulder and had to swim back. The second time he tied two ropes together, but they came out of the throw bags too fast and he couldn't fight the drag of the line in the current. The third time he made it to the boulder and was pulling the boats across when he slipped and fell heavily, spraining his ankle and ripping the nail almost entirely off his right big toe. He recovered, and kept control of the boats, but his toe was bloody and the nail on it was flapping from a little hinge at its base.

He wrapped his headband around it as a tourniquet, tested his battered ankle, and went back to work.

The first ghostboat caught the current and Mike watched it bounce right out of the Boh Constrictor and disappear around a bend. He gave a cheer as it headed to the right, away from yesterday's keeper eddy.

A few minutes later, while he was sitting down in the second boat, coiling some ropes, he heard Sylvie scream. He looked up and leaped to his feet. The boat he was sitting in had come loose and was floating right into the rapids! He ran to the back of the boat, dove upstream, and made it back to the boulder, but just barely.

Exhausted now, and in pain, Mike prayed that the second boat would also make it through the Boh Constrictor without any problems. He watched it hit the big hole, drop in and bounce around, then pop out and veer to the left. Damn! To the left, around the bend, right into the keeper eddy. There was nothing to do but to make his way down to the eddy, where, sure enough, the boat was trapped. This time it was no fun belly-crawling beneath the trees and making his Tarzan leaps.

Meanwhile, Dave had found the first ghostboat stuck in a logjam. He dove into the water and managed to get to it, and then, forever a boatman, he climbed in and took off, heading almost immediately for a rock. He fell into the rapids just as the boat shot up.

Back in the land of the buzzing furies, we all looked up when we heard the shout and saw Dave in the water, coming downstream just behind an overturned boat. Gary, in an instant, dove into the river and caught the boat while Raymond whirled the rescue line and threw it. It was off the mark, about ten feet behind Dave; Raymond had just one more chance. This time the rope landed right in Gary's hands.

We were all helping right the first boat when Dave gave another shout. It was the *second* ghostboat coming down in the water, also unannounced. This time both he and Gary dove into the water and Raymond's first throw was good. Dave's face was beaming when he emerged from the river, and I wondered if it was the euphoria of a survivor, or his idea of a good time.

It seemed to take Mike and Sylvie forever to make it down to us, but when they finally showed up, we realized why. Sylvie had rigged up an outfit for herself that consisted of green plastic garbage bags tied around her legs and arms and fastened at the ankles, thighs, wrists, and elbows with rubber bands and scarfs. She'd draped a sarong over her head and tucked it into a rain jacket that was zipped and buttoned up to her chin. She looked like a garbage-bag monster from a low-budget horror movie. Leech-fear had turned beauty into beast.

We ate lunch in about three minutes because the bees were so bad now we had to be in constant motion, dancing and waving our hands to keep them off our food. Sylvie threw her food down at one point and ran toward the water. Then she screamed and dove in. When she came back she said, "I couldn't take the bees anymore and wanted to get in the river. But while I was running to get there—I don't know what happened. Maybe I ran too fast. They attacked me. I got about ten stings."

She looked on the verge of tears. "I hate this," she said. "I'm going to have a nervous breakdown."

We were all, by now, just barely coping. Fortunately, we all wanted to be good sports, so none of us gave in to the impulse to throw ourselves down on the rocks and have a tantrum. But we did throw our cheese and crackers in the food bag and get back on the river in less than five minutes. It was still possible that we'd come through the last of the bad rapids and would have enough time to find a sandy campsite and maybe even the Mahakam.

As Gary oared us downriver through the next few twists and turns, I looked for signs of the canyon walls widening, or an abandoned hut—anything to indicate that people had been able to get this far up the Boh from the Mahakam. But mostly the river felt eerie, as if we had reached the eye of the storm. The misty light fluttered through the trees; the water was a deep, dark green. Then we saw Mike up ahead pull over to an eddy and heard the ominous rumble of white water. Gary cursed, pulled into the eddy, and stormed out of the boat. It was to be his signature gesture: we'd reach some big rapids, and he'd storm out of the boat saying, "Shit!"

31

"We call this a pinball rapid," Mike said. "It's full of rocks and boulders but it's runnable. It will just require a lot of fast maneuvering."

Although Mike and Dave were still making an effort to deny their frustration, Gary couldn't hide his. He didn't complain about his feet, but I knew from seeing them last night that they were hurting. Even worse, he seemed nervous about the river. He was more cautious than Mike or Dave, but with good reason. He had the non-self-bailing boat. He also had us—John and me. We were uncomplaining but we were not strong. Mike had told me earlier that on this trip he had a nightmare image. It was of John in the rapids without his glasses, not knowing where to swim or when to try.

I wondered if the same nightmare had presented itself to John.

The Dayak word for rapids is *bemberum,* and that's the way I heard it now: the roar of the river, alive and unrelenting.

I asked Gary exactly how dangerous it would be if we ended up swimming, and he said we'd bounce around on the rocks and get bruised, but the flow probably wasn't big enough for a hole or a whirlpool to hold us under. Of course, we could get caught in a sieve, he said, get sucked under in an instant and held there forever.

Dave called out the order that we'd run the rapids: first Mike's boat with Raymond and Sylvie; then the paddle boat, with Mimo, Howard, Stuart, Bill, and Linda; then Gary with John and me. We took off without time to do anything more than strap on our helmets.

Although our boat was last, we were already in the water, heading for the top of the run, when we saw Mike's boat make some pretty fancy turns up ahead and then go through a chute, hit a drop, and become invisible in the spray. The boat disappeared for a very long moment and finally exploded up—twisting, straining, then becoming completely airborne. For a second it was poised on the edge of turning over and then it came crashing down. I was just counting three heads upright and still in the boat when Gary shouted, *"There goes the paddle boat!"*

We could hear Dave yelling commands—*"Forward! Stop! Backpaddle!"*—and then, as the boat went down the drop, we could see all the paddles in the air, flailing. When it popped up, everyone was tumbling in the center of the boat and suddenly, like a diver making a jackknife, it flipped.

"Oh, no!" I heard myself screaming.

"Get down and hold on!" Gary cried.

I saw Howard and Bill and Dave in the water and then we took off. I concentrated on clenching the ropes with all the strength I could muster while trying to relax enough to take some big bounces, and Gary did a few nifty maneuvers, handling the boat with precision. He found the still points in the churning water and positioned himself correctly for each move. For a while it seemed we were running a slalom course. But then, in an instant, we picked up speed and took the drop. At the bottom of it was the hole that must have caught the other boats—a tremendous, whirling eye with water pounding into it from all sides. We were heading right into it, and although I was hanging on to the ropes for all I was worth, I was preparing myself mentally to bail out and swim. But then the back of the boat took off to the right and somehow we whipped around the edge of the hole, backward. I remember feeling my jaw still open wide with admiration when we emerged downstream, upright.

We hadn't taken a drop of water. It was class oaring on Gary's part and I applauded as he pulled into the eddy.

But something was wrong. Only Howard and Stuart were there to grab our throw line, and the expression on their faces was serious.

"Linda's gone," Howard said.

"She swam the second rapids," Stuart explained. "She disappeared around the bend."

It seemed that when the paddle boat had flipped, everyone ended up underneath it, churning in the boiling current, a tangle of flailing arms, oars, legs, and buckets. But not Linda; when she came up she was in front of the boat, and just as she looked to see what was behind her—*boom!* The boat crashed her into a rock, ripping off both her helmet and glasses.

Dave, who was also in the water, only about twenty feet away from her, yelled, *"Swim left! Swim left!"* But to the left was another rock and she didn't want to get between it and the boat again, so she swam away from the shore and ended up right in the middle of the current, heading for the second set of rapids.

Bill saw her in the water, picking up speed, looking disoriented, and as soon as he made it to the eddy he stood up and shouted at her to swim to shore. She cupped her ear; she couldn't hear. He knew she couldn't see without her glasses. He stood in the water for a moment, paralyzed, watching the river take her away from him. He could see the splash of white water behind her. He knew the image of her face in the water would stay with him for the rest of his life.

Then Dave yelled, *"Grab a rock!"* and Linda managed to swim to one and hang on while the water tugged her downstream. Dave groped beneath the overturned boat to find a throw bag, and Bill looked at Linda's fingers slipping inch by inch off the rock.

Then she made a convulsive move, as if to hurl herself on top of the rock; but she slipped, and was gone.

Bill's legs were shaking as he ran after Dave, who was scrambling to the top of a rock to try to see around the bend. He scanned Dave's face and saw him shake his head no. Then no again. Then Dave yelled, *"I see her! I see her!"*

"Is she alive?"

"Mike's got her! She's all right!"

When they got to Linda she was sitting on the bottom of Mike's boat, spitting up water. She was crying, but she was also laughing. For a moment all Bill could think of was how much his entire body was reeling and how he thought he might faint. Then he said, "Linda, oh God, Linda. I thought you were dead."

"I'm pissed," she said, "but I'm alive."

When Gary, John, and I arrived, maybe three minutes later, she was still teary.

"How *are* you?" I asked.

"Beat up," she said. Her voice rang out like a rifle shot.

"I'll bet."

"The phrase 'pinball rapid' finally makes sense. I felt like one."

"You must have been scared."

"If I could have talked, I would have been swearing."

Later Linda told me that just after Mike and Raymond picked her up she had the quintessential Raymond experience.

"We got to shore, and I was exhausted—I could still barely get my breath. I was sitting on the floor of the boat having . . . I don't know, the dry heaves, when I heard Raymond yell at me: 'Pick those clothes up! Don't let them get wet like that!' I looked down and saw a sarong or something of Sylvie's sloshing around in the water and couldn't believe it. That guy, I mean, something is seriously wrong with him to be so completely lacking in sensitivity."

32

Camp that night was a short way downriver on a boulder-strewn spit next to a small tributary stream. Because it was flat enough to actually pitch our tents, it looked like paradise, a sure sign that our luck was going to change. Later I found out that Dave had decided to camp there only because the guides were too exhausted to go any farther. It was a stream channel and we were totally susceptible to flooding. If it had rained hard that night, we might have lost the boats.

Not that camp was actually pleasant. It was great to get the tents out and set them up for the first time, but the bees were still around, and when we opened up our dry bags we discovered that most of them (including John's and mine) had taken in water. Once again I spread my wet underwear, notebook, and T-shirts on a rock, some primordial instinct driving me to repeat, over and over again, an activity that was completely useless.

After we'd set up our tents, we retired inside them to escape the bees and check out our feet. Mine now hurt constantly, even when I wasn't walking. It wasn't too bad, but I worried about the next day and the day after that. I found Gary and asked to borrow his Tenactin, an antifungal cream.

"Okay," he said with a sigh, "but we don't have much."

"I'll use just the tiniest, tiniest bit," I promised, hating, once again, to be so dependent.

Raymond and Mimo cooked dinner that night, hoping, in vain, that an artful mixture of freeze-dried meat and vegetables, Indonesian spices and rice, would combust spontaneously into actual flavor. Mimo, who had continually teased Dave about the quality of the food, was as dispirited as I'd ever see him when his own concoction turned out to taste like the same old pasty sludge. I didn't mind it; after eating freeze-dried meals for years on backpacking trips, real cooked rice tasted great. Besides, my food fantasies weren't about perfectly cooked vegetables. They were about ice cream. Ice cream and hot fudge. Ice cream and hot fudge and toasted almonds. And a root beer float. And lots of crispy animal fat. Duck skin and pork fat and an entire pound of bacon.

After a while we all noticed that Mike and Sylvie were missing. Earlier, just after the pinball rapid, I'd seen Mike lying down in the boat with his eyes closed. Sylvie was sitting next to him, running her fingers through his hair and stroking his forehead. There was something intense about it all, a hushed tone to the scene that made me wince. Romance is fine, but I was uncomfortable treating it as sacred. Now Dave explained that Mike had collapsed. He thought he might be having a malaria attack.

"He'll be okay," Dave said. "He got it in Africa several years ago and knows what to do. He has his medicine. But he may be out of commission for a couple of days."

That night Sylvie metamorphosed into the Boh River's nurse goddess; she'd emerge every now and then from her and Mike's tent, come almost shyly over to where we all were sitting, and arrange a plateful of food to take to him.

"How's Mike?" someone would say.

"He's sleeping," she'd reply, and then quietly go off into the night, back to her wounded warrior. Once we saw her in front of the tent with her video camera; once she went down to the river to wash something—it looked like a headband—and once she came back to the fire to rummage around the food bag for tea. Of all of us, she was the only one still with dry clothes. She had packed all her clothing in plastic bags within plastic bags, pressing out the air, folding everything flat. Even her underwear was gorgeous. She wore a blue shirt unbuttoned down to her bra, which was white and lace-trimmed. Next to her tan skin it looked like some kind of hypercolor. Next to our mildewed, dirty T-shirts, it seemed as if the whiteness had somehow been beamed down from outer space.

When Dave finally appeared in camp that night, feet bandaged and walking gingerly, he confided that all the guides were in pretty bad shape.

"Mike's down, Gary is almost crippled with foot rot, and I'm hobbling from rot and bruises plus I'm exhausted. If we don't make it out of the gorge tomorrow, we may be in an emergency situation."

Somehow the word emergency perked me up. If there was such a thing as "an emergency situation," clearly there was an emergency plan.

One of Dave's emergency plans had been to bring along three gallon jugs of hard liquor, and tonight, after dinner, he made a pot of Tang and gin and urged us to drink. It worked. We spent an hour or so telling war stories—encounters with grizzlies and guerrillas, and Bill's near death from a poisonous snake. Then Dave told a story about the worst trip he'd ever had. It started with a brutal forty-eight-hour nonstop ride in the back of a truck on a dirt road in Peru. And that was just the beginning. While the guides were rigging the boats, some kids on the cliffs above the river started showering them with rocks.

"It was dangerous," Dave said. "The rocks were hitting the boats and ripping right through the rubber. We tried to get them to stop—we even climbed back up the cliffs to tell them how dangerous it was—but they didn't care. They were just incredibly hostile. Finally we had to throw everything in the boats and take off before we had them fully rigged.

"Then we actually had a couple of nice days. We went down the river and camped at night; the rapids were no problem and the sun was out. But about the third night, while everyone was sleeping, it started to rain, and we woke up when the water started to flood into our tents. We had to scramble out of our sleeping bags, roll up the tents, grab our clothes and the food, secure the boats, and climb fifteen feet up into the jungle—all in the dark in a hard rain. No one slept that night at all, and by morning half the group had foot rot.

"We continued on the next day, but our first priority was to find a place to rest and dry out and get a good night's sleep. Finally we found a beautiful spot—an island in the middle of the river, a small, sandy hill. But again that night it started to rain and again the water started to rise. Only this time we had no place to go. The water got higher and higher until finally we had everything piled up on a little hill about fifteen feet square. Then the entire island disappeared underwater and we had to throw everything in the boats and spend the night floating downstream in the rain, in the dark. The next morning more than half the group hiked out."

"What! No bees?" said Stuart.

"No malaria?" cried Linda.

"At least you could hike out," I said.

His story restored, for a moment, our group macho. With a few more bad rapids the Boh might move right up there to the top.

33

I went to my tent that night oddly awash with forbearance. Somehow I didn't connect Dave's story about rising rivers to our campsite, which was not only next to a stream but backed up against a high, water-carved rock wall. I didn't know that the guides, that night, were getting up every hour or so to check the water level. Even Mike was sleeping lightly, unable to suppress the image he saw before collapsing in his tent: some hornbills flying overhead against an eerie, orangish rain cloud.

As far as I knew, the river was calm where we were, and that's all that mattered.

Alone and safe in my tent, images flooded in from other rivers, most of them in California, where I had spent many happy hours riding through rapids in inner tubes and small, inflatable kayaks. And then a memory welled up, a new one, as vivid as if it had happened yesterday. It was of my very first encounter with white water. I was about four years old and standing with my mother at the edge of the Pacific Ocean. She had a firm hold on my hand and was lifting me up whenever the surf got up to my head. Then, suddenly, she grabbed the straps of my bathing suit and said, "We're going to have to dive, Tracy, at the count of five." I saw the fear in her face, and then I saw the enormous wave coming in. She counted and I dove, but it didn't matter. I bounced and tumbled in the wave, gulping water, eating sand, careening into my mother's legs, bouncing off her knuckles. I felt one of my straps fly out of her hand at one point and that was it—my first memory of absolute terror. I didn't really know what was happening; I just knew that if she let go of my other strap I'd drown.

It was not an entirely unpleasant memory, I realized. After we got out of the surf we sat on the beach for a while, reliving the experience. I felt proud to have survived what felt like a test of adulthood.

I picked up *Lord Jim* and read some more of it by flashlight, feeling like a kid reading secretly under the bedcovers, and then, because I didn't want to use up my batteries, I turned the light off and drifted out of time, on my own personal journey, back to the secret places where words were without human weakness and I first fell in love with them.

Words were vessels back then—big words, small words, mysterious words, words I could not yet understand. They all held people and places, a real world that existed in the realm of imagination. Words were not artifice, they were the quintessence of things, and when they came together to create a mood or a feeling that seemed exotic or strange I rode them in my bed, under the covers, as I rode the Boh River, hanging on for life. Words were my ticket to a world that existed beyond my imagination; proof of life on a higher plane.

When I woke up in the middle of the night with a hot flash and heard the rain coming down softly on the tent, I decided to make the best of being awake and go down to the river. I got out in the soft rain and walked quickly and surely in the mist, my face and chest flushed with heat, the breeze cool on my skin, my flashlight poking a tiny hole in the blackness. The canopy was dripping water, but in the slice of sky overhead I could see brilliant, twinkling stars. For a moment I felt the sweet glow of being somewhere extraordinary, the presence of an intangible, undefinable force that breathed down upon me from the wet, lush, almost hypertrophied vegetation of the rainforest.

Then the wet tropical air brought back another infusion of

memory, this one less pleasant. I remembered a dream I'd had the night before about the sore in my mouth. It had gotten worse and my gums looked as bad as Gary's feet. Three teeth had actually toppled over and were hanging by tiny threads. I didn't know what was wrong with my teeth, or why they had fallen out, but I remembered knowing for certain that the condition would get worse, and that I would have to keep the whole thing a secret. How would I talk for the rest of my life? I'd wondered. How could I fake it?

It was clear that the dream had been about menopause. I was confronting a transition in life for which my culture had somehow conspired to keep me completely unprepared. I didn't know if all women got hot flashes, or how often, and had no idea if mine were normal or abnormal. I'd heard that emotions were often altered by the change in hormones; could it be that something chemical was making me cautious, even fearful?

I was amazed, then outraged to find myself in such uncharted emotional waters. Why hadn't I read about women going through menopause? I tried to think of female characters in Western literature who were middle-aged, and couldn't come up with a single name. No wise woman; no benignly powerful woman; no free spirit; no one attractive or successful. Where were all the heroines who were over the goddamn hill?

I'd heard, of course, that menopause can be linked to depression, and I knew that some cultures (rural Ireland, for instance) think it causes insanity. But I wasn't prepared for the embarrassment, for the feeling that I'd crossed some invisible line. Yesterday I had been young; today I was middle-aged. A few years ago I would have been on the rocks with the guides, helping them with the boats, and now I couldn't even control my own temperature. Like my teeth, I was beginning to lose things that had seemed part of me, essential to my life.

In the seventies, when I was about to turn thirty, I took off for Mexico and Guatemala with just five hundred dollars and a backpack. I wanted to prove to myself that I was still a free spirit, that nothing had changed. For three months I traveled happily, first with a girlfriend, and then alone. Because I was speaking mostly very simple Spanish, I had no idea if the people I was meeting were smart or educated; simply connecting with them at all seemed magical. I became attuned to the basics: their generosity of spirit, our shared impulse toward laughter.

Then one day, when I was hitchhiking in the Yucatán, an American kid from Florida picked me up. He was traveling in his van, which he'd equipped with a tape deck, ice chest, Coca-Cola holder, and roach clip. We shared a joint, listened to some rock-and-roll, and he told a long, boring story about surfing on Isla Mujeres. Finally he looked at me and said, "And what about you? What's your major?"

I remember saying something about being nine years out of college, but I also remember knowing, then, that I'd reached my limit. Within a week I was heading home. I didn't want to be what I had become: merely young again. I wanted more. I wanted to move on.

On the Boh, my personal journey was now taking me right up against the same kind of limit, only how was I going to move on when all I could think about were the things I was going to miss? I'd miss looking good and having men pay attention to me; I'd miss being physically confident enough to go at life full tilt. And even worse, some of the things I'd miss I hadn't done well enough yet, or with enough purpose or understanding. It was unfair that just when I was in a position to have great adventures, my time had run out.

Despite the soft tropical night, the facts were coming into focus. Like the river, the world around me sailed on independent of my desires. If I wanted to define myself by facing challenges, I had better stop making them physical. I could take on spiritual challenges, intellectual challenges, emotional challenges—but how, and where, and which ones? The thought loomed up more monstrous, even, than swimming another set of rapids.

It did occur to me that there was something about the moments of happiness and contentment I was feeling on the Boh that might be key. If I was going to reinvent myself, turn menopause into some sort of rite of passage, I would have to look inward.

I heard the rain start to fall softly again and thought of Sylvie and Mike, body surfing in their tiny, moldy tent—sweating, panting, exploring, loving. And although it had a certain fecund appeal, it also seemed like an incredible amount of bother. Suddenly I felt a rush of love for my husband, who, unlike me, had been prone all his life to various fears and terrors. When I have insomnia, he actually likes to hold me in his arms and rub my head and tell me stories until I fall asleep. He may be afraid to go on an exploratory river trip, but he has the courage to offer great love.

34

Miraculously, the river hadn't risen all night, even though it had rained. "The Dayak prayers were with us," Dave said the next morning. We had slept in blissful ignorance. Over breakfast—last night's rice fried in margarine and spices—Gary and Dave talked about the river, an incessant topic of conversation among the guides, who tried to chart our progress down it each day as best they could. We had only one map—the white piece of paper with the snaking blue line Gary had told us about—which looked as if a child had tried to draw some capillaries and a vein. The rapids were penciled in, then erased, then penciled in again. The guides spent hours, it seemed, talking about where we were on the squiggly blue line and how many kilometers we'd come. Everyone was taking the Dayak trip seriously now, especially the "big mountain" Pelanjau had warned us about.

Seeing Raymond and Dave alone together reminded me that they were both American expatriates, both extraordinary men willing to try out new lives. Dave lived in Indonesia because he had found his life's passion—river running—and Indonesia was a country where he could live on the $12,000-a-year salary it typically brought in. Raymond's choices were more negative. I never heard a good word from him about the United States, or about any other country, for that matter. And although he was trying to lead a meaningful life, which I admired, nothing ever seemed to be good enough. To his credit, Raymond had not given up his search: his screen was large, his appetites unlimited. But I imagined him at fifty, brittle and cynical.

Dave was by nature a softer person, more accepting and less critical. He was able to live in America and Indonesia, in two very different worlds, by living two lives, both separate, both equal. He was the only person in our group to ask me to keep a secret about himself, and I came to respect his privacy. To take away Dave's ability to move with caution and discretion would do him a great injustice. He was a gracious man, not prone to gossip, and although he played his cards so close to the vest that he discouraged great intimacy, he did have respect for a wide array of ideas and people. He was larger than Raymond in that way, larger than most people.

John, another mystery, was sitting silently on a log by himself that morning. I noticed him now, running his fingertips gently up and down his feet; even at a distance I could tell something was wrong. I went over to bring him a refill of coffee and saw that his feet were covered with rot. There were raw spots between his toes and blotchy, prickly red dots all the way up to his ankles.

I gave him my best pep talk about caring for his feet, but he didn't respond; he didn't lift an eyebrow. Almost like an autistic child, he rocked back and forth, moving his fingertips around the sores, up and down, up and down. It was conceivable, I realized, that John might not ask for help until he could no longer walk.

Mike was back with us that morning, saying he'd either had a mild case of malaria or had simply been dehydrated from diarrhea and exhausted from working so hard. He and Sylvie sat and ate breakfast together like two old lovers. Mike's body, like Sylvie's, was a source of genuine pleasure. He looked like a well-fed animal. He was extremely well muscled but also perfectly proportioned—head, neck, shoulders, thighs. And his skin was brown and smooth, bulging but supple. With his longish, sandy-brown hair, headband, and wire-rimmed glasses he looked classic: a Greek god with a drawl. I looked at the two of them and remembered the power and glory of sheer physical attraction. Earlier I had seen Mimo with Sylvie's video camera, shooting her teasing and hugging Mike.

After serving up our fried rice that morning, Raymond came over and sat behind Mike and Sylvie. He picked up a shirt Sylvie had tossed down on a rock and carefully folded it and laid it on the ground next to her. It was the act of a ghostly lover.

Sylvie, I noticed, seemed to have developed an existential rapport with the bees. She was wearing, this morning, nothing but a strapless bathing suit and a sarong wrapped around her hips, and she sat motionless while bees crawled all over her shoulders, legs, and back. Raymond stared at the bees as they drank up the sweat on her neck. He watched as she gathered up her hair, gingerly to avoid being stung, twisted it into several loops, then tied it with a scarf and stretched back, arching her body, as if the tingle of tiny feet had overwhelmed her with exquisite delight.

Bill and Linda were mostly quiet now, worried about getting out of the gorge in time to make their plane flights. Bill's classes were important, but Linda had an additional problem: she hadn't defecated since our first day in Balikpapan. Everyone had brought pills for diarrhea but none for constipation, so amidst all the rot and mildew around us she was dreaming about backed-up plumbing and overflowing swimming pools. She wasn't eating much, but her stomach was distending—percolating with deng deng and rice, she said. The forces inside her were fermenting. She felt like she was going to explode.

Howard and Stuart remained tried and true: strong, a help to the guides, uncomplicated and unassuming. Alongside the rest of us with our strange passions and bursts of turmoil, they seemed like a row of corn, or a line of fence posts.

We were on the river early that morning since the guides reported that it had finally started to rise, and the first half hour or so restored our good moods. The rapids we sailed through were a pleasant Class III, and we took them perfectly. Mostly we drifted.

Gary even remarked that the canyon up ahead seemed to widen and the walls were getting lower.

"I hate to say it *again*," he said. "But by this afternoon we just may be on the Mahakam."

Remembering the enchantment I'd felt reading last night and hoping to share it, I asked John and Gary if they wanted to hear a passage from *Lord Jim*. It was a literary impulse that had already faded by the time I got the book out of my ammo can, but I searched for a boat scene, one that I remembered as being stylistically thrilling.

She held on straight for the Red Sea under a serene sky, under a sky scorching and unclouded, enveloped in a fulgor of sunshine that killed all thought, oppressed the heart, withered all impulses of strength and energy. And under the sinister splendour of that sky the sea, blue and profound, remained still, without a stir, without a ripple, without a wrinkle—viscous, stagnant, dead. The *Patna*, with a slight hiss, passed over that plain, luminous and smooth, unrolled a black ribbon of smoke across the sky, left behind her on the water a white ribbon of foam that vanished at once, like the phantom of a track drawn upon a lifeless sea by the phantom of a steamer.

Every morning the sun, as if keeping pace in his revolutions with the progress of the pilgrimage, emerged with a silent burst of light exactly at the same distance astern of the ship, caught up with her at noon, pouring the concentrated fire of his rays on the pious purposes of the men, glided past on his descent, and sank mysteriously into the sea evening after evening, preserving the same distance ahead of her advancing bows. The five whites on board lived amidships, isolated from the human cargo. The awnings covered the deck with a white roof from stem to stern, and a faint hum, a low murmur of sad voices, alone revealed the presence of a crowd of people upon the great blaze of the ocean. Such were the days, still, hot, heavy, disappearing one by one into the past, as if falling into an abyss for ever open in the wake of the ship; and the ship, lonely under a wisp of smoke, held on her steadfast way black and smouldering in a luminous immensity, as if scorched by a flame flicked at her from a heaven without pity.

The nights descended on her like a benediction.

As I was reading, a little embarrassed by the passionate prose, we heard someone in the paddle boat up ahead give a shout. I looked up and saw Mike oaring out to an eddy.

"Shit!" Gary said.

"What's wrong?"

Gary oared into the eddy and tied up the boat without saying a word. Then he got out his knife and took off for a scout downstream despite his painfully swollen feet. The rest of us sat silently in the boats. None of us grumbled; we didn't want to jinx our good luck. We just waited. All of us, by now, had developed our own reptilian mode. Finally I took *Lord Jim* out of my ammo can to distract myself but unfortunately came upon this passage:

There are many shades in the danger of adventures and gales, and it is only now and then that there appears on the face of facts a sinister violence of intention—that indefinable something which forces it upon the mind and the heart of a man, that this complication of accidents or these elemental furies are coming at him with a purpose of malice, with a strength beyond control, with an unbridled cruelty that means to tear out of him his hope and fear, the pain of his fatigue and his longing for rest: which means to smash, to destroy, to annihilate all he has seen, known, loved, enjoyed, or hated; all that is priceless and necessary—the sunshine, the memories, the future; which means to sweep the whole precious world utterly away from his sight by the simple and appalling act of taking his life.

I recognized that purpose of malice, that unbridled cruelty. I'd felt it tumbling underwater in the rapids and also in those nightly hot flashes. My life was halfway over. Time had given me a nudge.

35

When the guides returned from the scout they were exhausted. Their hands were aching from chopping with machetes, their feet were raw from walking in wet shoes with foot rot, and they had blood trickling all over them from cutting off leeches. Mike had cut the entire top of his right tennis shoe open and was wearing a cupped rubber bandage that completely covered his big toe. Mimo had given it to him, calling it a "finger condom."

Gary reported that there was a six-foot waterfall in the middle of the river, and no way to get around it. We'd have to ghostboat the paddle boat again and line the oar boats down the opposite riverbank.

"The Dayaks told us the gorge was an evil place," he said. "Maybe we should have listened to them."

Later, when I thought more about what he said, I had to get up and walk around to take some deep breaths. It was a frightening belief, that there might be such things as evil spirits.

Once in India I'd had an undeniable encounter with a force that was beyond my imagining. It didn't change my life, as I thought it might at the time, but whenever I remember it I still get the shivers. Actually, my husband had the encounter first and then I went back to see for myself. He was approached by an old man in white robes in a beautiful park near the tourist office in Jaipur. The man was a fortune-teller.

For some reason my husband agreed to have his fortune read: he had time to kill; the man seemed pleasant; he wanted to sit down.

So he and the fortune-teller sat down on the lawn, and the old man asked him to think of a flower. He thought of a daffodil.

"Tell me how many letters it has and what letter of the alphabet it begins with."

"It has eight letters and begins with *d*."

"Daffodil."

"Right."

They did this with about seven more flowers and then the man asked him to throw some dice and add up the numbers. This went on for a few minutes, while my husband added up the numbers in his head, and finally the fortune-teller put his hands in a prayer position and said, "Now I am going to tell you the day you were born."

He took my husband's hand, counted on his fingers up to eleven, and said, "November." Then he counted again, this time up to six.

"November sixth," he said.

"Right."

"Now I will tell you the day you got married."

He counted again on the same hand.

"September."

"Right."

"September nineteenth."

"Right."

"Now I will tell you about your family. You have two daughters."

"Right."

"One is not living with you."

"Well, sort of."

"Now I will tell you the name and age of your mother."

After a few more rolls of the dice and adding up numbers, the old man wrote something onto a piece of paper, folded it up, and gave it to my husband. On it was written, *Jane, 66.*

His mother, Jane, was sixty-six.

"This time," said the fortune-teller, "I want you to think of an enemy."

My husband thought hard, but no name came to him.

"Maybe a long time ago. Ten years. A short person. Short and fat."

"Okay. I have one."

The fortune-teller wrote something down on another piece of paper and handed it over. It read, *Jann Winner*.

The person my husband had thought of was Jann Wenner, the editor of *Rolling Stone* magazine who had fired him eleven years ago.

Back in our hotel room, I got the whole story: his mother, the kids, the piece of paper on which "Jann Winner" was written. And not only that, the fortune-teller had predicted that my husband, a writer, would have a book published within two years.

I raced back to the park and found the man he had described to me, wearing white robes and thick glasses. He was talking to a German man who seemed dazed. The German looked at me and said, "Be careful. This man knows everything."

The fortune-teller and I sat face-to-face on the lawn and everything happened just as it had with my husband: the flowers, the dice, my birthday, my anniversary, my mother's name and age. But I couldn't think of the name of an enemy, even when he suggested that the enemy might be short and fat.

"Wait a minute, that's my husband's enemy," I said.

"Okay. Then think of the name of someone who may be thinking about you right now," he replied.

I thought of an old boyfriend about whom I felt some guilt.

The old man wrote something on a piece of paper and handed it to me. I opened it up, and there was the name. It was a difficult name, but it was spelled correctly.

"This person," the fortune-teller said. "You . . . you were very intimate with."

"Right."

"I mean . . . intimate. Do you know what I mean?"

"Yes."

The fortune-teller smiled.

Then he told me my future. I would have twin boys. I would write a book. Some man would give me $51,000, either as a gift or for work. I could barely contain my delight.

"How do you do this? How do you know these things?" I asked, and he reached in a pocket and took out a picture of a blue Hindu god.

"Krishna," he said, "comes to me. He comes and gives me . . . a little . . . push."

For days afterward, I thought that I would have to accept the idea of fate, that my life was preprogrammed and all I could do was live it. Then I decided that the man had simply read my mind: when I couldn't think of an enemy, neither could he. Still, it was an overwhelming thought. How could anyone have entered my mind and read it? That afternoon on the lawn, facing the fortune-teller who could not know what he knew, I felt the breath of another world; I felt an ancient wind that held within it the power of the supernatural. Did I believe? No. Did I *not* believe? I couldn't say.

An evil river spirit, however, was something else. It was not benign. Even if it was just a symbol for some extrasensory way the Dayaks had of sensing danger from the sounds and sights and smells of things, we had been warned. Perhaps the Dayaks' story hadn't made sense because they didn't want to tell us how they knew what they knew. Perhaps Pelanjau showed us the photograph because he thought it was the only thing we'd understand.

I did ask Gary one more time about the evil spirit. Who had seen it, and what exactly had Pelanjau said?

"I'm not sure who saw it, Pelanjau or Ferguson, but I know Pelanjau was frightened. We started to offer him more money but stopped because it was clear nothing was going to make him change his mind. He was afraid of the gorge. Something about it really scared him. And so far, everything he told us about the river has been exactly right . . . although he did say the river went underground at one point."

"What?"

"I know. It's hard to believe. He said the river disappeared into the ground."

For a moment it felt as if I were in some disaster movie and had just realized that all along the town idiot had been telling the truth. It was possible that anything was possible, that unimaginable things lay ahead—things as unforeseeable as the end of the world, the suspension of gravity, a rent in time.

I sat, for a moment, entranced with the notion that our small group might be voyaging into some heart of darkness. Then, abruptly, I heard Dave call.

36

Dave had set up a traverse down the wall of the gorge to the end of the rapids, so once again Sylvie, Linda, John, and I made our way downriver, walking on muddy roots, grabbing hold of trees and shrubs—"vegetable belay," rock climbers call it. I was surprised to see Howard join us after a little while. After a quarter mile or so we reached a rope that Dave had tied to a tree, and made a short rappel down to an enormous, flat rock ledge that jutted into the river. It was a magical spot, a throne overlooking the gorge. If we could have forgotten that we were stuck in the middle of nowhere, the next hour might have been sheer joy. We had ringside seats to watch Mike, Gary, Stuart, Bill, and Mimo line the boats down the other side of the river, over rocks and a small waterfall.

Mike's boat was the first to appear; he'd decided to avoid the main drop and take it down a "sneak," a small waterfall at the edge of the current, perhaps four feet wide, that poured with some force over a ten-foot drop. At the bottom of it was a churning pool of white water and a good-sized rock.

Mike, Gary, and Raymond pushed the boat to the top of the sneak, and the boat tumbled down the waterfall into the pool, bounced back up, and almost made it completely over the top of the rock. Almost. Suddenly, in mid-flight, it stopped. We could see its front end hanging down the front of the rock, almost in the water, but the back tube was bent back in the other direction, pinned to the rock by tons of falling water.

"It's a wrap," Dave said. "A classic wrap."

It could have been worse; there could have been six people in the boat, and the boat could have been wrapped on a rock in the middle of some rapids with no way to get to dry land. So we watched as the guys unloaded the boat and then, for over a half hour, tried to get it off the rock. Mike attached ropes, figured angles, had everyone heave and ho at the count of three. Then he stood by himself on some submerged rocks, with water racing over his feet and ankles, and tried lifting, pulling, and shoving the boat's trapped rear end. He leaped in and out of the boat, on and off the rocks, and at one point he walked right into the waterfall and disappeared behind it. We could see his arms poking through the water as he tried to get another purchase on the boat, then his entire head. He was Indiana Jones and Sly Stallone; certainly he was the hero of the video Sylvie was shooting next to me on the ledge. Her camera rarely stopped whirring.

When I took my eyes off Mike and looked back up the canyon, I was startled to find that the scenery had changed, as if a curtain had suddenly dropped. There was an oddly cold wind and the river was pewter-colored. Within minutes, it started to rain. We retreated to a narrow space beneath an overhanging rock and began to look at each other with anxiety. The wrap now seemed ominous, and, even stranger, we were shivering.

"I can't believe I'm two miles from the equator and cold," Howard said. Linda's teeth were chattering. Dave told us to do jumping jacks, which we did, and finally we heard Dave say to no one in particular, "Good, Mike's got it. He's going to let some air out of the chamber."

And sure enough, when Mike finally did deflate one section of the four-chambered raft, a coordinated effort at pulling and shoving got the boat off the rock. I asked Dave why Mike hadn't tried deflating the chamber earlier, and he shrugged and said that maybe Mike had been enjoying himself. I laughed, but later it occurred to me that he was telling the truth. Mike was an athlete and a born outdoorsman. In the winter, when he wasn't river running, he cross-country skied in Alaska. He'd built a log cabin in one of the coldest parts of the state and explored the back country in −50-degree weather.

We didn't notice the water level until about twenty minutes later when Gary's boat came around the bend. It was raining hard now, but we could see everyone struggling with the ropes.

"Where's the rock?" Howard suddenly cried out.

"My God," I said. "Did it break loose or what?"

"The water is rising," said Dave with unusual grimness. "And quickly. We had better get out of here."

The river had completely submerged the boulder that Mike's boat had wrapped on. It had risen at least five feet in twenty minutes.

As Mike and Gary oared their boats downstream to an eddy around the bend where we couldn't see them, Dave left to run back up the river and kick the paddle boat into the current. We continued our jumping jacks beneath the gray, clammy sky.

At last we saw the ghostboat bounce around the bend and "surf" at the top of the falls, dancing in place for several seconds as if it were gathering courage. Then it took the plunge and was stuck in the keeper wave at the bottom for what seemed like several long minutes, bouncing around like popcorn in a hot-air popper. Finally it bounced out, and we watched it disappear around a bend where Mike, Gary, and the others were presumably waiting to pick it up.

By the time Dave got back to us, we were all cold and glum, still huddled under the overhang, shivering. Our mood didn't pick up when he told us that to get to the boats downstream we'd have to climb down from our ledge, using a rope, and jump into the river, which was now silty and rising fast. I thought of the ALLWET team looking at the Boh in high water and saying that it was instant death. Maybe we should be cautious. Sylvie asked if Dave was *sure* the guys would be there to pick us up, and although he said yes, it wasn't much comfort.

"How does he know?" Sylvie muttered.

"Now we'll really be cold," added Linda.

Normally I like the notion of riding a current. I'm a good swimmer, and on other river trips I've loved plunging into big, fast-moving water, especially with the blessing of a river guide. But the Boh, now a bilious green in the hard rain, seemed dark and ominous. I looked at John and Linda and Sylvie and they looked at me. Their faces were blank, their mouths slack. I knew the feeling.

Just then, two heads rose up over a boulder about ten feet below us.

"Taxi!" Gary called out.

Sweet blessed Jesus! Gary and Raymond had pushed and pulled a boat upstream to get us. In five minutes we were all together again, teeth chattering, voices quivering, making small jokes about the monster gorge, the black-hole gorge, the gorge that wouldn't quit.

"Let's get going," said Dave, interrupting our black humor. "We can make good time with the water at this level."

And so we sped down the Boh under a leaden sky, heading, it seemed, into darkness. The gorge, rather than opening up, was getting narrower until finally the tree canopy completely enclosed us. Although we looked through the rain for signs of logging or fishing, it was in vain. We were in a tunnel of rain and gloom. Overhead and up very high Bill pointed out two eagles, and closer, some hornbills dipping and squawking in the gray light. I could see that not only did they have tails over a foot long, but a kind of square knob on the top of their bills. The Dayaks believe they are magical birds and see omens in their flight patterns. I watched them fly in a loose V straight down the river canyon and wished I knew how to read them. We could use a little help from the supernatural.

After a while we passed from opaque light into a world of foreboding gray. The air in my lungs turned cold, clouds blew into the canyon, and then the rain started hammering at a slant into the water. We watched with amazement as the river turned browner and darker. As we continued to float cautiously down the river, clouds of mist rippled out from the canyon walls and mingled with the gray of the boats; rain, whenever the canopy opened up, dripped from our faces, soaked our hair, filled up our shoes, and ran down our necks. I had borrowed a rain jacket from Gary and now hunched down into it protectively. The only way the world could get wetter, I thought, was to completely submerge it.

This is what the earth must have been like when the rain forest was created. It must have been what most of the world was like one hundred sixty million years ago when rain forests covered land as far from the equator as England and Alaska.

Then we heard a yell and saw Mike up ahead start to oar frantically, pulling hard to the right bank. Dave shouted out instructions to the paddlers—*"Right! Right! Hard forward! Stop! Right!"*—and Gary swung into action, straining on the oars to make the eddy.

When I started to say something, Gary shut me up. "Listen!" he barked.

And we heard it: the whine of white water. The distant rumble.

"Shit!" Gary's face was red and contorted. "I am getting mad!" He grabbed his knife, tied up the boat, and took off with Mike and Dave to scout.

The rest of us ate lunch under some trees; we were down to the deng deng, which was beginning to turn green, a few stale crackers, and the last of our peanut butter. In two more days we'd be out of lunch completely. I thought of Redmond O'Hanlon's description of the fish that inhabit Borneo's rivers: small, tasteless, and bone-filled. Eating them, he said, was like eating a hairbrush caked in lard.

The guides came back after only a half hour or so, muddy, full of leeches, and strangely calm. Gary stood up in our boat and made an announcement:

"The whole character of the trip has changed," he said, his voice carefully controlled. "What we've seen up until now—*everything* we've seen on the river until now—is child's play. Up ahead are ten-, twenty-, thirty-foot waterfalls, and the river is still rising. We're going to have to pack everything up and head for high ground. This is a flood."

37

*I*t seemed like the right time to make a call to the twentieth century, to cry uncle or just say, "We give up!" What about that helicopter Dave had arranged to come looking for us? Wasn't now the time, we asked the guides, to admit defeat and wait for it? Wait for someone to come and lift us out of this mess? This was our sixth day in the gorge; we were already expected in Samarinda.

"First of all," said Mike, "if Indonesia is anything like Africa, there's almost no chance a helicopter will actually come looking for us if we're only a week late. They'll start to think about it then. Next they'll try to contact Sobek, and after Sobek gets on their case they'll try and find a helicopter. But then the helicopters will all be over in Irian Jaya, or they'll be broken down waiting for parts, or the sultan of something or other will have commissioned them. You don't count on being rescued unless you're absolutely desperate."

"And even if a helicopter did manage to find us," added Gary, "I don't see how it could land here."

"Well, why did Dave bother to arrange for a helicopter rescue," asked Mimo, "if it's impossible?"

"Forget about the helicopter," said Dave. It was the first time I had heard him speak sharply. "Just forget it. What we do is go on until we can't go any further. That's the nature of the game."

The good news was that the rain had let up and it looked as if we could easily get to high ground right across the river. The river took a sharp curve just before the monster rapids, and the gorge at that point rose rather gently, it seemed, to a plateau at about three hundred feet.

"We're lucky, is the actual truth," Mike said. "If the gorge had been too steep to climb here, like it is most of the time, we'd be down to—I don't know what. Plan Z, I guess."

"Maybe the Dayak prayers are with us," said Gary.

"We'll cross the river, unpack the boats, and carry as much as we can up to high ground," said Dave. "We'll probably have to leave the boats in the river tonight. Let's get moving."

Earlier I'd joked with Dave that in order for me to have a really good story, someone would have to die on this trip. We'd both laughed, but then Dave said very seriously, "If someone dies on this trip it will be the end of my career."

It comforted me now to remember this.

While Dave and then Mike were taking their boats and crew across the river, Gary talked again about Pelanjau's warnings.

"We didn't trust him because of the photograph, and his story about the three-headed monster. But now we know the Dayaks did get at least partway down the gorge. Yesterday on our scout we saw some machete marks, and they looked about eight months old, which is just about the time the Dayaks would have been here. So now we believe they did make the trip, and that they did do some portages. I think the big mountain they portaged may have been the one we just passed, and the rapids up ahead are where the river disappeared into the ground. It's a huge drop and there are house-size boulders. In low water the river could easily go under them. But a lot of things still don't make sense. A lot of things."

"Maybe Ferguson lied to Pelanjau about the photograph," I suggested, "and Pelanjau hasn't seen enough photos to be able to tell."

"I know the Dayaks weren't exaggerating about one thing: they said the rapids were dangerous and they were right."

Everything we thought we'd known about the gorge was beginning to seem irrelevant, if not wrong. The river was supposed to be Class III and it had turned out to be Class VI. The ALLWET team claimed to have portaged all of it but instead faked it for television. The Dayaks claimed to have made several portages and in fact did make some, although not the ones they showed us in the photographs. Dave Ferguson had either seen a three-headed monster and become incoherent, or he'd made the trip successfully, which is what he told Sobek. He was either a delightful Brit with a genuine love of Dayaks or a man who told lies and saw demons.

Even worse, there was either a big mountain up ahead that we still had to portage . . . or there wasn't.

38

We didn't start making camp until five o'clock, which meant we had an hour to take everything off the boats and haul it to high ground. After that the gorge would be completely dark. John picked up our heavy dry bag and began to stagger up to camp with it. I took as many lightweight life jackets and helmets as I could hold, and, looking like some sort of plastic bubble monster, carried them up the rocks until I came to the forest. Then I dumped half of them on the ground, clipped the rest to my life jacket, and continued on to camp through the brush. Within minutes I broke into primary hardwood rain forest. Suddenly it was easy to walk.

After a while I ran into Raymond, who barked at me: "Get the tents and start setting them up!" For once I was glad for the order and raced back down to the boats, running past the pile of helmets and jackets. By the time I found the tents and walked back up, dark clouds had settled into the canyon and rain, once again, seemed imminent. We all worked in silence, finding firewood, cutting it, starting a fire, setting up a kitchen area with an overhead tarp, putting up tents, cooking dinner. For the first time we ate dinner (instant chicken soup, rice, and hot peanut sauce) without Gary, Dave, or Mike. We knew they were down by the river, worrying about the rain, still trying to secure the boats.

Dave and Gary finally did appear, just as the sun was sinking. Mike was still working on the boats. They'd had to keep tying and retying the boats as the river rose, getting them fixed to rocks, then roots, then trees. As soon as they got one boat secure they had to scramble back and retie another. Now the problem was the debris that comes hurtling down rivers during a flood—boulders, logs, branches, even uprooted trees. Trees fall constantly in the rain forest since their roots are so shallow (in camp, we were actually in some danger of being beaned), and a tree coming down the Boh could puncture a boat or rip it loose.

Dave said they'd taken everything off the boats, including the extra oars and paddles, so if one boat was lost we'd be able to continue on with just two. "We've done everything we can," he said. "All we can do now is hope the ropes hold."

My flashlight was now next to worthless, a dim, faint glow. It had eaten up twelve batteries so far, which was all I'd brought. From now on I'd have to go begging.

There was still a little light, however, and I headed into the forest to try to see the river. The sky was overcast, but the moon must have been out; the trees looked like shadows on a flat, silvery backdrop. Only twenty yards or so away from camp I abruptly stopped: I could see lines of splashing water through the tree trunks. The river hadn't been there when I was looking for places to set up the tents, when it seemed as if we were in an endless forest sheathed in quiet. But now it surrounded me on three sides, frothing and silvery in the twilight. And loud. I walked toward it to get a better look, and when I came to the edge of the forest I gasped. It was as if I'd come upon something savage.

The river had risen so far so fast, and was so loud and frightening, that it seemed almost improper to witness it—like rubbernecking a gang rape or a knife fight. The twenty- and thirty-foot waterfalls had filled up, and there were no big drops or eddies, no forks or sneaks. It was just one solid onslaught of water filled with branches and logs, racing down the canyon. I stared at it for several minutes, fighting the urge to turn and run.

Dave was the first person I saw back in camp.

"The river's right there. I can see it."

"I know. I know. It rose twenty feet in less than an hour."

Howard and Bill left to take a look.

"What if it keeps rising?" I asked.

"Look at these big hardwood trees," Dave pointed out. "They've been here for at least a hundred years."

"What do we have to do?" said Linda. "Climb one?"

It was then that I remembered the gaggle of life jackets and helmets I'd left on the rocks. In my rush to set up the tents I'd forgotten all about them. If the river had risen twenty vertical feet, they might be on their way to Samarinda by now, bobbing halfway down the Mahakam. It was a horrible image. Life jackets were absolutely necessary on the river; if we hadn't been wearing them when the boats flipped earlier, some of us would have drowned. I raced down to the tree line in the dying glow of my flashlight, and saw the river, now just twenty feet way. The boats had become toy boats, bathtub boats, boats bobbing at the edge of the flood like pathetic rubber duckies. The Boh was raging at about fifty thousand cubic feet per second, twice as big as the Colorado in the Grand Canyon.

The life jackets were gone.

It was, I think, my worst moment on the trip. We would all die on the Boh and I would be responsible; mass murder, they'd call it. Or worse. I looked around for a while, experiencing a much-magnified rerun of how I'd felt at the Jakarta airport: unwilling to believe this had actually happened. Then I ran back up to camp to make a life-jacket count. The first person I ran into was Bill, who said, in his low-key, always calm manner, "Yeah. I think Howard picked them up."

Howard was still under the kitchen tarp, drinking tea with the rest of the group. He nodded casually when I asked him if he'd taken them. "Yeah, I picked them up much earlier," he said. "They were right on the trail."

"Where are they?" I cried.

"They're here." Dave laughed. "Everything's fine."

Everything was not fine, but it had stopped raining, night had fallen, and all we could do now was try to relax. We sat by our tiny fire, which didn't do much to dispel the darkness. Dave had brought two kerosene lanterns, but left the kerosene itself behind at the airport. So we listened to the river. Bill and Linda hadn't eaten dinner and were in their tent, which was ominously quiet. Sylvie and Mike lay on a sheet of plastic, their gorgeous brown legs entwined. Raymond and Mimo talked desultorily, and Stuart, Howard, John and I sat silently in the black night. Gary, who had announced earlier that his feet were in constant pain, was lying with his legs in the air, like a beaten dog.

"I hate to take pills," he said, "but I need one. Does anyone have a pain pill?"

I had a bottle of Percocet, the pills my pharmacist had registered as a narcotic, and I gave him five of them. He took one, lay back down, and said in his precise manner, "My feet feel like they are in the middle of a fire. Right in the middle of a fire."

None of us wanted to get into our tents before we were tired enough to fall asleep instantly, so we huddled under the dripping tarp, under the canopy of the rain forest, under the stormy equatorial sky, and listened to the roar of the river and the thud of tumbling logs and boulders. All of us had told stories of our other lives, but at that moment everything that wasn't on the Boh seemed phony, or trivial. The magazine editing job I had just left seemed as far away as a blue porcelain washbasin. So we waited. We waited for the rain to stop, for the river to fall, for the boats to stop straining at their ropes, for the night to end.

We could hear the rain pounding on the tree canopy, but it only fell in drips on the tarp above our heads. Bill explained that the canopy broke up the biggest droplets, which then fell down to the layers of vegetation below and were absorbed by mosses, lichens, bromeliads, climbing palms, ferns, liverworts—all of which acted like a big sponge.

I wondered how Borneo's rain forest could ever have burned— how the huge fire of 1982–1983 had gotten so out of hand—

and Bill said it was a combination of logging, which left a lot of dead wood in the forest, and a freak weather pattern. For nine months the wet air coming from Asia missed Indonesia completely. Instead of the normal hundred inches of rain during that period, Borneo had no rainfall at all. Animals flocked to the rivers, and leaves dropped off the trees.

Finally Gary announced that the Percocet hadn't done anything to kill the pain. Nothing at all. "You said you had something," he said to Mimo, and Mimo got up and returned with a plastic bottle full of dozens of different colored pills.

"What you need is heroin," Mimo said. "I had some once on a trip, and it actually saved a person's life. It's really silly that we can't use it as a painkiller. But here, this will help."

Gary took the pill and lay on his back again, still keeping his feet in the air; the only way I could think to help him was to massage his face and neck. In Bill and Linda's tent several yards away the light flickered intermittently, and at one point we could hear them quietly talking. For once Bill's voice was louder: I heard him say, "Linda, listen to me. It doesn't matter."

39

Since we were short one tent (one had a missing rain fly), and since Mimo and Raymond had claimed the only single-person tents, John and I had to sleep together that night. We walked through the wet leaves with his flashlight, which was now almost as dim as mine, and when we reached our tent he took off his shoes, got in it, and lay down on Mimo's flimsy sleeping bag. "Good night," he said and closed his eyes.

I had miles to go before I could sleep. I had to take out my contact lenses, find my water bottle, find toilet paper, locate my stupid flashlight, stuff some clothes into a pillowcase to make a pillow, put on my dry T-shirt, find a case for my glasses . . . thank God John was oblivious. He slept beside me in our tiny, airless dome without moving—calm, blank, almost breathless.

Finally there was nothing left to do, and I lay down in the hot, clammy air, now rank from John's socks, and listened to the trees dripping on the tent. The air suddenly seemed bereft of oxygen and I took some deep breaths. After having had an asthma attack as a child, I discovered that I could terrify myself by becoming aware of my breathing. Lying in bed, or in a classroom, and once in an experiment with a friend, I would concentrate on each breath and imagine sucking oxygen in and out of my lungs until it felt completely unnatural, and after a while I'd end up hyperventilating. I did this as a kid, I suppose, to learn to control my fear, but it was also a way of passing the time by getting high on adrenaline.

I think I must have gone to sleep, because when it happened it felt as if I were somehow behind it just one step. It was a little like climbing a tetherball pole when I was six and suddenly having an orgasm. My body was slippery with sweat, and the sheets were wringing wet. I sat up, gasping, dazed, my heart pounding. I was afraid. I hoped for a while that the tent was somehow at fault, that it had created its own hothouse effect. Only there was John sleeping next to me, calm and dry.

Then I remembered: a hot flash. Every time I had one I was still surprised.

I put on my shoes and stumbled outside, but there was no such thing as fresh air: sweat dripped from my nose and water splattered down from the trees. There must have been a moon— I could see a bit—and to distract myself I looked up at the canopy. Most of the animals and birds were up there, in the leaves, on the vines, inside hollow tree trunks, but around me the forest seemed wrapped in mist and a deathlike silence. Insects were quietly on the march, lizards waited for them like stones, and here and there something seemed to flit by like a shadow. I knew most of the larger animals in a rain forest are nocturnal, and all have places to hide, but I couldn't even sense them. A rattan vine scratched my arm and stuck in my T-shirt. Damn! I remembered the leeches. I had to keep moving.

For five minutes or so, until the hot flash subsided, I paced around the perimeter of the tents, very much alone, just me and my secret. I thought of all the times I'd missed my period and feared and then hoped I was pregnant. I thought of Sylvie and Olatz and envied them not only their beauty but their youth: they had time, still, and money enough to do everything. For a moment I tried to think rapturously about sex, but quickly gave it up.

Back inside the tent I lay down on the air mattress, and dreamed about a maniacal three-headed river demon. It looked strangely like a life jacket.

It was that night, I think, that I grew fond of John. I had two more hot flashes, two more moments when I awoke in what seemed like some sort of slimy underground torture pit, two more episodes of careening out into the night, gasping and panting for air while John remained sleeping quietly beside me, a true friend. He allowed me to have my flashes and fits in private. While I tossed and fanned, flapped wet bedsheets, and zipped and unzipped the tent, he lay calm as death. His was the cold neutral eye I needed, now, to cast upon the world, the one that encountered growing old with acceptance. My childbearing years were over, I told myself, and there was no longer any biological reason for me to be able to attract younger men. In fact, survival of the species would have been impossible if young men were attracted to older women; God would have made a mistake.

For a moment I considered declaring my old age and basking in the courtesies that might be extended. In most tribal cultures women gain privileges once they are infertile. If I were a Dayak woman going through menopause I would be free to take part in the world of men. I could act as a peacemaker between rival villages, even set myself up as a prophet.

I knew there must be an up side to menopause in Western culture, but given the circumstances, I couldn't think of it.

In the morning when I woke up, John was gone and the tent was suffused with a soft glow. I put on my shorts and muddy white sandals and staggered out into the daylight. The forest was greener than I'd remembered; the water on the leaves glistened. I stood for a moment and listened to voices around the kitchen fire, and then looked up at the tree canopy and felt a rush of emotion. Way up there, above the trees, there was brightness.

The sun was out.

When I walked down to the edge of the forest to have a look at the river, I noticed that Sylvie had already spread her Balinese sarongs and tiny bathing suits out on a rock. The colors were glorious—purple, white, red, chartreuse—and all over and around them were hundreds of butterflies, dancing, swooping, and flittering. We had seen lots of butterflies on the Boh—on the rocks, by the water's edge, perched on our bags and life jackets—but it was hard to take much joy in them. They were, after all, flying insects with tiny proboscises and little tickling feet. After they'd crawled around on your sweaty skin for a while, you felt like swatting them into oblivion.

But now, next to Sylvie's sarongs in the early-morning sunlight, the butterflies seemed like a cache of jewels. I climbed down the rocks to get a closer look and saw that there were hundreds of tiny white ones, their wings opaque, like old silk, and flying among them like great, muscled dancers were Brooke's birdwings, perhaps the most spectacular of all of Borneo's butterflies. Named after Sir Charles Brooke, the much beloved "white rajah" of Sarawak on Borneo's east coast from 1868 to 1917, they have a wingspan of five to six inches and are velvet black except for a curved band of iridescent green spots extending from wing tip to wing tip. Their beauty was almost brazen—like a shooting star, or a sunset. I had to laugh, they were so obviously dazzling.

As I stood in the sunlight by the butterflies dancing, I did some stretching exercises and after a while began to feel good in my body again. My back was holding up, I was getting leg muscles from all the rock scrambling, and for some reason I was limber, perhaps from all those muscle-warming hot flashes. I took in the small cloudlets of butterflies, listened to the *bemberum* of the rushing water, and thought about the bulging middle of the earth where I was standing now: the equator, the 25,000 mile strip of the world where the earth spins the fastest, gravity is weakest, and day and night are forever perfectly balanced. Overhead 22,300 miles into space, a necklace of communications satellites was hovering, traveling at the same rotational speed as the earth, intercepting and relaying television pictures and telephone calls.

I felt suddenly, inexplicably, connected. I couldn't be lost. I was right here on planet Earth.

40

*A*t breakfast Dave announced that despite the rain the river had miraculously gone down during the night. Early this morning the guides had found the boats high and dry, hanging from their ropes at a 60-degree angle. Today we would make the portage, carry everything perhaps a half mile through the forest, short-cutting across a bend in the river to the bottom of the rapids. As he talked, I noticed that all of us had gradually started waving our hands and walking around in circles as if we were characters in *Last Year at Marienbad:* the bees had finally found us in the forest, pursued us even in the shade. The sweat bees I could understand. They fed on carrion and we probably smelled a lot like rotting meat. But we still had no good theory as to why the stinging honeybees were torturing us.

The reason we weren't being attacked by mosquitoes, Bill explained, is that mosquitoes normally feed in the canopy on birds and monkeys and other animals. They don't bother with humans unless something disturbs that balance (like the trees being felled). But he was still upset that he couldn't figure out our honeybees. Bees make their nests in the very tallest trees of the forest, he said, or in holes high up in vertical rock walls. There was no reason for them to come down to us. Something must have gone wrong.

Although Bill was sticking to his salt deficiency theory, the rest of us had our own ideas. There was the color theory, the mildew theory, the sugar theory, the heat theory. We had lots of time to speculate about what was driving us to the brink. We considered putting some bees in a jar and bringing them home, since they might be a hitherto unknown species, but none of us got around to it. The bees were destroying our will.

By midmorning, last night's turmoil was very far away and our camp seemed almost homey. The guides had strung a sheet of plastic from tree branches and we all sat beneath it. Around us were plastic jugs of water, two big boxes of food, our small, foot-high table, a medicine box, and bundles of life jackets and helmets. The rocks, down toward the river, were covered with drying clothes. The bees were still buzzing, but around us the world was leafy, green, and wet.

It was hard to believe that we had been talking about hypothermia yesterday afternoon. I was hotter now than I'd ever been in my life. I knew I must be having hot flashes, but now it was hard to tell when. The minor ones would start somewhere in my head and spread out to my neck and shoulders, but occasionally the sweat would pour out of me in bursts and I'd have to stop whatever I was doing and lift up my T-shirt and find something to use as a fan. But the sweat was pouring off everyone, particularly the men. With a humidity of 98 percent, there was practically no evaporation, nothing to dry up all those bodily excretions, no relief by cooling. We just accumulated layers upon layers of smells and muck.

I envied the Dayaks, who have adapted to the rain forest by minimizing sweat. Researchers have found that for some reason the natives of Borneo generate little body heat. They are also short and small, which means they have a large surface area for dissipating heat in relation to their bulk.

By three that afternoon the sweat bees were dancing in ecstasy around my rotting carcass and I had a total of four honeybee stings still festering: one in my armpit, one on the back of my knee, and two on my neck. Four beestings in seven hours, my overall personal best. When the hormones kicked in I knew how

Mimo must have felt when he ran that fever: a pariah exiled to the world's outer edge.

During one of the bee attacks I fled into my tent to escape, which turned out to be a bad idea. The tent now smelled as if something very large had decided to decompose in John's socks. Holding my breath, I reached down to the bottom of his duffel, grabbed the socks, and carried them to the river where I scrubbed them and scrubbed them until they smelled like soap. Then I lay them next to Sylvie's sarongs in the sun, where they failed to glisten or shimmer. The butterflies, I noted, gave a sniff and ignored them.

Oddly enough, the best part of the day was the portage, carrying the loads through the forest. Heads bobbing, arms loaded with gear, feet tapping to find firm ground, we walked on a barely discernible trail like ants carrying loads of plastic and rubber. When our adventure didn't look scary, it looked ridiculous.

The guides had marked the trail by blazing a few trees with machete marks, but for someone like me, with no sense of direction, it was definitely possible to get lost. After the first trip, I was usually on the trail alone and had to look for tracks to get me from one mark to the next—find a skid mark in the dark compost, a bent leaf, a cut vine. It was amazing how little the forest had been marred by our walking through it. There were no footprints in the black mass of resilient vegetable matter, and the vines and leaves that we moved aside sprang back instantly, unmarred. Even the ants I stepped on seemed to survive by sinking into the compost. Occasionally clouds of butterflies floated up like muted fireworks.

This wasn't the kind of landscape that I'd ever found visually exciting. In California, I loved the desert and the high mountains. I loved great folds and rumples in the bare earth and the rocky landscape above tree line. I loved open spaces and brown- and purple- and peach-colored vistas. I loved the earth sculptures left by massive cataclysms.

Here everything was green and close, transitory and soft. I

knew the river was about 150 feet away, but it might as well have been on another planet. My world was a thirty-foot circle, and all I could see in it was green plants. The light was soft and opaque, dimming and brightening for unseen reasons, and although time seemed a distant concept, I had the feeling that I had to keep moving, or get smothered.

The nomadic tribe of Dayaks, the Penans, call this shadowy world home. You can spot them in coastal cities, it is said, by the way they walk, staying in the shadows of buildings, crossing the street to avoid the sun. I was getting more and more comfortable in the rain forest, but I still felt as if I was in someone else's private place. I remembered the attic of an old wooden one-room schoolhouse that an older girl had taken me to when I was six years old. There was no floor to it, just exposed beams, and except for a single stream of light coming in a dusty, cobwebbed window, we were in pitch blackness. We walked in silence, tiptoeing along the beams, barely able to see and with no idea of what we were going to find.

The rain forest was like that: the world's dark and secret attic.

One of my favorite travel writers, Peter Fleming (brother of Ian Fleming), wrote a best-selling book, *Brazilian Adventure,* about an expedition to a remote part of South America in 1932. In it he remarked that being the first white man to see someplace was "quaint rather than impressive . . . like being married in an aeroplane." I agreed with him, but even so, the knowledge that everything around me as far as I could see was exactly how nature had intended it was thrilling—like coming upon a lost treasure or stepping through a looking glass.

As I became more and more at ease walking the trail, slipping less and less in the mud, it became easier to see the rain forest as Bill did: here was the oldest, richest, and most stable environment on earth, and also a kind of evolutionary hothouse. The climate was moist and hot with a perennial growing season, and the plants and animals had had millions of years to develop. Being on the equator had saved the jungle from various ice ages, and being on the island of Borneo, one of the oldest pieces of land on earth, had given evolutionary forces a particularly long time to experiment.

And God knows there was enough to look at, even on our tiny half-mile trail. By the time I'd made three trips back and forth, carrying ammo cans, paddles, helmets, and bags of food, I began to see the forest as an exotic garden. There were spiky plants and broad-leafed plants and trees and vines and fungus; everything was wet-green, with the occasional variegated leaf standing out like a patch of sunlight. Moss and lichen were everywhere, along with unknown splotches of things—wet tassels dripping with goo, random spongy lumps, and soft, oddball plumes. Most exotic of all were the epiphytes. I was so used to seeing these strange plants sprouting magically from a piece of bark hanging on someone's living room wall in California, that they looked odd at first, growing in abundance on tree trunks and branches. But they actually made up a miniature garden high above the forest floor. Some looked like cacti, with long, spiny, twisted spikes; others were like bunches of grass. When I looked for them, they were everywhere, their leaves collecting rain water and litter from the canopy. They made up an entire ecological niche, supporting colonies of cockroaches, earthworms, salamanders, and even snakes.

I was glad to see that the Tarzan movies hadn't been completely fraudulent. There were plenty of lianas weaving through the forest like a giant web. They grew up from the ground, using trees for support, until they reached the canopy, where they branched out and flowered, or so I'd read. On the equator the forest is supposed to flower and fruit all year round ("You may be the fortunate ones," my guidebook proclaimed, "if you happened to watch with your bare eyes these orchids in blossoming"). But here in the gorge we couldn't even find any petals on the ground. We were in a bee warp, an animal warp, and now a flora warp.

Trying to identify, or even distinguish, the trees along the trail was an exercise in frustration. I knew it was unlikely that any two trees I passed by were the same species, but their trunks were covered with vines and epiphytes and the leaves were so high up in the canopy I couldn't see them. I could distinguish the giants of the rain forest, the huge diterocarps that were prized by loggers. Their trunks were as straight as flagpoles and mostly bare. But everything else was pretty much indistinguishable except for one tree with a great flying buttress, and a stand of bamboo with stalks the diameter of dinner plates.

There was also an immense tree with a hollow center that Bill identified as a strangler fig. It had started out as an epiphyte in the canopy but had sent out long roots and eventually killed its host. Every type of fig tree in the forest has its own wasp, he said, each with a strange abdomen adapted just for pollinating it.

For a while I considered the possibility that our bees thought we were fig trees, that maybe we had a weird kind of abdominal adaptation. But then I remembered Bill hadn't said bee, he'd said wasp.

I sat down gingerly on a log after testing it for slime, thinking I should stop and smell the rain forest for a few minutes. But as soon as I did, I heard a rustle in the compost, and when I turned over a leaf there was a white furry nest attached to it and a band of ants already up to my wrist. I shuddered to think what a short time it would take for me to be covered with mold and fungus and eaten by bacteria and insects. Within a few weeks I could be recycled into the nutrients that feed the rain forest and hold the earth in balance, that keep the lights of man's empire blazing and its cars speeding through the night.

41

*L*ate in the afternoon, Bill, Stuart, Howard, and Raymond came down the trail carrying the first of the three rolled-up boats. They were sweating, slipping and staggering under the weight; it didn't look like fun. Then came Sylvie, carrying a heavy rubber dry bag slung over one arm and two heavy wooden paddles balanced like skis on her shoulders. Her legs were muddy and she was sweating and dirty; I was thoroughly impressed.

Later, when I saw her ask Mike to look down the back of her tiny bikini bottoms to check for leeches, I realized that her attention to her body and the casual sexiness she displayed was not only very French, but very practical. She hated leeches.

"I went out of the tent to pee very carefully last night," she said. "I had my feet only half out of the tent, just trying to aim outside, you know? And when I got up this morning—phe-e-eh! I found a huge leech, filled with blood, right between my toes."

"I don't know how you can think about romance," I said.

"It is almost," she admitted, "impossible."

At one point I had started to confide in Sylvie—tell her about my hot flashes—but then I changed the subject. She was too young; the confession wouldn't interest her; she would start treating me like her mother; she would be turned off. Also, no one realized I was over forty, and I couldn't think of anything to gain by telling them.

Linda was having the toughest time of all of us. In addition to the obvious miseries, she'd been in rain forests for two months by now and was homesick. That afternoon she told me she and Bill were having a hard time.

"I haven't told this to him," she said, "but I know it's over between us. I can't stand to talk to him. I can't stand to kiss him. I can't stand to touch him."

"What's the matter?"

"His whole life is the rain forest. You don't understand about Bill. He loves the rain forest. He couldn't live without it. It really is his whole life."

"Yes, but . . ."

"I *hate* the rain forest. I never want to see it again. I never want to hear about it. It's a terrible place."

"I think he feels the same way now. We all do."

"No. It wouldn't be fair to live with him feeling like this. I'm a New Yorker. I like art; I like flash. I want to be in a nice white studio; I want bright lights and buildings."

"Maybe—"

". . . I'm going to have to get rid of my apartment, go back to New York, start all over again . . . it's so depressing. And the thing is, I'll really miss Bill."

I gave Linda the obvious advice: don't make any decisions now about the future. But that night I noticed that she stayed in her tent again instead of eating dinner, and that Bill came out only to eat briefly, then went back to be with her. I felt sorry for them both.

Dave and I talked about writing. I owed Sobek an article about the trip for its catalog, and I joked that it was already book length.

Dave was going to write about the trip also, he said. He'd noticed that the only explorers anyone remembered were the ones who were writers. I agreed. Then I told him that when my article was published he would probably be disappointed.

"It will tell my story," I said, "and not yours. It will make you mad because I'll leave out your experience."

* * *

When I came back to camp after carrying the last load, the gin and bitters bug was already singing, and it was fast getting dark. Sylvie and Mike, looking clean and happy, said they'd just taken a bath in the river, and I begged some soap and raced down to do the same. The river was big and churning, the huge waterfalls around the bend were loud, and the sky was gray with clouds and just a tinge of pink. As darkness fell I stood alone at the edge of the river, soaping, rubbing, washing my hair, my ears, my crotch. The water was warm, the air was warm, the bees had gone, and the soap smelled pure and sweet. Soaking wet in the moonlight, my skin looked as if it had been dipped in oil.

Earlier I'd asked Dave, Mike, and Gary what the best part of the trip had been for them so far.

"It's getting better and better," said Dave.

"You mean the challenge?"

"Yeah."

"I wouldn't say this is fun," added Mike. "There are too many things to worry about—too many dangerous situations."

"But I've seen you enjoying some of those cowboy maneuvers," I teased.

"Well, in the heat of the chase, yeah. A raft is stuck, someone has to get it—that's nice. But the problem is we're not working at top level because we're crippled. The foot rot has gotten to us."

"And the bees," added Gary.

I knew the frustration of not working at top level; in fact I knew the frustration of knowing my top level was forever gone. But now, cool, clean, and alone in the river, I realized that the best part of the trip for me had changed. If I could no longer dazzle myself or anyone else with physical prowess, I could at least savor small private moments. So I stayed in the river awhile, watching the overcast sky dissolve into black, and then I stood there for a moment longer, trying to commit to memory the smells and sounds. I knew that later, when it was all over, the experience would seem unreal, and I wanted to remember the details of a time when I had been someplace extraordinary and come face-to-face with extraordinary things.

42

*T*he next morning at breakfast Dave announced that the river had risen three feet during the night, and they'd had to retie the boats again. He'd decided not to run it at that level because it might be impossible to find an eddy. Also, the guides could use a day to rest and dry their feet. So unless the river fell by midmorning, we'd spend another day in camp.

It wasn't what we wanted to hear.

He also announced the beginning of food rationing, which we'd avoided so far only because he'd brought enough food for seventeen people and there were only twelve of us. From now on there would be no seconds. Leftover rice for breakfast, the loathsome deng deng and stale crackers for lunch, rice for dinner. It wasn't much, but it was better than the alternatives.

When Tom Harrisson, the English ethnologist, traveled in Borneo's rain forest in the early 1930s, he ate only what his guides could find: birds' eggs, frog legs, goat moths, caterpillars, fat crickets, toadstools, orchid pods, camphor-bark nuts, water vines, wet moss, horseshoe bats, and the occasional partridge chick. Charles Miller, that adventurous Hollywood cameraman, wrote that his guides carried dried monkey meat, which swelled and turned white and green when wet. They ate it putrefied, he said, by swallowing it without chewing.

When Richard Bangs hiked with some of the men from Long

Lebusan, he carefully avoided the usual offerings of maggots and grubs. He did, however, swallow "an unidentifiable wad of mush" that tasted like spinach but turned out to be sweat bee larvae. Redmond O'Hanlon tried that other staple of the rain forest, monitor lizard, whose flesh, he wrote, "was soft and yellow and smelled like the stray chunks of solid matter in the effluvia one sees in England on an unwashed pavement outside a public house late on a Saturday night."

So many food choices in Borneo.

It was clear that if we were stuck in the gorge long enough, we'd starve. I'd been hunting once in the rain forest of Central America with two Mayan men, their dogs, and a German anthropologist. We were on the Usumacinta River on the border of Mexico and Guatemala, a very long way from a butcher shop. We left at sunset in two canoes and paddled downriver mostly in darkness, accompanied by so many cicadas and frogs roaring and singing in the river canyon that it felt as if we were in an enormous engine room. The racket was so loud and monotonous that the rhythmic drip of water from our canoe paddles seemed comforting: soft and intimate amidst the cosmic din.

We followed the sound of the dogs barking in the jungle until we heard a splash in the water up ahead of us, and then the men began to paddle our canoes furiously. I couldn't see what it was in the darkness, but finally we came up to it: a small deerlike animal trying to swim across the river, its head trailing a soft wake in the current. It was no contest. Paddling leisurely, we stayed alongside the swimming deer, and for a moment I didn't understand what was going to happen. I kept looking at its eyes, which were beautiful doe's eyes, fixed on me and brimming with terror. Its churning legs, tiny and thin, could barely make headway across the current. Finally the Mayans, acting on some unspoken command, grasped the animal's small horns, one man to a side, and firmly pushed the head down below the water. The water rippled, but there was no splashing, no sound. In a couple of minutes they lifted the drowned deer up and flung it into the boat.

I had mixed feelings about hunting. I know that most hunters understand animals and respect them, but there is a ghoulish side to the sport, a side that is disrespectful. Peter Fleming, for instance, writes with maddening nonchalance about the carnage left in the wake of the hunting party he traveled with in Brazil in 1932. At one point he complained that the alligators they came across didn't put up a fight.

"We acquired so great a contempt for these unenterprising creatures," he wrote, "that after we had killed well over one hundred in a month, we almost gave up shooting them."

I'd also read Oscar Beccari, one of the great naturalists and travelers of the nineteenth century, who hunted orangutans in Borneo. Since the orangutans responded to him with curiosity, he would simply wait in the forest until they came to have a look at him. Some he merely wounded and carried out alive; others he wounded but couldn't retrieve; and still others he killed and cut up into parts to ship back to Europe. When he left Borneo, he took with him "portions of just twenty-four individuals."

Hunting in Borneo even today, according to my East Kalimantan guidebook, is not particularly subtle. You don't even have to get out of the car to do it:

"You do not have to go inside the jungle. Just ride your car along the road and park somewhat further at the roadside. Or you can take a lift, at a log cargo truck heading to the jungle then stop in some quite place. The next move is to wait your hunting deer pass by in group. So many and so tame they are that you may aim your rifle at the one you want to shoot."

By midmorning the river was still high and roaring monotonously all around us. The guides left early to go downriver on a long scout and I went back to the tent to read: I was almost through with *Lord Jim*.

But now it was not only hot and claustrophobic inside the tent, it was dark, too dark to see the words on the page. The sky was gray, we were under the tree canopy, and the tent had only one opening to the natural light. Since using a flashlight was out of the question—mine had about three minutes of light left in it—and since the bees and leeches made reading in the open air impossible, and since going for a walk by myself would be dangerous, I had nothing to do.

It was a startling discovery. I'd never spent an entire day doing nothing. I thought of Gary going reptilian. I thought of John and his unconscious hand waving. I thought of all those hours I'd spent as a teen-ager lying motionless next to guys on the beach. I thought about books.

The nineteenth-century European explorers who wrote about Borneo weren't great writers, but they were close observers, and I'd come to admire their straightforward story-telling. They had traveled at a time when there were no airplanes or outboard motors, no dried or canned food, no malaria pills, no way at all to contact the outside world should they need help. And all of them were amateur scientists. They learned the language, collected plant and animal specimens, studied the indigenous culture, and in general were curious about whatever they found around them. They spent months traveling upriver to places like Long Lebusan, and all seem to have genuinely enjoyed the Dayaks they spent time with.

I thought about one man, a Norwegian, who spent over a year in Borneo's rain forest and never got used to the darkness, which he claimed had "a depressing effect" on his spirits. His solution was to have his porters cut down a large circle of trees whenever they made camp, thereby creating a patch of light in which he could read and write. When I'd read this I'd considered it an appalling waste of trees, but now I understood. I couldn't imagine spending a year without writing or reading a book.

Books have always been an essential part of travel for me; wherever I go, my armchair adventures commingle intimately with actual ones. On this trip I was traveling with *Lord Jim*, but also with other people's memories, half-remembered phrases, scenes from novels, and especially the river trip Spenser St. John, the British explorer and colonial administrator, had taken in British Borneo in 1858. It was the most extraordinary and dangerous adventure in Borneo that I'd read about, and now it seemed remarkably close to our own experience.

Like us, St. John had been warned by the natives about the dangers of traveling through the forest: "warned of head-hunting Kayans, the wandering Pakatans with their poisoned arrows, the strange aborigines who had never seen a white man or even a Malay, the dangers of the river that imperiled our boats, and the wanderings in the jungle that threatened starvation." The Limbang, he was told, was "too full of cataracts, rapids and huge rocks to be descended by rafts."

Like us, St. John ignored the warnings.

He and "his men"—Dayak boatmen and porters—had come up the Limbang River from Brunei in longboats, which they had to abandon along with some of their provisions when they hit a long series of rapids. Now St. John wanted to return to the boats by the river rather than by foot, and instructed his men to build four rafts: three from bamboo lashed together with rattan, and one twenty-foot raft made of a double layer of lashed-together logs.

The first rapids they came to destroyed all three bamboo rafts, and although the large log raft made it through carrying St. John and the provisions, he fell off it and had to be rescued. Fortunately, his hair had grown long, he wrote, and a Dayak had been able to grab it and pull him ashore.

In the second major rapids St. John's raft was hurled against a rock and then caught in an immense whirlpool, where it circled for over ten minutes before the wreckage of one of the bamboo rafts crashed into it and drove it out.

In the third set of rapids the center trunk of the big raft was pounded from its place and the logs started to unravel. St. John, riding it alone, careened downstream, holding on to the bucking logs for dear life. Finally, he came to another whirlpool, where he circled long enough for his men to reach him and pull him out.

At the end of this white water drama, St. John explains why he kept having to be rescued: he couldn't swim.

After the third rescue, St. John's men convinced him to give up on the river and head inland, on foot, over a mountain. And so they did, with only a day's worth of food left. The first day they walked from dawn to dusk, climbing a mountain "so steep that we had to place our rifles and guns before us as far as we could reach, and then pull ourselves up to them." That night they camped "on a ridge not three feet broad." By noon the next day they had eaten their last chicken, and each man was given a final ration of rice: one cup.

By the third day one of the Dayak leaders had a high fever and many of the men felt ill, so St. John asked five of the strongest men to push on for the boats so they could bring back some of the provisions he'd cached in them. St. John was now walking barefoot along with everyone else, and his greatest torment was "leeches getting between my toes and crawling up my trousers, reaching even to my waist, where the tight belt prevents their farther progress."

The men walked for a total of six days, eating nothing but thin rice water and cabbage palm, and on the sixth night St. John took out his bottle of opium "to deaden the pangs of hunger." But before he took it, one of his men came back with some fruit and a bees' nest. By noon the next day they reached the boats.

There, St. John found the five men he had sent ahead "looking fat and well." They said a bear had eaten all the provisions, but St. John found evidence of cooked meals. He had a fit of rage, and calmed down only after finding a tasty jar of pork fat.

If St. John went up the Limbang today, he could follow the red dirt logging roads. Although not all of the trees have been cut down, the canopy is open and secondary growth has taken over. The river itself is full of motor boats.

43

*T*he sound of the conversation coming from Bill and Linda's tent was rhythmic: varying intensities of *tum-tum-TUM, tum-tum-TUM, ta-TUMTUM,* punctuated by occasional high squeaks and basso moans. At one point I tried to notate it as a sort of jungle symphony, but although I could get the notes more or less in order, I had no idea how to indicate texture—tinkles and growls. Finally, when I grew sick of passing time by myself, I went over to their tent to see if they wanted to play cards. I called out to them as I used to call to my childhood playmates:

"Li-i-inda. Bi-i-ill."

"What?"

"Want to play cards?"

"No," said Linda, "thanks anyway."

"Are you okay?"

"Just my knees are all banged up, I'm out of cigarettes, the food is shitty, I haven't gone to the bathroom in nine days, nothing will get dry, my tongue hurts, we've missed our plane . . ."

"Well, if you want some company . . ."

"Maybe later," said Bill.

Our camp looked deserted, and it was now deathly quiet. Everyone was in his tent, zoning out or napping. Only John seemed awake, and just barely. He was sitting on a log in perfect camouflage. Since his tobacco had gotten too wet to smoke, he had perfected the art of being absolutely motionless. I had mistaken him earlier for a moldy tree stump. But now I saw that he had taken his shoes and socks off and was once again looking at his feet. They had been covered with red spots and cracks, but now they were hideously swollen, so swollen they looked inflated. His ankles were as big as his calves, and his toes looked like little puffballs on the end of two stumps.

"My God," I said.

"Yeah."

John hadn't brought any antifungal cream and he hadn't asked to borrow any, and now, as I stood and looked in horror at his monstrous appendages, I felt a surge of anger and frustration. Why didn't he take care of himself? But then I looked at him and realized that, like all of us, he was doing the best he could. So I borrowed some cream from Howard, got the pair of socks I'd washed and laid out yesterday to dry, and retrieved his shoes from the tent and put them in the sun as well. To my surprise, John seemed truly touched and grateful. He thanked me softly, and I left him gently pressing his swollen toes.

Clearly, a day "relaxing" in the jungle wasn't going to bring us together as a group: the oppressive clamminess made us turn inward, turn morbid. Everyone was alone, trying to cope.

I remembered the first book I had ever read about a rain forest, Peter Matthiessen's *At Play in the Fields of the Lord*. He had called it "a cathedral of Satan" in a paragraph I had once thought was particularly melodramatic:

He touched a tree, dismayed anew by those dark, twisted amphitheaters, the hanging ropes, the quaking rot beneath his feet that breathed its reek with every step. He stumbled around in small half-circles. . . . In the dark tunnels of the rain forest the dim light was greenish. Strange shapes caught at his feet and creepers scraped him; putrescent smells choked his nostrils with the density of sprayed liquid. He fell to his knees on the rank ground and began to pray but instantly jumped up again. He had wandered into a cathedral of Satan where all prayer was abomination, a place without a sky, a stench of death, vast somber naves and clerestories, the lost cries of savage birds. . . .

I found it easy, now, to imagine the triumph of Satan. In a place where natural forces are so ever-present, I could see why the Dayaks believed in evil spirits. Certainly transcendence seemed out of the question: a prayer spun from a Buddhist flag would get tangled in the canopy; a monk copying sacred texts would rot before he finished. There was no sublimity in a rain forest, no voice in the thunder. There was only living and dying in ceaseless repetition.

I tried to take a nap and finally relaxed for an hour or so into a kind of hallucinatory doze; at one point I looked up and saw a fire in the tent, flickering in a corner. Then, as if on cue, all my bites and infections and poison pus came alive in a frenzy of stinging and itching. While I scratched and squirmed I remembered the researcher in the Amazonian rain forest who had undertaken a study of the three-toed sloth. He had counted the number of vermin (moths, beetles, ticks, and mites) living on its skin and in its fur and come up with several hundred in addition to a film of algae that completely camouflaged the sloth green. Baby sloths, it is said, urinate and defecate right on their mother's stomach.

Just then John came inside and lay there alongside me with his blown-up feet. I realized then that if we stayed on the Boh much longer we would all eventually puff up. I wasn't afraid—I believed we'd get out—but I had a healthy respect for what would happen if we didn't.

A little later I heard a soft roar, way up high in the canopy: it was raining again. I went to take a look at the river, which, as I had feared, was rising, already filling with silt, debris, and boiling currents. The huge twenty- and thirty-foot drops were filling up, and the river was again becoming one monstrous mass of water. When I ran into Linda, who'd come out of her tent to pee, she said Bill had reassured her that there was an American army base near Balikpapan and that if we needed to be rescued and Sobek was too cheap to do it, the army would come in. The thought reassured me as well.

I tried to cheer her up and handed her some of the last of our packaged biscuits, but she nibbled one and said they were the worst biscuits she'd ever eaten. I told her a story about some stale biscuits I'd survived on in Papua New Guinea, and she said she never wanted to see a biscuit again. "I'm just pissed," she said at last. "I'm not fit company. I don't want to eat. I don't want to talk. I just want to cry."

There was nothing to do, finally, but wait out the rain in the thick, cloistered haze of our tents. John and I exchanged comforting noises, but nothing outside our tiny camp seemed real. The Boh had closed in on us and we had closed down. We were in a hall of mirrors, looking inward, and among all the reflections the vastness of the unknown ahead seemed like another world, another lifetime.

44

At dinner that night—two cups of rice and a dried boullion cube—Dave reported that he had good news. The guides had made a long scout that morning and hadn't seen any more unrunnable rapids. Also, their foot rot had benefited from an afternoon of airing and Mike's big toe looked like it was going to heal without getting infected.

"We're hoping to be out of the gorge soon," said Gary.

"We're almost out of antifungal cream," added Dave, "and we've begun to ration our pain pills."

"Did you really see a gibbon?" Mimo asked.

"Yeah," said Mike. "It was just cruising through the trees, peeking down at us."

The conversation went downhill from there, at least for me. We started talking desultorily about our "other" lives: Stuart about politics in Australia, Mimo about a room in an Italian villa where he had slept in a bed slept in by Napoleon, Mike about how unhappy he'd been working for the Department of Forestry. They were probably interesting stories, but none of us pursued them. Talking about the world we'd come from seemed jarring, almost disrespectful. Of all of us huddled under the blue tarp that night, only Sylvie and Mike, nuzzling and stroking each other, seemed anything but numb.

Then Howard brought up one of his favorite subjects—Australian bourgeois materialism—and someone mentioned yuppies. Raymond joined in the conversation, which was a little unusual. He said he had a sports car and a house in Jakarta with a swimming pool and five servants but did not consider himself a yuppie.

"Well, you're a young urban professional. You're spending money. That's the demographic definition," I said.

"I haven't had this conversation for six years," Raymond snapped, "and I'm not about to have it now."

His words hung there in the night as if Count Dracula had suddenly appeared by the fire and uttered them. I was used to Raymond's random ill-tempered bossiness and figured he made up for it with a lot of hard work. But the idea of him insulting the quality of my conversation was too much.

I sat perfectly still, reeling with anger but unwilling to pursue it. I didn't want to fight. I didn't want to defend my remark and I didn't want to apologize. Like everyone, I was just trying to make it through the night.

The silence lasted for maybe thirty seconds until Dave finally cleared his throat and said, "Well, that's *that*," and got up and went over to the fire. I followed him. Then I saw my white city sandals—the only shoes I had besides my wet tennis shoes—melting in the coals. I'd propped them up on a rock to dry near the fire and someone must have knocked them over: the white plastic straps were shriveling and turning black.

The tent I had grown to hate so much suddenly seemed a refuge. I crawled into it and in the faint glow of my flashlight I noticed that my right forearm had swollen up almost as grotesquely as John's feet. But it didn't itch, and it didn't particularly hurt; it just looked as if my arm had sprouted a two-inch tumor. Then I checked my other forearm and saw that it was swollen in exactly the same place. Both had tiny black marks in the middle where something poisonous had probably been injected.

I was sitting in the dark, marveling at the coincidence of two ants or spiders biting with such precise symmetry when John came in and said that he'd heard me use the phrase "one day at a time." Was I, he asked, a friend of Bill Wilson?

A close relative was a member of Alcoholics Anonymous, I said, and John confided that he'd been in A.A. for eight years.

I had pictured John doing many things, most of them having to do with oddball private obsessions like designing computer games or writing historical monographs. But I'd never imagined him to be a drinker.

"I was a lot of things in my youth," he said (John was almost forty). "I used to be very political, very right wing."

"You were a Republican?"

"I was a member of CREEP."

"CREEP? You mean the Committee to Re-elect the President? During Watergate?"

"Yes. But as I said, my political views have changed."

"How? Less conservative?"

"Yes."

"Why?"

"I realized that some people actually do need help."

They do, we all do. After a moment I said, "What do you think went on with Raymond tonight?"

"I think Raymond was being a jerk."

I laughed and blew him a kiss. I was growing fond of John, who was probably very smart and certainly kind. Somehow he had learned to live contentedly in the world without getting much support or even attention. I hadn't seen anyone on the trip show the slightest bit of interest in him, but I sensed he had learned to deal with that years ago. I wanted to ask him how he managed to be happy and almost invisible, but I couldn't figure out how to phrase the question. So I went to sleep thinking about my husband. Earlier in the evening Howard had asked me about marriage, and I'd told him that I had come to believe in it in the old sense—for better or for worse. For the first time in my life, I said, I knew I'd stick with my husband even if he somehow became a burden.

"Unconditional love?" Howard had asked.

"Well," I replied, "not if he becomes a sadistic murderer. But I'd stick with Jon if he became ill or feebleminded or bedridden." I was still selfish, I said, but now I believed that a long-term marriage was in my self-interest.

I could hear my husband in my head: "If you're loved enough, why are you there?"

Before I went to sleep I made a written inventory of my physical condition:

Feet: Covered with red spots, particularly under my left arch. Dark red sores between my toes with stinging, broken skin. Foot rot arrested, but not gone.

Ankles: Right ankle swollen for some reason; left ankle has an open sore on it—have to beg some antiseptic.

Legs: Four dark bruises on my left leg and a huge welt behind the knee (a spider bite?). Two dark bruises and a bump and gash on my right shin, plus a line of poison something on my calf, oozing and itching like crazy.

Arms: A new rash on my right arm; hope it isn't the same poison thing. Two immense bites, one on each arm, still swollen about two inches.

Hands: A splinter festering in my thumb, eight fingernails broken.

Mouth: The sore on my gum neither better nor worse.

Mind: Mildewed, lethargic, maybe rotten.

Heart: Love you, Jon.

45

*T*he next morning Dave reported that the river had miraculously gone down during the night, even though it had continued, on and off, to rain. Mike and Gary were at the bottom of the rapids already, pumping air into the boats, and we were to pack up camp and carry everything down to them as soon as possible. The river was low and fast; today, our ninth day on the gorge, was the day we'd sail out of it.

Down by the boats, in the hot sun, the bees were once again on the attack. The honeybees were stinging now for no apparent reason, and the sweat bees were seething on our skin, T-shirts, and life jackets. It was a little unnerving to think of the bacteria the carrion-eating sweat bees were introducing into our open gashes and sores, and it was seriously maddening to get stung. The hour or so it took us to load and rig the boats was an exercise in endurance. With the bees and the heat and the waiting and the hot flashes, it was, for me, one of the most miserable hours of the trip in terms of pure discomfort. I was attracting so many clouds of bees that Stuart wondered if I had a fever. I just shrugged. I remembered what I thought about women over forty when I was his age, and I still had illusions of my own. One of them was that I was not conceivably old enough to be Stuart's mother.

But at last we got in the boats and pulled out into the current.

To my amazement, I didn't feel relieved. I remembered what it was like to head straight down into a drop, be hit in the face by an enormous wave of water and suddenly have the world go dark. I remembered that the river could flip me into an underwater nightmare as easily as I could put my finger on one of the tiny ants that was crawling up my leg and squash it.

Not surprisingly, the Olympic sport of the Dayak world turns out to be holding one's breath under water—a sport in which I had, unfortunately, never been coached. One of the books I'd read described a contest called *Besalam,* which, when I thought about it, seemed pretty astonishing. Whenever two Dayak families had a serious dispute, they'd each hire a renowned "diver" in the area to compete in a *Besalam.* On the appointed day, everyone would go down to the river, and the two divers would go in the water, accompanied by their "handlers." At the signal, they'd dip their heads underwater and the feuding families would wave fighting cocks at each other and throw around saffron rice.

I'd assumed the winner would be whichever diver surfaced last, red-faced and gasping. But the Dayaks had taken the sport to a higher level. Both men could stay underwater until they passed out. The winner was whoever was hauled out of the water last by his handler—unconscious but not yet dead.

The first rapids of the day proved easily runnable, even though Mimo fell out of the paddle boat and had to be dragged back in. The white water looked rough, with plenty of hydraulic terrors—drops, chutes, and holes—but there turned out to be routes through them. It was nice to see Gary relaxed and confident.

Then the river widened and we cruised through some riffles as the canyon walls angled out. The river was letting go of us, it seemed, flowing fast but calmly below the logs and debris left on the riverbanks by yesterday's flood. The eddies lapped quietly against the rocks. We'd still pull out every ten minutes or so, whenever we couldn't see ahead, but now the scouts were brief. Most often Mike would scramble to the top of a boulder, glance for a moment or two at some easy Class II white water, and then pull out almost immediately into the current. Gary started whistling as he oared; John took off his shoes and dried his monster feet, and I got out some sunscreen and lay back on the boat and closed my eyes. Up ahead I could hear everyone in the paddle boat laughing. I could feel the knotted muscles in my back begin to uncramp.

Then Gary stood up and muttered his now infamous line: "Oh, shit." I looked ahead and saw a white line in the river ahead of us, and in a matter of minutes we heard the roar.

"This river has us by the balls," Gary said.

"Fruit bats!" Dave called out as we oared into an eddy. We passed a tree black with hanging bats, but none of us cared. Even Bill gave only a cursory look.

After a twenty-minute scout, the guides returned and said we were in luck. The rapids were big, and full of huge standing waves, but there was a run. "Put on your helmets!" Dave cried out.

Then Gary stood up to make an announcement:

"I feel I should tell you," he said, "that those who want to can get out of the boats. There's an easy walk here along the rocks to the eddy where we'll be pulling out."

Linda, Sylvie, Bill, and John got out of the boats immediately, and I watched them head off downstream. My inclination was to conquer my fear and take the ride. I knew I'd feel good afterward; I'd enjoy the thrills and feel better about myself. But I also remembered the promise I'd made to my husband. He'd made me say it out loud: "I promise to take every opportunity to be safe." I knew he'd never find out if I walked this stretch or not, but finally I couldn't betray him. So I got out of the boat, stood on the rocks, and watched everyone make it through the rapids safely, heard the whoops and shouts.

"Boy, that was fun," Stuart said, as the paddlers pulled up into the eddy.

"That was a fantastic run," said Howard. "Really great."

"You missed the best," Mimo said, shaking his head. But to my amazement I wasn't completely sorry I'd cast my lot with the wimps. It felt good to send a message to my husband, to keep a promise I didn't have to keep.

After lunch—crackers, and jelly (Mimo said he was saving the deng deng for Dave)—the gorge changed even more dramatically. The water became extremely calm. Suddenly we could see reflections: the jungle rooted in the water, the spin of soft, gentle whirlpools, the bright flicker of the river goddess as she floated just below the current. Also, we seemed to be in permanent shade. The walls were moss-covered and dotted with ferns and waterfalls, and the canopy was closing up over our heads. It felt as if we had entered an immense grotto, cool and dark. On the riverbanks vines crawled over the rocks, and even more promising, there were no bees. During a scout, Bill went into the jungle with his snake stick and came back saying he'd heard the call of an argus pheasant.

For about a half hour we floated downriver looking for monkeys and birds, and scouting the banks for evidence of logging or fishing. Gary told us to look for a major tributary coming in from the right; a mile or so after it we should run into the Mahakam. Up ahead I heard Sylvie and Mimo laughing and talking in French; Mimo had joined her in Mike's boat and they were throwing things at each other again.

Gary started talking about his plans for getting out. He wondered if he was going to be able to make his flight to Singapore and then to Papua New Guinea. If he didn't, he'd lose a job as a guide for Sobek on the Watut River and money he was counting on. John and I protested that it would be unfair of Sobek not to pay him. It would be like punishing him for having to work overtime on the Boh. But Gary said that in all his years of river rafting he had never heard of a company paying a guide for a trip he was unable to take. The only good thing about missing the Watut, he said, would be seeing his wife, Ginger, who was also a river guide. They'd been married only a year and had spent the summer apart, working different river trips.

Then, up ahead, I saw Mike stand up in his boat and look downriver. "Rapids," said Gary. Then, "Shit."

It seemed somehow impossible. There couldn't be more rapids. Already we'd been nine days in the gorge instead of three, and even Dave said we'd come at least eighteen miles. But Mike was holding his boat against the current, and the rest of us floated down to meet him. We all looked at each other but didn't say anything until finally Dave said, "Let's go scout it." As we pulled into the eddy we could hear the angry voices of arguing rapids.

"It could be," said Gary as he tied up the boat, "that the Boh isn't through with us yet."

After a while, Mimo went downriver to see the rapids for himself and returned in about twenty minutes: "It's immense," he said. "There's no way that I can see to run it. There's a huge tree lying right across the river, and at the end of it there's a waterfall with an enormous hole at the bottom. You should go look at it. It's awesome."

None of us wanted to look. We had seen enough awesome white water. We sat waiting until Gary returned and confirmed that the rapids were unrunnable.

The only good news was that we didn't have to portage: the guides could line the boats down the river alongside the rocks. It was possible, Dave said, that we might be able to clock some kilometers in the late afternoon and find a better camp.

Once again we listlessly grumbled. Days ago all of us had missed the plane connections made for us by Sobek's travel agents, who had evidently been unaware that the Boh River itinerary was just wishful thinking. By now people back home were worrying about some of us: thank God my husband wasn't expecting to hear from me for another ten days. I hoped Sobek hadn't called him.

46

*T*he rapids were as bad as Mimo had reported, and by five-thirty, just a half hour before nightfall, the guides had managed to get only one boat down. We'd have to make camp where we were for the night. Since we now knew better than to camp next to the river, we climbed to high ground and pitched our tents in the muddy forest litter in the dark. John and I did it without a flashlight as both of ours were now producing only dim yellow beams.

While Mike and Raymond cooked dinner, Dave made the vodka Tangs. He'd found a trail near camp, he said, that probably led to the village Pelanjau had told him about. It was out of the question to try to follow it, since the village was a three-day walk away and the trail was little more than a few machete marks. But it was the first sign of civilization and we welcomed it. I was surprised that I wasn't worried anymore about being rescued. Something in me was beginning to like the forest. My foot rot was almost gone, the bees weren't at their worst, and I had learned to live with the poison-oak-like oozing and itching spots all over the back of my calf. At night, when the canopy closed overhead, I felt safe.

Dinner that night, Mike said, would be a surprise he and Raymond had found at the bottom of the rice bag. "We put it down there at the beginning of the trip and forgot about it," he said.

"Oh, come off it," said Stuart. "I saw the package. It's bloody freeze-dried mashed potatoes."

"I guess that's why we put it down there."

I remembered eating freeze-dried mashed potatoes on a backpacking trip in the Sierras. They tasted like polyester pillow-filling. I'd had a touch of altitude sickness at the time and almost immediately threw them up. It was like throwing up library paste, and for a few horrible moments I'd thought I might suffocate.

But miracles are unexpected, and that night the freeze-dried mashed potatoes turned out to be a gift to us from heaven. They came with instant gravy, margarine, and freeze-dried beans, and tasted so good that we grew silent, savoring the flavor. There was something overwhelmingly sensual about the taste of meat and grease and salt. We licked our plates; we licked the spoons. We even licked the pot.

"This is the best meal I have ever eaten," Sylvie announced.

"This is better," said Bill, "than real potatoes."

I thought of some friends who'd gotten lost hiking in Argentina and gone from half rations to quarter rations to eighth rations to no food at all. When they finally stumbled into an *estancia* at around ten o'clock at night, they bought an entire sheep from a rancher, slaughtered it, carried it down to the river, and roasted it over a fire. They ate for three hours, they said, finishing at four in the morning, and went to sleep covered with grease in a pile of the discarded bones.

Linda was in particularly good spirits, even before dinner, which surprised me. Then I noticed that she was getting drunk, and I remembered earlier what she'd said about not being able to socialize, not feeling up to cracking jokes. When Bill finally helped her negotiate the muddy trail back to their tent, I sympathized. She was trying to get over her depression, but a hangover wasn't going to be much fun.

That night I woke up hearing something rustling outside the tent. John was in his usual comatose state next to me and I could hear no voices, so I figured it must be someone going to take a leak. I decided to do the same myself, although it was going to be hard without a flashlight. The forest was black, broken only by vague shadows, and I felt my way behind the tent bit by bit until I ran into some vines and heard a noise. I stopped and stood motionless for a moment and then saw a human figure about forty feet away, moving fast but with amazing stealth. It stopped, or was gone, and I didn't call out. It wasn't one of us. We weren't able to move that quietly without a light.

It thrilled me to think of someone at home in the forest, able to move so remarkably in the darkness. I thought of the path Dave had found leading away from the river; perhaps it was a village man come to watch us. I wasn't afraid. Dayaks have always been friendly to outsiders, even at the height of their headhunting.

Headhunting was an aspect of Dayak culture that I had been inclined, at first, to dismiss. War is war, after all, and people everywhere get killed. So what if Dayaks used to cut off the heads of their enemies and hang them from the rafters? Why is that worse than burying them, or leaving them on the ground to rot?

But then I read some eyewitness accounts of the ceremonies that took place after Dayak raids, and I realized that headhunting was not about warfare at all, it was about something else. It was a religious rite, and a particularly gruesome one.

In the enormous pantheon of Dayak spirits, the most powerful spirit of all was believed to reside in a human head. A fresh head wasn't sought in anger, but because a person, or a village, needed spiritual strength. If kept warm and fed grains of rice, a head would make a village strong and bring it wealth. It would re-plenish the spirit that leaves a village after someone in it dies. It would even bring strength to its captor in the afterlife.

It wasn't until sometime in the nineteenth century that head-hunting began to get out of hand and threaten the Dayaks' very survival. While it used to be that a fresh head was needed only when someone died, by the 1800s fresh heads were required for almost all male rites of passage. A head had to be taken in order to name a male child, to send a boy on his first headhunt, and to declare a young man eligible for marriage. Every male in a village had to get three or four heads, and to get them they eventually had to attack whoever they could sneak up on and surprise—women gathering berries, children playing games. Occasionally, they'd even get a head from a corpse.

When, exactly, headhunting became an excuse for wild, drunken partying is not certain, although clearly that was the case by the time the European explorers arrived.

Charles Miller described an official headhunting celebration, a nine-day *mamat ulu,* that began when the village men returned from a hunt with several heads. First they told the story of their victory to a cheering audience and then they danced the famous headhunting dance, parts of which we'd seen in Long Lebusan. After the dance, the heads of a few chickens were cut off and someone ran about dripping blood all over everyone, and finally the headmen of the village impaled the new heads on the ends of sticks and marched around the longhouse so that everyone could touch them while their spirits were most potent.

"The rush to be the first to touch the heads," Miller wrote, "is beyond description. Men have had their throats cut and women have had their brains bashed out in the melee. In this case, one old man was so badly trampled that his throat was crushed and he died two days later."

The women in the village participated in the *mamat ulu,* and some say they were particularly bloodthirsty, grabbing the bloody heads and licking and biting them. The old men took the heads down to the river after everyone else was through with them, and dipped them in water and let the runoff flow over their genitals.

Sex was forbidden during the nine-day ceremony, Miller reported, but around day seven the nightly dancing turned lusty.

"Now they became personal movements, utterly shameless in their suggestive rhythms. Men and women alike picked up the rhythms of the gongs and small drums . . . any continued barrage of sound from those compelling instruments would unleash a surge of passion that would sweep the kampong into homicidal frenzy. Red-eyed with repression, the warriors circled the women hungrily and glared at each other in inflamed jealousy. Every now and then a warrior driven beyond self-control would explode into a group of dancers and begin a solo burst of wild dancing in which his whirling *mandau* would endanger the lives of all within reach."

On the seventh night Miller started taking a loaded gun to bed with him. On the eighth day he attended an all-day feast during which the women fed the men "until they could not stand." On the eighth night there was "an exhibition dance where the men got possessed and leapt over the verandah railing." One man, Miller reported, had "a bloody froth" on his lips caused by "clamping his filed teeth over his tongue in an ecstasy of self-torture"; another came close enough to Miller with his *mandau* to make Miller fear for his life. He responded by shooting a flash with his camera that "set everyone to wailing."

On the ninth and final night of the victory celebration, the headhunting party turned into an orgy. It was time for the women of the longhouse to "absorb the powerful spirits the warriors had accumulated from the headhunt."

"Here was not a case of brutal men attacking frightened women," Miller wrote. "Here was a case of men and women meeting on an exalted level of overpowering mutual desire."

Missionaries and European administrators worked hard to eradicate headhunting, but the British, at least, did understand its place in the larger culture. Anthropologist Peter Metcalf writes that whenever the British government took heads from rebellious longhouses, it kept some in stock to lend to the villages after someone died. He imagined "a district officer sorting through his collection, looking for a nice head to give to a favorite chief, and then noting the details on a file card for future reference."

By the time Miller came to Borneo (at the beginning of World War II), most of the Dayak chiefs had denounced headhunting and the practice was all but gone. It was revived briefly when the British parachuted into the interior during the war and encouraged the Dayaks to take up arms against the Japanese; but after the war it subsided again. Miller may have witnessed one of the last of the Dayak *mamat ulus*.

"Maybe the night was just a disgusting exhibition of unleased lust," he wrote. "There are many who think so. And then again the Dayaks may find something sublimely elemental in their festival of mamat ulu. Blood, death, spirits and sex, the powerful essential of primitive life, all mixed up together in a barbaric ritual that does not end until every person in the kampong achieves the ultimate of physical relief and spiritual satisfaction. When it is over, all desire in gone. No religion can do more."

Back in my tent I remembered the old woman who had tried to tell me about the Dayak spirits back in Long Lebusan. I could see her face, feel her grip on my arms. I wished I could have thanked her. I hoped that in her place, I'd do the same.

Once again I wondered who had convinced us that we knew more about the rivers and rain forest than the Dayaks did.

47

*T*he next morning, while waiting for the guides to get our boats downriver, I decided to torture myself: I borrowed Sylvie's mirror and looked into it. My hair was dirty, limp and stringy except for a few frizzled, permanented ends, and my skin was spotted and wrinkled. There were lines around my mouth, lines in my forehead, lines everywhere when I squinted or smiled, and in the few places where there weren't lines there were entire fields of blackheads. My nose was a thousand shades of red, and the skin on my neck looked reptilian. I handed the mirror back to Sylvie and felt like going into hiding. I was simply too ugly to inflict myself on anyone.

For the past few years I had complained that photographs of me were generally unflattering. But I knew the truth. I had always thought I would be perfectly happy with wrinkles and had never paid much attention to my face. I had looked in the mirror and it was fine and that was that. I rarely even bothered with makeup. But now it wasn't fine, and I felt a little as if my bluff had been called. I was prepared to die, but not to look dreadful for the rest of my life.

I had once tried to come to terms with the subject of female beauty, back in the early seventies, when women's confessional writing was all the rage. I'd pitched an article about it to *Cosmopolitan* magazine, mostly because beauty was something no one else had written about. In my query letter I said I wanted to use an example from my own life. In college some fraternity house had wanted me to compete to be their "queen" and I had refused, saying I thought beauty contests were demeaning. But I certainly didn't refuse the other perks that came my way from guys who found me attractive: the help with physics and chemistry, swimming and skiing; the special treatment on backpacking trips; the invitation to a celebrity party or a movie set.

An editor from *Cosmopolitan* called me and said that she could never publish such an article.

"First of all, you can't say you got all that attention," she said. "Women don't want to hear it. *Cosmopolitan* operates on the belief that most women are down. They think they're ugly, they think they're fat, they think they're unlovable. We start from there and *then* try and bring them up. We'd publish an article about how you thought you were ugly but then you put on some new clothes, or got a massage or whatever, and ended up being transformed.

"And also," she added, "this story about college. It sounds conceited."

I had felt terrible at the time, mortified at being called conceited, terrified that I'd meet the *Cosmo* editor someday and she'd find out that I wasn't *that* pretty. Not pretty at all, in fact. Two months later when I came to New York I avoided her, although I had another encounter with an editor at *Esquire,* who listened to my pitch for California stories and finally interrupted me to say that none of them interested him. But he did have another proposition. Before I'd arrived, a cover shot had come in that was supposed to be of an attractive woman. But the model had "huge tits," he said, and looked too obviously sexy. He wanted someone "with . . . you know, ordinary tits." Would I be interested in posing?

I remember bristling with outrage. I was a writer, I said, not a model. He backtracked hastily: "Of course, of course . . . I just thought . . . of course. You're a writer, yes, indeed."

Now, whenever I tell this story to anyone, including my stepchildren, they can't imagine why I refused his offer. Who wouldn't want to be on the cover of *Esquire?* they ask. And I have no good answer except that my ambitions were larger back then.

As I sat there in camp it dawned on me that it was not entirely my fault that I was unprepared for losing my looks. I hadn't been able to admit to having them in the first place; that would have been far too conceited. Consequently I had come to believe I actually deserved all the attention I had gotten from men. I had a special personality. I had a special inner soul. What could I do now, in my forties, to compensate? Become more witty? More wise? More interesting?

In my journal I wrote, "Maybe I've always been courageous on these adventures because I knew someone would look after me. This is not a comforting thought. What do I do now, on this trip, when I am very much alone?"

48

*I*t had taken the guides over three hours to get Gary's boat down the rapids by pulling and pushing it over enormous piles of rocks. Now there was one more boat to go: Mike's. When Dave added up another three hours plus lunch, he announced that we would probably have to stay put today and make camp just below the rapids.

Another day, another few hundred yards.

Dave looked exhausted, and Gary, I knew, was both anxious and pissed off. I had seen his feet that morning and although they weren't as fiery red as they had been during the portage, they were pocked with small inflamed craters. Between the rot and the leeches and the grit in his tennis shoes, walking was not fun. Raymond, for once, had not been helping with the boats. I saw him reading a book by Scientology guru L. Ron Hubbard.

Then I saw Mike down at the river, studying it as if he were planning a run. Dave went down to join him, and then the two of them started pointing at things and making swirls and loops with their arms. The rest of us sat in the shade, awash in a quiet, somnolent malaise.

A short while later, Dave came up to us to report that Mike wanted to run the rapids alone in his boat. "Considering everything," he said, "including how exhausted we are and our dwindling supplies, I agreed to let him."

Mike, we discovered, had wanted to run these rapids all along.

Gary was against it, and Dave, although he thought it might be possible, was somewhere in the middle. Yesterday he'd been conservative; today he'd changed his mind.

"There's a run," Mike said, when we all went down to the river to watch him take off. "I just have to be completely accurate."

The rapids looked impossible to us, as Mimo had reported. They started out with a series of big waves, and then, in the middle, where an enormous tree had fallen across three quarters of the river, they became truly dangerous. If Mike hit the tree, he might be sucked under it. If he went around the tree, he'd have to go down a ten-foot drop where the river gushed around its roots and poured over a rock into a tremendous hole. Gary's boat had overturned in the hole yesterday, when they were lining it, and Mike could easily get into trouble. I had no idea if it was a keeper hole, but from the look on Mike's face I knew it could be dangerous. Also, there was the problem of getting too far over to the right. If Mike avoided the drop altogether, it looked as if he'd end up at the edge of the river where it dashed into a pile of rocks.

With Gary and Dave stationed at the end of the rapids, prepared for a rescue, and Sylvie on a rock in the river with her video camera, and the rest of us standing on a ledge with a bird's-eye view of the run, Mike took off. For the first several hundred yards he moved like a kayaker, finding places in the churning white water where he could hold still for a moment and plan his next move, dancing down the river sideways, backward, powering directly into the big waves. Then, suddenly, he was in the air, almost in a flip.

I watched as he let go of the oars and flung himself to the high side of the raft. The boat landed upright, but by the time Mike regained control he was heading at high speed right for the fallen tree. I was certain he was in serious trouble. But then he executed a maneuver so quick and precise that the boat spun to the right and careened around the edge of the tree like a whirling teacup, his oars shipped (straight in front of him), his head disappearing for a moment beneath an overhanging root.

Then the drop caught him and he plunged into the hole, bounced off the rock, pulled hard to the left, and the rest was a whirl of gray, yellow, and orange in the spray. Finally we saw him sail out of the hole, upright and cheering. He threaded through a few more rocks and disappeared around the bend, where Gary and Dave were waiting for him.

It was a beautiful performance, and great for our spirits. It meant we had another chance to get out of the gorge by nightfall. We all picked up our ammo cans and raced down to the boats.

"I was scared," Mike said later.

"I'll bet you were," said Dave.

"I knew it was just a matter of absolute concentration."

"Whatever you did, it was right."

After deng deng for lunch, which now tasted exactly like old linoleum, we were on the river again. But within moments the sky clouded up and suddenly the breeze started getting cold; the air felt almost as it had just before the flood. We were already fearing the worst, when suddenly we saw the river end. In the distance was an immense mountain, and the river didn't seem to go around it.

"Maybe that ridge before Fungus Falls wasn't the big mountain," Gary said. "Maybe this is it."

"Or this is where the river goes underground," I said. Then, more tentatively, "That was a joke."

Gary gave an unconvincing laugh. "I think we aren't dismissing anything now. All bets are off."

We floated slowly downstream, the guides standing up in the boats to see ahead, until suddenly we saw it: the middle of the mountain opened up a crack to reveal a steep, narrow canyon about twenty feet wide. The river funneled right into what looked like one of those horror-movie caverns where the walls begin to close and there's no way to get out.

I was shocked when Mike didn't stop to scout it, but we entered the canyon cautiously, and instead of finding raging, foaming rapids, the river was eerily calm; it was almost as if the viscosity of the water had changed and it was now flowing heavy and thick. There was no splashing, no white water, just a ribbon of muddy water, narrow and deep. Mike took the lead and oared standing up. At each bend he either stopped to stand on a rock and scout, or made an okay sign with his arms circled over his head. Gary, John, and I kept our voices low. It felt almost as if we were in a church.

Then the rain came. It was a drizzle for ten minutes and then a steady, gentle downpour. Once again we were cold and wet and scared. In such a narrow canyon a flood could strand us for days, and this time with little food. Also, it looked almost impossible to get to high ground; the walls of the canyon seemed to rise straight up.

There were no bird calls now, no signs of light or opening in the sky overhead. The air was gray, the rain was gray, the canyon was gray. All we could think of was getting out. We watched Mike up ahead of us raise his arms at each bend in the river to give the okay sign. The sight of those bare arms rising slowly from his sides to make a wide circle over his head, fingers touching like a ballet dancer's, is something I'll never forget.

Now I was afraid Mike would stop, which might mean another set of major rapids, but I was also afraid that he wouldn't stop, which might mean we'd come around a bend to see the top of another twenty-foot waterfall. I was afraid it would keep on raining; I was afraid that even with rivers there was a calm before the storm.

"I am feeling dread," I said to no one in particular.

"You're not the only one," replied Gary.

"Kierkegaard's concept of dread," said John, "was one of my favorite notions in philosophy."

I loved the fact that when John did speak he was oblivious of the context.

"You mean the leap of faith?" I asked.

"Sort of. It postulates that man was given free will and that free will brought with it the experience of dread. It compares dread to Adam looking into a chasm and being unable to see the bottom."

"Whew," Gary said, and once again we fell silent.

It seemed like forever that we went on this way, floating down the deep river in the high canyon, hunched over in the rain, shivering from a combination of cold and muted terror. Even when the rain stopped there was a Tolkien quality to the experience, as if we were traveling through an evil kingdom—a sense that something supernatural had power here.

By now anything seemed possible; there were clearly worlds beyond our wildest speculations. I thought of the evil Dayak spirits and wondered if they were subject to some larger, darker force: a monster in a cave, a troll on a throne. Who knew? I certainly didn't. Then, up ahead, we heard a shout. It was Dave. Gary grabbed the oars, prepared to pull out into an eddy, and my heart sank.

Suddenly, farther ahead, from Mike's boat, we heard a great big whoop. It was Raymond. Or was it a monkey? Then we heard cheers from the paddle boat and saw Dave turn around and shout back to us, his hands cupped around his mouth:

"Logging! To the right!"

We looked over and Gary cried out, *"Yes!"* He threw back his head and let the oars flop. *"We're out!"*

"See that light green hillside?" he said. "It means a boat was able to come up the river and get the logs down. That means there are no more big rapids."

I looked at John and saw that his face was lit up with a smile so sweet and simple it looked beatific. I wanted to hug him but refrained.

Mimo and Sylvie were yelling at each other up ahead in Italian and French, and Linda gave a cheer that boomed across the river like a foghorn, and Howard and Stuart yelled something about Bali and beer. We drifted together in the dark, deep canyon and it was over. Just like that. I looked around and saw a beautiful stage setting, exactly as if I were in a theater, with luminous rock walls and a river the color of rich jade. The mist was drifting out of the canyon, leaving two buttermilk jet trails, and the sky was now clear, transparent, diaphanous. Overhead a hornbill gave a short announcement: *cawk cawk*. A heron stood on a flat rock looking for fish; a large deer with magnificent antlers posed like a statue on the riverbank.

We stayed together in the middle of the river to celebrate and then, as if to remind us that we were still at the mercy of the river, there was a loud, harsh noise just behind the paddle boat: *kersplat!* It sounded as if someone had dived off Dave's boat and landed in a full-tilt belly flop. But when I turned around and looked I saw all six paddlers in the boat and Dave and Bill standing up, staring down into the water.

"Who jumped?" I yelled.

"No one," Dave yelled back.

"What was it?"

"We don't know."

"You don't know?"

"No."

"That was pretty big," said John, "to be invisible."

"What was that?" yelled Mike, who was farther downstream.

"They don't know."

"They don't know?"

"Everyone's still on the boat."

"Didn't they see anything?"

"I guess not."

There was a tree branch arching over the river, but Gary pointed out that any vegetable matter that might have fallen from it would probably have been too light to sink. And what animal would dive in the river and never come up?

"Maybe it was a freshwater dolphin," yelled Dave.

"Maybe it was the three-headed river spirit," Gary ventured quietly.

"Maybe it was the three-headed river spirit!" yelled Mike.

I liked the idea of the river spirit making one last attempt to get us before we left the gorge. It was a great end for my story.

"That's a great end for your story," called out Dave.

But of course we still had four hundred miles to go.

49

We went about twenty-five miles on the Boh that afternoon, traveling as much in three hours as we had in ten days. I hadn't realized how anxious Gary had been until he suddenly started becoming garrulous. I had thought him tongue-tied, but now I realized he had been silent for the same reasons we all were. He asked John about lawyering, me about writing, and talked about the Colorado River where he and Ginger had honeymooned just a year ago. They'd spent six weeks in the Grand Canyon, he said, exploring the side canyons, finding new streams and waterfalls, discovering Indian petroglyphs and hidden grottos.

Although I was interested, even curious, I felt uncomfortable. I didn't want to hear about another river, I didn't want to talk about corporate law, and, most of all, I didn't want to talk about the magazines I'd edited, the stories I'd written. Gary asked about my husband, but all I told him was that he was a newspaper columnist. I wanted to hold on a little longer to the awe.

I was glad when Gary yelled, *"Snake!"* and we looked over to see an enormous black snake, maybe twelve feet long, swimming in the water just in back of us. Its head was enormous and it was heading for the shore. Dave came oaring back up the river toward us with Bill standing up in the boat holding his snake stick like George Washington. But by the time they got to the riverbank where the snake was heading, it had disappeared into the bush.

"*Did you see it?*" yelled Gary.

"No," Bill answered.

"*It was enormous.*"

"*I still haven't seen a single goddamn snake.*"

At about four o'clock we stopped to make camp in a broad, flat marshy area next to a tributary stream and a strip of sandy beach. The sky had cleared and the sun was just hitting the tops of the trees. We pitched our tents on the beach, as far from the river as we could get, and I sat for a while in the late afternoon glow feeling the soft breeze on my arms. There were no bees!

It was only when I went back to the cooking fire that I felt the silence and realized something was wrong.

"The river's rising," said Mimo.

Earlier he had planted a stick in the marshy area in front of us, and the water level on it had risen at least a foot. It was probably still raining hard back in the gorge.

"We'll wait and see how far up it comes," Dave said, "and if worst comes to worst we can take our gear and the tents and climb up to high ground. Or if the tributary stream isn't flooding, we can walk up it."

"Shit," Linda said.

"We're not out of here yet," said Dave. "If we had the Dayaks with us, there would still be a lot of chickens being sacrificed."

"Bill!" said Sylvie abruptly. "Will you take off that sweatshirt?"

Bill looked down at his shirt, which read, "Save the rain forest." It had drawings on it of animals and flowers, all brightly colored: tigers, toucans, monkeys, orchids.

"I don't want to look at it," Sylvie said.

"I hate the rain forest," I said.

"I hate it too," Linda said.

"Nuke the rain forest," Stuart said.

"Fuck the rain forest," Mimo said.

Next year, we all agreed: *Club Med! Club Med! Club Med! Club Med!*

We chanted to keep up our spirits and then started cooking the last of our rice for dinner.

Just after dark the water reached our cooking fire, and by nine o'clock it was six feet from our tents, which we couldn't move back because they were already up against a steep rock wall. Now we talked about the possibility of having to head for high ground in the middle of the night. We should go to sleep, Dave said, with our gear packed and our flashlights out.

"John and I don't have any working flashlights," I said.

Dave shrugged.

"What can we do?"

"I don't know. I don't have an extra one."

"We have to have some kind of plan."

"Stick close to someone else."

"If we're all scrambling for our lives up the canyon and you guys are dealing with the boats, no one is going to wait for us."

"Yes, they will."

"No, they won't."

I could feel my anger begininng to rise. I could see John and me trying to climb the slippery rock wall in the rain, in pitch blackness; I could see the river surging around our feet; I could see my notebook, my glasses, my gear spinning and tumbling in the current.

"I don't know what to say," said Dave.

"We can't count on other people to help us. It doesn't work that way on this trip."

"She's right," said Raymond. "It's every person for himself."

I was surprised at Raymond's support, but then remembered he'd said the same thing when he and Mimo had taken the only single tents, forcing me to sleep with John.

"I'll give you my flashlight," said Dave.

"But you'll need it."

"It's the best I can do."

"Why don't we just pitch our tents next to you?"

Later Mimo said he'd look at my flashlight to see if it was broken, but when I brought it up to him he stared at me and walked away. Tempers were still frayed, I realized. I thought of the flashlight and mini book light sitting in my duffel bag somewhere and wanted to tell someone that it wasn't my fault the flashlights in Balikpapan were so goddamn ridiculous.

After dinner, Mimo apologized and spent half an hour trying unsuccessfully to fix my flashlight. Later, Dave announced that he and Mimo had decided to stay up all night and keep watch over the river, which meant John and I could borrow his flashlight. I thanked him and read in the tent a bit, and then, around midnight, I awoke to hear Mimo call out that the water level was dropping. I crawled out of the tent to look and saw that the stars were out. For the first time in almost two weeks the soft wind in the trees was louder than the river.

Mimo had dried some of John's soggy tobacco, and I sat by the fire with him and Dave for a while, sharing a pipe and talking about Africa. Oddly enough, I wasn't ready for the trip to end.

50

*B*y midmorning the next day the Boh had turned into a generic jungle river: wide, flat, slow, and hot. Our only danger now was starvation or sunburn: we still hadn't seen a boat or a village or even a fisherman. Around noon we did hear the roar of a small plane and suddenly, up the river, flying low, came a tiny MAF two-seater.

"Don't wave, don't do anything!" yelled Dave. *"That way he'll know we're all right!"*

The plane passed overhead, then circled and came back a little lower. It was the moment we'd been waiting for, the one where we shout, *"Hello, Hello! We made it! We're all right!"* But we were not dealing in language or emotions now, we were dealing in signs and symbols. And so we just grinned and looked up, and the plane circled and passed over us again, this time so low we could see the pilot.

"He's counting bodies!" Dave called out.

We watched the pilot smile and wave to us and I had to sit on my hands. The urge to wave back was almost unbearable. It was like finding a lost child and not being able to give it a hug.

Then the pilot dipped a wing, nosed up, and banked off to the left. We didn't pick up our paddles until the sound of his engine had completely disappeared.

Lunch on the banks of the river was seriously bad, more of

Dave's deng deng which now tasted like rancid, crystalized sugar. But the place where we ate it was paradise: a wide sandy beach under a fantastically buttressed banyan tree. We were relaxed and joking again, but I was also beginning to feel strangely let down. The trip was almost over, and all that was left was a predictable tapering away of the experience: a float down the Boh to the Mahakam, a riverboat to Samarinda, a hotel and a plane flight to Balikpapan. We were safe, but safe for what?

As we continued down the river we kept looking for more signs of fishing or logging, but the river remained unpopulated. We found waterfalls and floated close to them and saw herons sitting on sandspits. I sat on the raft casually and confidently, swaying pleasantly in time to the boat's rhythmical lurching. It was humid and hot and quiet. I almost didn't notice it when we merged into the Mahakam.

We had expected the Mahakam to be full of motorboats, but it, too, seemed primeval. It was actually narrower than the Boh, and as we turned east toward the coast we picked up only a little speed. At this rate, about seven miles per hour, Long Bangun, the first town on our map, was at least three days away.

Around four o'clock it looked as if we'd have to camp one more night on the river, maybe two if we couldn't pick up a river taxi before Long Bangun. But just as we were arguing over where to pull out, we saw a small landing for boats on the right side of the river, and in the undergrowth above it several huts. We pulled in, and Dave and Raymond got out to see if they could buy some food. A few minutes later we heard a motor in the distance and a longboat came into view. Mike and Gary stood up and waved and yelled, and although the boatman continued on past us for a while, he finally turned and headed back.

The boat was about twenty feet long and five feet wide. It didn't seem big enough to hold all twelve of us and the rafts in addition to its cargo of some heavy metal drums and a family of five Dayaks. But it did have two big outboard motors, and Dave and Raymond began negotiating with the captain.

In a few minutes, Dave reported that the captain had agreed

to take us to Long Bangun. He was charging an outrageous amount of money—the equivalent of six hundred dollars—but Sobek, Dave said, would just have to eat it. We cheered. There was one other problem. There were some rapids below us that had to be run before dark, so we'd have to unload the rafts, derig and deflate them, roll them up, and get everything transferred to the longboat in a half hour.

"Let's go!" shouted Mike.

From start to finish, we were out of the rafts and into the longboat in twenty minutes. It was, Dave said, a world record.

And so we sped down the Mahakam to the roar of two motors, dragging a wake behind us like a long skirt. We made it through the rapids and for the first time since leaving Samarinda we saw the moon. In the gathering darkness we passed some smaller boats with shadowy figures in them and exchanged waves and greetings. The world was back on schedule now. The scaffolding of stars was in place in the sky, and the clouds were speeding across the heavens. The boat was moving fast in the calm, dark water, and it was a more or less straight shot to the twentieth century.

After a couple of hours we saw, like a mirage, the lights of Long Bangun coming up: a row of tumbledown houses on stilts over the water, a collection of ragged boats rooted to their dull reflections, and up on the riverbank some fifty flickering lights. But we passed it by and headed for the river's left bank, pulling in next to a battered wooden boat about fifty feet long and ten feet wide, with two rusty smokestacks and a covered hold. It looked Conradian, but it also looked like a piece of junk.

There was a logging camp here, Dave said, and he was going to see if we could spend the night. Our boatman had told him most of the men were away doing survey work, and it was our best bet for finding a place where all of us could sleep. We scrambled up the muddy riverbank and walked up to a clearing.

The camp was a collection of wooden huts lined up in three rows and a large open-air room that was lit with kerosene lanterns. We gathered in the light and Raymond went off to try to find someone willing to cook us dinner. Soon a Chinese woman appeared and unlocked a door, and we followed her inside. It was a tiny store (the Chinese have been the merchants of Borneo since the seventeenth century), and we bought warm beer and bags of peanuts. I bought a flashlight. It was a return to civilization of sorts, but our attempts to celebrate were not successful. The camp was a forlorn place—dirty and poor—and the few people left in it seemed broken and unsmiling. There were no children and only one woman, the Chinese store owner who seemed more concerned with counting money than with socializing. When we'd heard there were bathrooms we perked up, but when we found them we wished we hadn't.

All around us were the ghosts of the men who called this temporary encampment home, men who had left behind their families and their culture. This was where they started: capitalism's bottom rung.

Dave came up from the river saying that the rustbucket we'd tied up next to was available for hire. For six hundred dollars the captain would get us to the coast in two days. We'd leave tomorrow morning, run through the night, and arrive in Samarinda the following afternoon. It wasn't the greatest of boats, he said, but it was ours, now, if we wanted it.

We did.

51

*T*he sound in the distance was clearly of someone throwing up—violently and often. Howard, it turned out, was sick. He sounded alarmingly bad. Stuart went to check on him and came back saying he had overdosed himself on medicine. He'd had cramps and diarrhea and had taken a good dose of Lomotil plus an antinauseant. "Howard has an entire medicine chest with him," Stuart said. "He had a bad reaction but I did some deep breathing with him and he's calming down."

I felt sorry for Howard. With his tremendous stake in being self-sufficient, it must have been terrible to have a violent reaction to something in this godforsaken place—to have your heart race, your blood pound, your saliva flow, your legs shake, and not know what was going on. I went out to find Howard and sympathize and saw him slumped on the ground surrounded by Mike, Gary, Dave, Sylvie, and Mimo. I hung back for a moment to see if I was interrupting anything.

"This is a private party," Mike called out.

I was angry for a minute; since when were Sylvie and Mimo Howard's close friends? But there was another explanation for the remark and I decided to believe it. Howard did need privacy, and Mike's remark would comfort him.

*   *   *

That was the night of Fred, the moth: a moth so gigantic it required a name. Fred landed on Stuart's right shoulder and stayed there for about a half hour, surveying us with insect blankness punctuated every now and then by a mysterious shudder. He was brown and ragged but as large as a parrot; the tops of his wings reached above Stuart's ears. When Fred finally flew off it was odd to see him head for the light and flutter stupidly next to the normal-sized insects. But then he came back and brushed Stuart's cheek with an audible *whoosh* before heading into the darkness. He flew like a moth in slow motion, his great wings flapping in jagged dips and soars.

Dinner was wonderful: stringy chicken fried in a delicious batter plus mashed potatoes with lots of spices and a leafy green vegetable. We were so sleepy afterward that we figured we could deal with the bunkhouses by collapsing. We'd peered into them earlier and fled in horror.

But by flashlight the houses looked, if anything, worse. Immense cockroaches scattered for cover. There were newspapers and random pieces of plastic on the dirt floor, cobwebs everywhere, and no beds. We had to put our sleeping bags right on the ground with the roaches. Once again John said he didn't need his air mattress, and I told him to call me anytime, anywhere, if he needed someone to save his life.

I spent the next few hours trying to ignore the rustlings on the floor and the smell of other people's sweat. The room was hot and dusty, so I opened the wooden shutters for a while to try and catch a breeze, but then the mosquitoes came in and I had to get up and close them. I opened and shut the shutters half the night, trying to find the right balance between itching and sweating.

Through it all, I remained eerily calm. On the Boh I had learned to do things I did not like, and even more important, I had learned to do them over and over and over again. At least for a while, my world had fewer demons.

Around two o'clock in the morning I heard the rain, and

minutes later a cool breeze rushed in the open windows. Then the rain turned operatic; it became a genuine tropical downpour, pounding so loud on the tin roof that it sounded as though we were inside some kind of steel drum. Even John woke up. I worried for a moment that the earth would turn to mud beneath us and our little wooden house would slide down into the Mahakam, but after a while, to my amazement, I relaxed in the cosmic din. I lay on the air mattress with my heart racing, and then the noise simply hammered me down into sleep.

At dawn I awoke to see a cockroach the size of a Snickers bar clackity-clacking across the floor next to my face.

The trip down the Mahakam on our own personal rustbucket was like a long bus ride. We read; we napped on the linoleum floor; we sunned ourselves; we unrolled the canvas curtains when it rained and played cards. We stopped at one tiny village to buy food, and Mimo cooked a dinner of pasta, garlic, onions, and some disgusting Day-Glo red liquid that came in a can labeled *Tomatoes*. Sylvie, Linda, and I took a girlish shower in the back of the boat, soaping up nude, trusting the men not to turn around and watch. We laughed together about our leech marks and our crotch rot, and Linda said she was feeling better, and Sylvie said, "I guess I'll never forget this trip."

"I can't believe I'm saying this," Linda said, "but I feel almost afraid to leave the river—afraid that . . . I don't know; that everything after this is going to be a letdown."

I knew what she meant. The moments of greatest intensity in life—whether they come from facing danger or falling in love or being carried away with some kind of work—seem almost surreal when they are happening; they take place in slow motion and seem to crowd our ordinary reality. But then, when they're over, they seem to have happened to someone else. Even on the Mahakam, when I thought back on the last ten days, I had only a dim sensual memory of what they'd felt like. Mostly I had a bunch of stories, a trace memory of dreamlike images, a feeling in my bones. What had seemed like another lifetime was about to become just another ten days in the discourse of ordinary life.

That night we hummed down the Mahakam, sleeping deeply while the gently rocking boat left a white band of foam on the dark smooth water and the steam from the smokestacks disappeared into the sky. Although the engine ceaselessly clattered and drummed, there was a marvelous stillness and immensity to the experience. We might have been one of those phantom steamers Conrad talked about that left no trace on the "circular stillness of water and sky."

When we awoke at dawn, everything had changed. The Mahakam had become a freeway, populated with boats of every conceivable description: dugout canoes, longboats, river taxis, logging barges, most of them as scruffy as ours. We passed village after village, all of which looked the same: a line of waterfront shacks on stilts, a row of wooden stores roofed in tin, and scuffed paths fanning out to shanties buried in the foliage. Occasionally a steeple rose above the rooftops, more often the dome of a mosque.

For the rest of the day I had plenty of time to think about what I would do after we arrived late that afternoon in Samarinda. We had lost a week in the gorge, taking ten days instead of three to get through it, and I had lost the week in Malaysia I'd planned to spend by myself, a week of leisurely sight-seeing, beach walking, and reading. Tomorrow I was scheduled to meet up with another Sobek group and run the Alas River in Sumatra's Gunung Leuser National Park.

Bill had taken the trip two years earlier and said I shouldn't even compare it to the Boh. It was relaxing and luxurious, with sandy beaches, fantastic food, lots of wildlife, and no serious rapids. But the truth was, nothing particularly enticed me. I wanted to prolong the adventure I was on; I wanted to shorten it. I wanted excitement; I wanted to relax. I wanted to meet some interesting people; I didn't want to be polite to anyone. I figured I'd end up flying to Sumatra for the same reason I'd flown to Borneo after losing my luggage: it was the easiest option.

52

*I*t was the first thing I saw when I opened the door to my hotel room in Balikpapan: the huge brown duffel bag right in the middle of the floor, a dark hulk, stuffed and bulging. It seemed like a cache of treasure that had surfaced from another world: so clean, so dry, so new. I went to it, knelt down, and drew the zipper back reverently. For a moment I flashed back to a guided dream I'd had under hypnosis. I was swimming underwater and had come upon a shipwreck with a trunk full of treasure. "Open up the trunk and tell me what you see," the hypnotist had said. I opened it, cautiously, and saw . . . a baby. The laughing face of a beautiful, apple-cheeked baby.

I remember even now drawing the zipper of my duffel back very slowly and then spreading it apart and reaching inside. The first thing I felt was a plastic Ziploc bag. I pulled it out. It was full of bottles and tubes and jars—everything I'd wished for to kill bacteria and fungus. Then I reached in and fingered the T-shirts, the cotton pants, the silky Lycra of my bathing suit, all neatly folded one on top of the other in a big, soft pile. I probed further and touched the rubber bottoms of my tennis shoes, a bag full of batteries, and, down at the bottom, a large black bag with camera and lenses.

I couldn't resist pulling everything out and piling it all on the rug. The T-shirts smelled so sweet and felt so soft . . . and there was my flashlight, my reading light . . . God, *my air mattress*! It was as if I had found a time capsule, treasures from another life. I spent ten minutes on the rug touching and feeling everything until I remembered, with a start, the hotel bathroom. I threw off my moldy T-shirts and shorts and rushed into a world of mirrors, lights, and glistening chrome and tile. I remembered Eric Hansen's blue terry cloth hand towel for a few seconds, but then I stepped into the shower and stood for a long time under a magnificent stream of hot, steamy water.

Afterwards, with a clean sundress on, and my hair still wet, I examined my face in the mirror. There were the same strong bones, the same large eyes, the same soaring nose, the same weathered skin. I turned on the fancy mirror lights, and found my small bag of makeup: an arsenal of tubes, compacts and pencils. First I took out the usual—mascara and blusher—and dusted my cheeks red, my eyelashes smoky black. The face in the mirror didn't change much. I took out a small bottle of skin-toned makeup and dabbed some of it on my nose to see if it would hide the redness. It did. I spread it out to my cheeks and then down to my chin. Now the face in the mirror was the face of a woman who wore makeup. It wasn't the face of an adventurer, the face of a woman who had emerged triumphant.

I grabbed one of the clean white handtowels, ran it under the hot water tap, and wiped the face clean. I looked at the towel: it was stained pink and black, almost as if someone had used it to scrub up a paint spill. It was a towel defiled, and I hid it under the sink. Then, at the top of my vision, something flashed, and I looked up. It was a gecko, a small green lizard, that had stopped in its tracks a few inches from the ceiling. It was looking down at me with stone cold eyes.

I put down the towel, lifted one bare foot up to the bathroom counter, and, in one motion, stood up. For a moment, the gecko and I were as still as death. Then I began to lift my arm slowly, past my hips, past my chest, up to my shoulders. The gecko blinked. I froze. Carefully, I shifted feet. Then my arm shot up just as the gecko turned and ran, and some new instinct within me calculated its speed and my arm changed direction. I caught it on the ceiling, my fingers curled around it like claws. I could feel its soft belly pulsing wildly in my palm.

Finally it shuddered and grew perfectly still.

I jumped down from the bathroom counter to the tiled floor, landing perfectly with both knees bent, and, still carrying my prey, I walked out of the bathroom, past the bed, past my duffel bag and out the door into the warm, hot air, with tropical smells drifting through it like slender waving reeds.

I looked at the gecko and wondered how it would taste flame-broiled, and then dropped it in a flower pot.

I had an hour to kill before meeting the group for our farewell dinner, and I ran back to my room, put on my charred sandals, grabbed my purse and walked out of the hotel into a world of cars, concrete buildings, and shops with big flat glass window panes. As the cars surrounded me like a mob of angry school children, I felt my fingertips tingle: the lizard's pulsing softness. Then I turned a corner and came upon the street of small stores where, just two weeks ago, I'd made that jet-lagged attempt to shop. They stretched out into the distance again like a row of baby birds, mouths open, wings aflutter, squawking. The clink and jangle of cash registers floated overhead again, and walls of small TV sets clattered rhythmically. I walked into the throng, unseen within the electronic din that filled the street, fearless as the noise started to tumble and boil and the steep walls of the shops closed in. Sometimes the noise parted and I sailed through it effortlessly; other times my skirt swirled around me like a whirlpool. When I heard the *eeeee eeeeee eeeeee* of the gin and bitters bug I turned expectantly, but it was the voice of a shop-keeper cradling a boombox. I saw his tongue go out as the noise poured into him, and watched him lick and bite the metal until the blood and the colors and the music dripped down his clean white shirt.

In the sky, the sun was on the horizon, sinking down into the Strait of Makasar.

53

*I*t wasn't just dark when I woke up in the middle of the night, it was pitch black. I propped myself up on one elbow on my air mattress to try to see, but there was nothing, only vague shadows. Black rocks. Black night. I could hear the river roaring to my right, but I couldn't see it. Even my hand was invisible in the blackness. I felt the ground—ah hah! There was my sheet.

But I'd missed something. Something was wrong. The rapids were close—I could hear the roar—but I was alone somehow. Everyone had gone for some reason. A thundercloud had filled the gorge and everyone had left, hiked up to high ground. They were miles away and no one had remembered me. I groped in the darkness for my glasses and felt something rubbery: a boat. Jesus! I was right next to the river; it had already begun to flood. I felt something hard—the food table! My flashlight was useless, so I didn't look for it, but I had no matches, either. How was I going to see? Where was everyone?

I could hear the river, but I didn't want to get any closer to it. I looked around to see if I could spot a line of tiny lights snaking up the side of the canyon. How long ago had they left? Nothing was coming into focus. I couldn't even see my hand.

I reached out farther into the blackness, feeling around for my glasses, and then I saw it, something shimmering faintly in the distance, almost like the northern lights. Was it the reflection of the river on a rock wall? I had to get up. I had to see.

Ah hah! My hands grabbed hold of my glasses and I put them on. The black shapes were clearer, but what was the shimmering? It was like moving water, only vertical.

I called out—Hello? *Hello?*—and the sound came immediately back. Something was wrong. My world was wrong. I was seeing things wrong. My hellos bounced back as if I were in a tiny room. I looked again at the shimmering light and reached over again to feel the boat. But it wasn't rubber—it was covered. Covered with cloth!

I found the food table and found the metal object on top of it, and then my fingers found the button and pushed it.

Light!

I was in my hotel room. The shimmering lights were curtains that had been fluttering in front of the plastic "blackout" shade. The river was the air conditioner rattling in the corner. The boat was another bed.

With the light shining and my heart pounding I sat on the bed a while to catch my breath. I was alone, but not really. I had never been really alone. I had always been able to see; I had always been able to find a friend. As bad as the river trip had been, it was never a nightmare.

54

*T*he next morning John came to my room to pick up his air mattress and we stood at the door to say good-bye. He was more talkative, more confident than I'd ever seen him, and I thanked him for being such a sound sleeper and a good river pal.

"Oh heck," I said, "I'll give you a hug."

To my surprise his face lit up and he held out his arms and said, "Oh good." He hugged me long and hard and for a moment I felt that I was swooning.

"There was a time when I needed to be looked after," he said quietly, "and I want to thank you for doing it."

"Thank you, thank *you*," I said, drawing back and looking at him. I was pretty much inarticulate in the face of his surprising warmth.

"I consider us friends," he said. "I have very much enjoyed being with you."

He gave me another bearhug and, overwhelmed, I watched him walk off down the hotel corridor and turn a corner.

Epilogue

*B*y the time I came home from Indonesia, all of my friends in the Bay Area knew more or less what had happened. I had called my husband from Balikpapan to tell him I was all right, and he'd written a column the next day called "The Wild Woman of Borneo: Part II" (Part I had appeared the day I left). It began:

> Oh my yes how amusing is this, because here is what usually happens: The beloved wife figure goes to Iceland or Mars and does something many people would consider to be foolishly dangerous but the wife considers to be big fun, and the husband worries comically and paces around like Desi Arnaz, and then everything is fine and ha ha on the husband!
>
> So my wife went to Borneo to raft a river never before rafted by humans, and I fretted. But this just in by telephone from Balikpapan: The trip turned into a disaster and confirmed all my amusingly expressed fears.
>
> It's the old switcheroo. Life imitates vaudeville.

I saw Richard Bangs back at the Sobek office in Oakland, and he said the trip sounded pretty exciting. Later, when I told him I had decided to write a book about it, he gave me the name of his agent and said to let him know if he could help in any way. I said I'd be critical of Sobek for listing the trip as average in terms of difficulty. He said the label was obviously a mistake, but as a writer himself, he believed in telling the truth. "Write what you want," he said. "Just don't accuse us of rape or murder."

A month before I finished the first draft of the book, he called up and said that Sobek was thinking of opening up a river for rafting in Angola. "You should come with us on the exploratory run," he said. "Angola has been closed to foreigners for years. This can be your second book. I can already see the movie."

John and I kept in touch for a while, and he sent a copy of the newsletter of the Primitive Art Society of Chicago in which he'd written about the trip in a section called "President's Notes." He didn't write about the river but about the destruction of the Kalimantan rain forest. He urged members to support people working to save it, saying, "Many of you, like me, spent your formative years in the sixties. Wouldn't it be ironic to be remembered as the self-indulgent generation that bequeathed an uglier world to our children?"

When I last spoke to him not much had changed. He was doing some pro bono work for the Indonesian community in Chicago and was still waiting for an answer from his girlfriend. He said his lawyer friends had all called him a fool for not suing Sobek.

At my hairdresser's, I saw a picture of Olatz in *Fame* magazine. It was a full-page vodka ad, and there she was with her wild black hair and full, sensuous lips.

Dave sent me a copy of an article on the Boh he had written for Garuda Airlines' inflight magazine. I was glad to see that he portrayed the trip as an ordeal, not just an exciting adventure. He wrote me a note, promising to get in touch when he came to the States so I could check some of the facts for my book, but he came and went without calling. Later someone at Sobek told me he'd flown from Jakarta to Los Angeles on a Friday, caught a flight to San Francisco that evening, driven three hours to Sobek's offices in Angels Camp, got a few hours' sleep, and spent all of Saturday buying twenty thousand dollars' worth of equipment for a new river trip he would be opening up for Sobek in Bali. The next morning he got up before daylight, drove back to Oakland, flew to Los Angeles, and connected with the sixteen-hour evening flight back to Jakarta.

I forgave him for telling me to go to sleep in the rain under a sheet of plastic.

I heard from Gary a couple of months after I got back. He wasn't doing well, he said. He had made it to Papua New Guinea in time for the Watut trip, but when he flew home to Arizona he found out that his wife had left him. He was about to teach one semester of English at a junior high school in Utah to see if he wanted to give up river running. We talked about our "swim" in the Boh and he said he went down very deep and for a long while thought he might actually be behind the falls in what's called a "drowning machine."

"I knew I'd have to conserve energy, so I put my knees up and my arms in front of my face, and I just waited. I had a lot of time to think. I'd had a strange, intuitive apprehension about the trip and now I thought that maybe this was the reason; maybe I was going to die. I thought about it in a detached sort of way, and then I began rising. There was light and then bubbles and I had a brief moment of fear—what am I going to come up into?—but finally I broke surface and I saw I was way downriver, about one hundred yards."

The last time I heard from Gary he was working out of Alaska with Mike, guiding on the Tatshenshini River.

I postponed calling Bill and Linda when I got back because I was worried that they might have split up. But when I did call,

Linda was as ebullient as ever. "Don't worry," she said when she heard the hesitancy in my voice, "we're still together!" Six months later she went with Bill on another river trip in the rain forest in Costa Rica. "I knew if I didn't get on another river right away I'd never do it," she explained.

Recently I got a T-shirt in the mail from her—a white one with black bees printed all over it. When I called to say thanks, she said she'd set up her painting studio in Palm Beach. "And guess what I'm painting?" she said. "The river. As I'm talking to you now, I'm surrounded by pictures of the Boh."

Bill said he'd also written up the Boh River trip and was thinking of trying to put together a book of his rain forest adventures.

Stuart sent me some prints of his Boh photographs and, later, a brief note saying he was getting married. A year after I'd written Howard asking for photographs, I got a tape from him in the mail in which he talked about the Boh trip while paging through his scrapbook. What he had loved most was the rapids, he claimed, especially his two white-water swims. "I was laughing with happiness," he said. "I enjoyed being in the rapids, thrived on it; I was happy when I opened my eyes underwater and saw it was dark and knew I was under the boat."

Howard's big news was that he was going to get married. That and the fact that he had just gotten his helicopter pilot's license. He and his girlfriend had gone back to Borneo and climbed Mt. Kinabalu, he said. They'd also taken a motorboat up a river not too far from the Boh. "We went to a longhouse built by the Malaysian government for the nomadic Penan Dayaks, and it was depressing, built out of concrete and sawn timber, with no character, no life. The people all hung out in a little kitchen they'd built for themselves." Through an interpreter, Howard talked to an old man, who pleaded with him to tell the rest of the world what was happening to the Penans, how they were being forced to live in concrete houses in a denuded forest. "He had tears in his eyes," said Howard. "I'll never forget that

old man, pleading with us, two white people, to help him. I'll
never forget that as long as I live."

Mike wrote up the Boh trip for an Alaskan newspaper, and
someone at Sobek sent me his ten-page manuscript. It's a good,
boatman's account of running the river, including the bees, the
flood, and the foot rot. This is how it opens:

> There's an old saying:
>   "All the true wisdom is to be found far from the dwell-
> ings of man, in the great solitudes, and can only be attained
> through suffering. Suffering and privation are the only
> things that can open the mind of man to that which is
> hidden from his fellows."
>
> IGJUGARJUK, an Eskimo, 1922.

I wrote to Mike asking him for his version of several events,
including his romance with "the remarkable Sylvie."

"Sylvie *was* remarkable," he wrote back, "but surely you can
see that under the circumstances, much of a romance was impossible. The companionship was there, and was helpful to us
both, but such a big deal it wasn't. Afterward in Bali is a different
story. But don't make too much out of nothing. Exhausted, sleeping on rocks with bugs everywhere, well, it's pretty hard to stir
up much action in those conditions."

When I talked to him on the phone in his cabin in Alaska, he
was making moose jerky and about to leave for Pakistan, where
he had been asked to set up river trips for an adventure travel
company. I asked him how his toe was, and he laughed. "You
should see it—it's retarded. I tore it again this summer. It's a
twisted stub." He says that whenever he tells the story of the
Boh River he always mentions how well the group welded together. "You could all have whined and bitched and panicked
but nobody ever did. Everyone seemed up for the challenge, and
a lot of people were working way above their capability."

I talked with Sylvie several times in New York, and she was always extremely friendly, although just about to leave for a fashion shoot in Jamaica, or Spain, or San Blas, or Paris. The Boh trip "was the most exciting thing I've done in my life," she said. "It was so far out, sometimes I wonder whether I actually lived it."

She agreed that nothing happened between her and Mike for the first three days except that "it was nice to sleep with some-body and have some warm, human comfort." They did make love once, she said, when we were all in camp during the flood, "but it was not very elaborate."

Later in Bali and then in Alaska, where she visited him, their sex life blossomed. "Then we had a great sexual relationship, I mean *really* good. More than just being attracted to each other. It really worked."

The last time I talked to Sylvie she said she and Richard had split as a couple but were living happily together as roommates. She hadn't heard from Mike in six months. "He was the one who had a problem with our relationship," she said. "You know, we were from such different worlds, blah, blah, blah. It was Mike who broke it off."

I never tried to contact Raymond, since I felt bad about not liking him very much, but Linda said she'd heard that he had organized a group of people in Indonesia for the express purpose of going on more exploratory river trips. I never wrote to Mimo, either, but only because I couldn't be sure of contacting him. Sylvie said Mimo had moved to Bali, where he's started up a furniture business. He's still with Olatz, who lives in Bali with him when she's not working.

Olatz, she was almost certain, had never done a vodka ad.

For a long while the mystery of the great splash in the river remained unsolved. The rain forest experts I talked to said it probably *was* the three-headed river spirit. But finally I came upon this passage in the second volume of Spenser St. John's *Life in the Forests of the Far East*. He is writing about his trip up the Limbang River, a few hundred miles north of the Boh:

> We were once much startled by a large animal springing from a high bough, and falling with a heavy splash within a few feet of our boat: it turned out to be a huge biawak, or guana, which, being alarmed, thus made his escape. The guana is a species of lizard, growing to a great length.

As for me, in hindsight I see that my own journey did not end with the Boh: the river was in some ways a metaphor for my voyage into middle age. Whether the river speeded it up or not I cannot say; I do know that writing about it helped. And so did the trip I ended up taking on the Alas River in Sumatra just three days after I came off the Boh.

The Alas was a beautiful, easy river with Class II rapids and sandy beaches. The water was so calm that one day I floated and swam alongside the rafts in my life jacket until I noticed that my skin had turned white and my entire body looked like a wrinkled bed sheet.

More interesting than the river itself were the people on the trip, especially two men and a woman over sixty-five. They were not blessed with youth and beauty, but they did have generous spirits and a wealth of life experience. They had philosophies based on what they'd seen for themselves and done, and there wasn't a subject they couldn't make interesting. With them, I felt young and competent again, but even more important, I had a glimpse of the emotional and intellectual journeys that lay ahead.

In memory, the Boh is still a jumble of images and confused feelings. Even writing about it hasn't allowed me to "relive" the trip or define it in a way that seems complete. Sometimes, when I have trouble sleeping, I close my eyes to see if I can get back to the Boh, see what images are there in the memory bank. But so far the journey is always the same. It starts on the Mahakam, on a river taxi, at dusk. I watch the villages fade away and the logging boats dissolve and then, when the river turns dark and quiet, I find myself on a longboat, standing up like Mike, trying to see what is coming. I am alone with the river and the hum of the motor and the heaving, breathing wetness of the rain forest. The water turns silvery in the moonlight and I can almost feel the soft warm air on my skin.

I can, with effort, get to the Boh—see the gorge building up, the rolling hills begin to crumple and steepen. But when I see the rapids actually foaming and frothing my journey stops. The boat shudders against the current, the light turns bright, and the detail is washed out.

It is as if someone sabotaged the film, overexposed the heart of darkness.

In some ways, of course, I never did reach the darkness; not the Conradian darkness, the unknowable darkness, the dark knowledge that has always fascinated me. Even traveling light, I was carrying too much baggage. I had a lifeline back to the twentieth century, and roots in a time and age that conquers and destroys whatever is inexplicable. When I think of the darkness in the Boh River gorge, I see an image of all twelve of us at the edge of the river, huddled in our orange life jackets and plastic helmets next to the toy bathtub boats. Whatever was primitive or savage inside us is still in the dark forest.

Instinctively, we seek the sun.

My personal journey is another story. At times, on the Boh, I lost track of myself. In the prison of the rain forest, with the bees like little furies and a group spirit that was not generous, I came to see myself only in that context: a woman over forty having hot flashes, physically handicapped, without my own clothes or medicine, and one of only two people on the trip without a friend. Women tell me it's a familiar trait—this blurring of our self-image by context—but I had never been so strongly tested.

I see, also, that the defenses I erected to protect myself and to remain independent were the very ones that kept me from reaching out to get what I wanted. I should have told Mimo and Sylvie about my bursitis, for instance, admitted to a weakness, worked out the misunderstanding. And I probably should have tried to understand Raymond. As a journalist I've learned that everyone has at least one good story, and I'm sorry, now, that I didn't make the effort to get his.

Would I go again on such a trip? I can't rule it out. On the Boh I learned that I could do quite well in a difficult situation on my own, and find moments of genuine rapture amidst the bees and the leeches and the foot rot. The story of the Boh that became a book is almost over, but I hope to keep with me the knowledge that even the most uncomfortable of journeys is tolerable. Sometimes it's better to trust fate than to keep from tempting it. As Ralph Waldo Emerson said: The wise man in a storm prays God not for safety from danger, but for deliverance from fear.